THRIVING TRANSITIONS

A Research-Based Approach to College Student Success

Laurie A. Schreiner, Michelle C. Louis,
and Denise D. Nelson, Editors

Cite as:

Schreiner, L. A., Louis, M. C., & Nelson, D. D. (Eds.). (2012). *Thriving in transitions: A research-based approach to college student success*. Columbia, SC: University of South Carolina, National Resource Center for The First-Year Experience and Students in Transition.

Production Staff for the National Resource Center:
Project Manager   Dottie Weigel, Editor
Design and Production   Elizabeth Howell

Library of Congress Cataloging-in-Publication Data
Thriving in transitions : a research-based approach to college student

success / Laurie A. Schreiner, Michelle C. Louis, and Denise D. Nelson,

editors.

p. cm.

Includes index.

ISBN 978-1-889271-83-5

1. College freshmen--United States. 2. Transfer students--United

States. 3. Student adjustment--United States. I. Schreiner, Laurie A.

II. Louis, Michelle C. III. Nelson, Denise D.

LB2343.32.T47 2012

378.1'980973--dc23

2012010294

Contents

List of Tables

Preface

Laurie A. Schreiner, Michelle C. Louis, and Denise D. Nelson

Higher education is at a critical juncture. Faced with unprecedented economic hardships, increased demands for accountability, and challenges from students, families, and the public to demonstrate the value of a college education, we must find new ways of helping students succeed not only in college, but in life. The tremendous strides that have been made in access to college have not translated to equivalent rates of success, as fewer than half of college students who begin a bachelor's degree ever complete one in their lifetime (Aud et al., 2010). Disparities in graduation rates, academic success, and psychological well-being across ethnic groups on campus (Hennessy, 2010) underscore that our traditional approaches to helping students succeed are not working—at least not for all students.

Even traditional perspectives that encapsulate student success in strong grades and degree attainment are open to question, as researchers are beginning to realize that the college experience includes more than the classroom and commencement (Kuh, Kinzie, Shuh, Whitt, & Associates, 2005). Engaging fully in that experience and benefiting most meaningfully from a college education involves potentially life-changing decisions, relationships, emotional reactions, social interactions, and psychological responses that transcend the behaviors we measure as GPA and graduation rates.

The construct of *thriving* as an expanded vision of student success provides a framework for conceptualizing new ways of helping students reap the full benefits of higher education. The very word thriving implies that success involves more than surviving a four-year academic obstacle course. Students who thrive are vitally engaged in the college endeavor—intellectually, socially, and emotionally. They experience what Tagg (2003) calls *deep learning*; they are investing effort within the classroom and managing their lives well beyond it. Thriving students are also goal oriented, applying their strengths to address the academic challenges they face. When they are thriving, students are connected to others in healthy and meaningful ways, and they desire to make a difference in the world around them. They also see the world differently. Equipped with a positive perspective on life, they are secure in the present and confident of the future.

Thriving is not a personality trait. Because it is comprised of psychosocial characteristics that are changeable within a person, interventions and environmental situations can make a difference. Thriving students are those who are able to experience life's transitions as opportunities that lead to significant personal growth. Yet, they rarely do so without support. Thriving students are typically surrounded by others who are thriving, and are often embedded in a community that provides them with a sense of belonging and competence. The very nature of college demands the successful navigation of a series of changes; thus, the focus of this book is on thriving in transitions.

The purpose of this book is to provide higher education faculty, staff, and administrators with both a deeper understanding of the nature of the transitions that students typically experience and a roadmap for helping them thrive during those transitions and ultimately succeed in life. As a result, each chapter outlines the research about students experiencing a specific type of transition, offering empirical evidence for what contributes to thriving during that period, and also includes practical suggestions for how educators can assist students so they remain fully engaged during difficult times of change.

Because the concept of thriving is a departure from the behaviorally oriented theories that populate the current student success literature, the book opens with an introduction by Jillian Kinzie, who places the student success theories in historical and theoretical context as a foundation for the exploration of thriving. The first two chapters then provide the framework for the book. In chapter 1, Schreiner describes the nature of successful transitions and outlines how the construct of thriving was developed and measured, as well as how it provides a helpful perspective for navigating transitions. In chapter 2, Louis and Schreiner highlight strengths development as the vehicle for helping students thrive in college. They include concrete descriptions of how integrating such a perspective might inform advisors, educators in the classroom, and student affairs professionals. As with each chapter in the book, the authors' focus is on practical strategies that can be implemented on a variety of campuses.

The remainder of the book highlights the successive transitions that students experience while in college. A chapter on the first-year experience by Nelson and Vetter delineates the hurdles students experience as they transition from high school to college, as well as the structures that institutions could put into place to support students during that transition. Paredes-Collins' chapter on students of color highlights the daily transitions that such students experience as they navigate a predominantly White campus. Sriram and Vetter continue the theme of continual transitions as they explore the experiences of high-risk students and what helped them succeed.

Sophomores receive particular attention from Schreiner, Slavin Miller, Pullins, and Seppelt in chapter 6, as the authors use the results of a national study of thousands of sophomores as the basis for their recommendations on how advising, student-faculty interaction, spirituality, and creating a sense of community in the classroom can foster thriving in the sophomore year. Transfer students and their ability to navigate a new institutional system are the focus of quantitative research in chapter 7 by McIntosh and Nelson, followed by Louis and Hulme's chapter describing an extensive qualitative study of high-achieving seniors who were followed into the year after graduation for insights on how such students were able to thrive as they moved from college into life.

The book concludes with a chapter by the editors that synthesizes all the recommendations from each chapter into a roadmap for educators. Recommendations are grouped into three main areas: academic, interpersonal, and intrapersonal thriving. The chapter ends with campuswide recommendations for establishing a culture that is conducive to this holistic vision of student success.

Throughout the book, our purpose is to balance empirical evidence about a wide variety of college-related transitions with practical suggestions for institutions as they help students address the challenges that accompany periods of change. For educational access to translate to student success, the rigorous inquiry described in this volume must be coupled with our best creative thinking to craft targeted solutions that equip all students to succeed. To that end, perhaps the most important principle we offer is that colleges and universities have both the power and the responsibility to help every student thrive.

References

Aud, S., Hussar, W., Planty, M., Snyder, T., Bianco, K., Fox, M., Frohlich, L. . . . Drake, L. (2010). *The Condition of Education 2010* (NCES 2010-028). Washington, DC: National Center for Education Statistics, Institute of Education Sciences, U.S. Department of Education.

Hennessy, E. (2010). *New data indicate educational attainment continues to flat-line.* Retrieved from the American Council on Education website: http://www.acenet.edu/AM/Template.cfm?Section=Search&template=/CM/HTMLDisplay.cfm&ContentID=38696

Kuh, G. D., Kinzie, J., Schuh, J. H., & Whitt, E. J., & Associates. (2005). *Student success in college: Creating conditions that matter.* San Francisco, CA: Jossey-Bass.

Tagg, J. (2003). *The learning paradigm college.* Bolton, MA: Anker Publishing.

Introduction

A New View of Student Success
Jillian Kinzie

Over the last two decades, concern about lagging graduation rates in postsecondary education has captured the attention of researchers and educational policy makers. In an effort to meet President Obama's goal of having the world's best-educated adult population by 2020, the call to increase higher education attainment rates has intensified (Bowen, Chingos, & McPherson, 2009; Nelson, 2010). However, despite increased access to higher education from a broader segment of the U.S. population, baccalaureate degree completion rates have remained below 60% for decades. Within community colleges, the success rate is even lower, as the percentage of students who earn a certificate or degree has hovered around 28% (ACT, 2010). Every year thousands of students withdraw from postsecondary education without completing a degree or certificate program. Moreover, according to the Organization for Economic Cooperation and Development (OECD) report, *Education at a Glance 2010*, which compares the proportion of students who began postsecondary education but did not complete a degree across 18 countries, the United States no longer holds a position of leadership in degree production. It has experienced growth in higher education participation rates, yet completion rates have not kept pace.

The OECD data, coupled with reports from influential higher education organizations such as the Association of American Colleges and Universities (AAC&U), make a strong statement that degree attainment rates are failing to grow fast enough to meet or maintain international economic competitiveness. In addition, the learning outcomes of graduates are not meeting society's needs in basic academic areas or in workforce readiness (AACU, 2002, 2005). These failings do not bode well, given that education beyond high school is now considered essential to earn a middle-class income, and as an increasingly diverse population with a wider range of academic preparation enters higher education. Although the postsecondary system has widened opportunity to numerous students from diverse backgrounds, this increased access has not resulted in higher degree completion rates or a better-educated workforce. Student success remains a vexing challenge in postsecondary education.

With graduation rates continuing to lag despite investments to increase educational attainment, there is a need for fresh thinking about student success. Why have graduation rates remained so stagnant for decades? Who are the culprits of depressed success rates: underprepared or unmotivated students or ineffective pedagogies and underperforming institutions? Is a success orientation something that could be encouraged in a student, or is this an unalterable student trait? Are traditional models of success simply deficient in that they neglect vital aspects of institutional practice, student attributes and behaviors, or emotional or psychological phenomena? Will current models of student success have any relevance for an increasingly diverse student population? Quite simply, what is missing from the extant student success research? There is no shortage of practical (and in some cases impractical) questions regarding the rather persistent need to enhance student success.

The contemporary challenge of student success demands more theorizing, advanced definitions, enriched models, and practical approaches and interventions to help more students succeed. A tall order for sure, but one that can be tackled given some fresh thinking in psychology, new perspectives on personal well-being, and the development of novel tools to assess student success. These fresh perspectives frame student success questions in more productive ways by inviting expansive thinking about the factors that affect student success. It is this evident need for an expanded understanding of student success and the potential of new thinking that is the point of departure for this book.

In the chapters that follow, the authors provide a comprehensive introduction to the notion of *thriving* as a fresh, research-based approach to student success. Conceptualized as optimal functioning in areas believed to contribute to student success and persistence, the concept of thriving emanates from research on psychological well-being and emphasizes the individual motivation and psychological processes that lead to student success behaviors. Borrowing from the field of positive psychology (Keyes & Haidt, 2003), with its emphasis on what contributes to positive individual and community functioning, the concept of thriving proposes to explain the difference between students who flourish in college, those who make the most of campus opportunities and fully invest in learning, compared to students who simply survive college by meeting requirements with a minimal investment in learning (Schreiner, 2010). The stark differences between students who thrive and those who merely survive college are recognizable to most educators in colleges and universities. No doubt, educators have wondered why students who seem to have similar backgrounds and potential for success have qualitatively different experiences at the same institution.

Thriving also draws from psychological models of student retention in higher education. These models propose that personality traits, such as self-efficacy and beliefs about locus of control, help students persevere when faced with academic and social challenges and that their interaction with the institution influences the development of a set of attitudes about being a student. These factors, as well as students' sense of commitment to the institution, result in persistence. The notion of thriving promises to explain the observable differences in how students approach, experience, and persist in college and suggests where theory can aid in the design of interventions to enable a greater percentage of students to thrive in college. Ultimately, thriving promises to make a novel contribution to the contemporary problem of student success.

In *Piecing Together the Student Success Puzzle: Research, Propositions, and Recommendations* (Kuh, Kinzie, Buckley, Bridges, & Hayek, 2007), the psychological perspectives that bear on the topic of student success were briefly introduced while extensive information about the practices that make a difference in student learning and success were presented. The authors of *Thriving in Transitions* add an important piece to the student success puzzle by effectively elaborating the psychological models of student success and demonstrating the power of measuring thriving. Even more, they describe the utility of this information to develop a predictive model for estimating student success and for designing practical educational interventions. Relying on an extensive body of research from Laurie Schreiner's Thriving Project (see www.thrivingincollege.org), this volume fully explores the conceptual foundations for thriving, presents empirical research on the predictors of thriving, and identifies approaches that help students thrive. The notion of thriving is explored in several chapters by examining its relationship to important college transitions, such as the first college year, the sophomore experience, and the transition during the senior year and beyond. The concept is also explored specifically for underserved student populations, including students of color on predominantly White campuses, transfer students, and high-risk students. Each chapter contributes to the development of a more nuanced understanding of thriving and offers practical educational interventions to increase student success.

Before delving fully into the concept of thriving in chapters one through eight, it is important to set the stage for this work and consider the foundational principles of student success upon which the concept of thriving rests and also builds. This opening chapter provides a broad introduction to the topic of student success. It begins by describing the national stage that is the scene for the current focus on student success and outlines some of the challenges associated with this emphasis. The theoretical constructions for traditional definitions of student success are then briefly discussed, and the frameworks for alternative models of student success are reviewed to provide a context for conceptualizing thriving as a new view of student success. The introductory chapter closes with a discussion of the ways in which the concept of thriving complements and extends existing research on student success and considers where this new view may lead us, given current and future concerns in post-secondary education.

Student Success as Degree Completion

The current national goal for a greater percentage of students to earn a college degree is ambitious. The combination of presidential mandate, rising concerns about college affordability, and stagnant graduation rates at the same time a college education is deemed essential to earning places significant pressure on administrators, educators, and policy makers to reduce the barriers to student success.

The contemporary emphasis on increasing educational attainment rates illustrates the most basic definition of student success: enabling students to gain access to college and complete a certificate or degree. Increasing the rate of college survival, or what institutions outside the United States often refer to as *throughput*, is the basis of arguments that emphasize increasing access, enrollment, and persistence (Bowen et al., 2009; Hauptman, 2007). In this definition, student success is equated with graduation.

The roots of student success theories are thus anchored in models of student persistence and graduation, as this definition of student success is foundational to all subsequent definitions. The conceptual framework for student success developed out of practical needs when campus administrators in the 1970s were generally concerned about students who departed, and in the

1980s when they realized that it was in their best interest to intensify efforts to retain and graduate the qualified students who had matriculated at their institutions. These interests led to research exposing the broad, complicated set of factors that interact to influence persistence. The persistence theories that have formed the basis of perspectives on student success reflect several different disciplinary frameworks, notably sociological, economic, organizational development, and psychological. This work is heavily based on Tinto's (1975) model of student integration, Braxton's (2000) framework of college student departure, and the economic models of St. John, Cabrera, Nora, and Asker (2000). Although all of these models address factors that influence a student to stay in college, they do so through competing explanations.

Sociological perspectives were evident among the first persistence theories. These theories generally involve a search for commonalities of behavior that distinguish groups of students who remain enrolled in an institution from groups of students who leave. They also emphasize an array of academic and social interactions that can be "portrayed generally as the notions of academic or social engagement or the extent to which students become involved in (Astin, 1985a) or integrated (Tinto, 1975, 1993) into their institution's academic and social systems" (Pascarella & Terenzini, 2005, p. 425). By far the most widely adopted sociological model is Tinto's (1975, 1993) interactionalist theory of retention that asserts student success is based on student-institution fit influenced by two independent, but complementary processes—academic and social integration—by which students adjust to college life. Academic integration represents the extent to which a student adapts to explicit norms, such as earning passing grades, and the regularizing academic experiences and values of the institution, while social integration represents the extent to which a student finds the institution's social environment to be agreeable with his or her preferences. Student persistence is a function of the quality of the relationships between the student and other actors within the college and their home community, and their integration with academic norms. Students most likely to persist are those whose values, norms, and behaviors are congruent with the dominant patterns on campus (Berger & Milem, 1999). Increased levels of academic and social integration are presumed to lead to greater commitment to the institution and to the goal of graduation (Tinto, 1993). These commitments, in turn, increase the likelihood a student will persist to graduate.

The second perspective dominating student persistence studies emphasizes an economic point of view. The primary determinants of persistence in
studies that employ an economic perspective include financial need, student
aid packaging, and adequacy of aid (Cabrera, Nora, & Castaneda, 1992;
St. John, Paulsen, & Starkey, 1996). Research using this approach has focused
on the overall effect of financial aid on persistence, the sensitivity of persistence decisions to grants, loans, and other forms of financial assistance, and
the effectiveness of different student aid packages in the retention of underrepresented students (St. John et al., 2000).

An economic perspective is also evident in retention theories that emphasize
the extent to which students consider the costs and benefits of staying in college and participating in various activities. These *price-response theories* focus
in part on students' analyses of the social and economic benefits of attending
college compared to the costs and benefits associated with alternative choices,
such as working full-time (St. John et al., 2000). If students perceive that the
cost of staying in school or becoming involved in educational activities, such
as a first-year seminar, internship, or study abroad, outweighs the return on
investment, they may forgo the opportunity and leave college prematurely
(Braxton, Hirschy, & McClendon, 2004). Although the economic perspective
has contributed to a deeper understanding of student persistence decisions, it
neglects the role that the institution and campus actors play in shaping those
decisions. Factors such as student support systems, interaction with faculty,
and affective outcomes associated with college, which are known to play a
role in student persistence (Pascarella & Terenzini, 1991, 2005), are rarely
represented in economic models.

Organizational perspectives that emphasize the institutional structures
and processes influencing student behaviors also inform the retention theories
that are foundational to any conceptualization of student success. Basic institutional features, such as enrollment, selectivity, residential facilities, campus
climate, and faculty-student ratio, shape students' attitudes and behaviors
(Pike & Kuh, 2005). From this perspective, a student's beliefs are affected by
experiences with the institution, which then evolve into attitudes about the
institution and ultimately determine a student's sense of belonging or fit. The
organizational perspective advances the idea that institutional structures and
processes, combined with students' perceptions of the fairness of institutional
policies and the responsiveness of faculty and staff members, affect decisions
to persist or leave the institution.

The final perspective employed in student success studies emanates from psychological theories. This focus views student persistence and success as largely influenced by students' individual attributes, perceptions, beliefs, coping skills, levels of motivation, and interactions with other members of the campus community. Psychological theories of motivation, attribution, and self-efficacy are foundational to this perspective.

Students' motivations are integral to psychological perspectives of college persistence. Ethington's (1990) model of persistence is rooted in expectancy-value theory (Eccles, 1987), the premise of which is that students' expectations of success combine with the extent to which they value the goal of degree completion to produce differing levels of motivation that determine the amount of effort they invest in the college experience. What students generally expect to happen when they enter college shapes their subsequent behaviors in college, which in turn affects their academic performance and social adjustment to college life (Howard, 2005; Kuh, 1999).

Students' levels of self-efficacy (Bandura, 1982), or belief in their ability to succeed in college, affect these postsecondary expectations, as does their sense of academic control (Perry, Hall, & Ruthig, 2005). Students who perceive the outcomes of academic tasks and challenges to be under their own control, rather than a function of luck or powerful others, are also more motivated to engage in the academic environment and invest the necessary effort to succeed. According to attribution theory (Wiener, 1985), those who are most likely to persist are those who attribute their failures to a lack of effort rather than ability. In the case of college students, this attribution enables them to seek new strategies and invest greater effort when they face challenges, so that they eventually complete a college degree.

Bean and Eaton's (2000) psychological model of college student retention incorporates these theories into a comprehensive portrait of student persistence. In their model, students' personalities, skills and abilities, beliefs, and motivation to attend college combine with their levels of self-efficacy, attribution, and coping skills at entrance to college to create a predisposition toward persistence or departure. Then, as a consequence of students' interactions with others on and off campus, their attitudes and sense of institutional fit are shaped. If the interactions bolster students' self-efficacy, increase their confidence, motivation, and internal attributions of control, and reduce their stress levels, academic and social integration are more likely to occur, producing a greater sense of institutional fit and loyalty, leading to a higher likelihood of persistence.

A psychological perspective of student success provides the conceptual underpinnings of the construct of thriving as a new way of defining student success (Schreiner, 2010). The concept of thriving explored in this book is rooted in the field of positive psychology, which emphasizes well-being and positive functioning, with specific connections to the construct of flourishing (Keyes & Haidt, 2003) that is manifested through positive relationships, rising to meet personal challenges, and engagement with the world (Schreiner, McIntosh, Nelson & Pothoven, 2009). This perspective expands on theories of motivation and individual psychological processes that can be influenced by practices at the individual, classroom, and programmatic levels, enabling more students to flourish in college. It also emphasizes the differential effects of interventions on student success. More specifically, it advances a measure of students' positive functioning in three key areas that are typically associated with student persistence: academic engagement and performance, interpersonal relationships, and intrapersonal well-being. The construct is somewhat more expansive than other psychological theories of student success because the measures of thriving involve individual attitudes; aspects of cognition and learning, such as self-regulation; and also students' experiences, interactions, and perceptions of the campus community.

Taken together, the different theoretical perspectives on student persistence account for most of the key factors that shape what students are prepared to do when they enter college, how they respond to the college environment once enrolled, and the meaning they make of their experiences. However, each perspective has its shortcomings in terms of advancing an understanding of student success. In fact, no one theoretical perspective can adequately account for all the factors that influence success in college. Instead, contemporary theories must incorporate a range of perspectives to address the complexities of student success and inform practice and policy on students' behalf.

Frameworks for Student Success

Although equating student success with increased completion rates is straightforward and essential to address current concerns, it also limited, offering little insight into the complexities of success. With its focus on the percentage of students who persist at a specific institution from year to year, along with grade point average as an intermediate marker of their progress to graduation (Venezia, Callan, Finney, Kirst, & Usdan, 2005), this definition conceptualizes the problem simply as reversing the dropout rate and increasing completion rates. Unfortunately, it also leads to the position that the easiest way to improve graduation rates is for colleges and universities to be more selective. Indeed, research demonstrates that students with certain characteristics, such as those who have strong high schools records, come from higher income families, and attend full time, are more likely to graduate (Adelman, 1999, 2006). However, such an approach of only admitting students whose background characteristics predispose them to graduate would not only fail to help the United States reach its ambitious goals for more adults with postsecondary credentials, but it also contradicts all the efforts to expand college access to a wider range of students.

The laser focus on completion may also overshadow other important college processes and outcomes, including the quality of students' experiences in undergraduate education, student behaviors and level of engagement in educationally purposeful activities, learning outcome attainment, preparation for the world of work and lifelong learning, personal growth and development, and many other desirable outcomes of college. The singular concentration on graduation rates also provides limited insight into the full scope of what may be contributing to lagging completion rates and, more importantly, what action should be taken to improve student success. Finally, the emphasis on simple survival to degree can eclipse important quality educational experiences that engage students at high levels and help them make the most of their college experience.

Although the current focus on increasing college completion rates is important, to make a real difference in a wider range of student success goals in U.S. postsecondary education, there is a need for more expansive and actionable definitions of student success. Expanded definitions still include graduation rates, but they also consider the attainment of other desirable outcomes and aspects of the educational experience itself. More specifically, expanded definitions attend to issues of the quality of the experience and the content of the learning environment, student perceptions and behaviors, the attainment of educational and personal objectives, what students accomplish, and how they develop while in college. Finally, these expanded views and definitions of student success must also help guide and inform action to improve such success.

Definitions of student success that move beyond the fundamental benchmarks of college completion rates and grades have emerged in recent years. Such expanded definitions have included learning gains, talent development, satisfaction and sense of belonging, and student engagement. The emphasis on student learning gains, for instance, has emphasized a definition of success focused on the attainment of various intellectual, personal, and social development outcomes, such as becoming proficient in writing, speaking clearly, and developing critical thinking skills. The attention to the attainment of particular educational goals is foremost on the agenda of many educators and organizations, including the Association of American Colleges and Universities (AAC&U, 2002, 2005). An emphasis on educational gains and learning outcomes as determinants of student success is emblematic of a learning-centered focus in higher education, which highlights conditions that produce learning. For example, in the learning paradigm college (Tagg, 2003), the focus is on ensuring the quality of exiting students and their learning skills. In this framework, student success results when colleges and universities develop students' talents and habits for learning and is gauged by the extent to which student learning is advanced.

Astin (1985a) advanced a theory of talent development that emphasized the institution's role in promoting student learning and success as a key aspect of student success in college. A talent development view emphasizes the educational impact of the institution on students and the extent to which the institution is able to enhance students' intellectual and scholarly talents to make a positive difference in their lives. This view of student success recognizes that every student can learn under the right conditions; therefore, the institution must organize its resources and create conditions for teaching and learning to optimize success. Ultimately, the talent development view is about increasing the institution's commitment to developing the student to his or her full potential.

This view of student success as developing student talent and potential has particular relevance to assuring success for an increasingly diverse student population. Such an approach emphasizes the need to embrace and address students' diverse talents and needs (Chickering, 2006). In this view, all students' talents and skills are considered *assets* rather than deficiencies. By adopting a talent development perspective and taking into account the backgrounds and characteristics of students, institutions develop approaches that are more responsive to the diverse learning needs of students historically underserved in higher education.

Students' perceptions of their experience in college, and specifically their sense of belonging and satisfaction, are also critical dimensions of student success. Astin (1993) proposed that an important aspect of student success is the extent to which students are satisfied with their educational experience and feel comfortable and affirmed in the learning environment. This definition supports the view that students' impressions of institutional quality, the degree to which they feel a sense of belonging and support in the college environment, their willingness to attend the institution again, and their overall satisfaction with their experiences are precursors of educational attainment and critical dimensions of student success (Strauss & Volkwein, 2002; Tinto, 1993).

Student engagement is another aspect of student success that has received considerable attention in recent years (Kuh, 2001, 2003; Pascarella & Terenzini, 2005). A substantial body of research indicates that once students start college, a key factor to whether they will persist and thrive in college is the extent to which they participate in educationally effective activities that have been empirically demonstrated to contribute to their learning, personal development, and eventual success and persistence (Kuh, 2001, 2003). The concept of student engagement originates from Pace's (1982) measures of quality of effort and Astin's (1985b) theory of involvement and represents two key components (Kuh, 2001). The first is the amount of time and effort students put into their studies and additional activities, leading to the experiences and outcomes that characterize student success. The second component of this perspective of student engagement is how institutions of higher education allocate their human and other resources and organize learning opportunities and services to encourage students to participate in and benefit from such activities. Because colleges and universities have control over the institutional conditions and practices that foster student success, this second dimension of engagement represents a point of influence for institutions.

The emphasis on the institutional perspective of student success is important. It has been argued that many more students would persist and succeed if colleges and universities intentionally and strategically designed themselves to promote greater student success (Kuh, Kinzie, Schuh, Whitt, & Associates, 2005). Quite simply, although student background characteristics influence persistence and completion rates as well as other college outcomes, engagement in specific educational practices increases the probability of success for all students. Essentially, successful students persist, benefit in desired ways from their college experiences, are satisfied with college, and graduate. In addition, the perspective appropriately places greater onus for student success on institutional conditions and action, rather than ascribing all the responsibility for success to students.

Another important consideration in the student engagement perspective on student success is that engagement does not happen the same way for all students. Research by Harper and Quaye (2009) and Bensimon (2007) elaborate the needs of historically underrepresented students in higher education and expose some of the problematic engagement trends among these populations. Views of student engagement and success must be expanded to examine differences among student populations and advocate for the creation of conditions in the learning environment that take into account the particular needs of diverse student populations. To address the contemporary challenges of student success, institutions must be intentional about creating educationally engaging learning environments for all students.

The aforementioned perspectives on student success are well established in the literature, and there is wide agreement on their practical importance. Notably, in recent years new elements of student success have emerged, representing novel dimensions, variations on common indicators, and harder to measure ineffable qualities. Examples of such indicators are an appreciation for human differences, commitment to democratic values, a capacity to work effectively with people from different backgrounds to solve problems, information literacy, and a well-developed sense of identity (AAC&U, 2002). Although degree attainment will likely remain the definitive measure of student success, strategies for advancing educational attainment are dependent on expanded definitions of success.

Expanded Views of Student Success

One of the objectives of the National Postsecondary Education Cooperative (NPEC), an organization of the U.S. Department of Education, is to advance the quality, comparability, and utility of postsecondary data and information to support federal, state, and institutional policy development. In 2006, NPEC sponsored a forum for exchanging ideas about what constitutes student success and what factors impact the chances of success for different types of students in various types of postsecondary institutions. This event and the research publications emerging from the project offered new perspectives, highlighted the multidimensional issue of student success, and offered distinct definitions, revealing the varied nature of the concept of postsecondary student success (see www.nces.ed.gov/npec/papers.asp for commissioned papers). Each of the major papers for the NPEC project adopted a different viewpoint to address the question, What is student success? In this section, the key points from these papers are summarized.

The new definition of student success offered by Kuh et al. (2007) is broad: academic achievement; engagement in educationally purposeful activities; satisfaction; acquisition of desired knowledge, skills, and competencies; persistence; attainment of educational objectives; and postcollege performance. The authors also proposed a depiction of the route to student success as a wide path that begins with students' precollege experiences; then moves into the college experience itself, which includes two central features: students' behaviors and institutional conditions; and ends with desired outcomes and postcollege indicators of student success. In contrast to the traditional educational pipeline image, this framework acknowledges the twists, turns, detours, roundabouts, and occasional dead ends that many students encounter in their college experience. This framework for student success also emphasizes the actions that institutions and other organizations associated with postsecondary education must take to improve student success.

Perna and Thomas (2008) specified student success as a generic term for an array of milestones ranging from middle school into adulthood. The authors reviewed literature on student success across four disciplines—economics, education, psychology, and sociology—and organized success into a chronological map of four transitions: (a) college readiness, (b) college enrollment, (c) college achievement, and (d) postcollege attainment. Their report develops a conceptual model to guide policy makers, practitioners, and researchers in their efforts to reduce gaps in success across income, class, and racial-ethnic groups. The model suggests that one of the key steps to close the gap in student success must include recognition that student success is a longitudinal process shaped by multiple levels of context.

Braxton (2008) explained that student retention and graduation are markers of student success, yet the meaning of student success extends beyond these two well-recognized indicators. He identified eight domains of college student success: (a) academic attainment, (b) acquisition of general education, (c) development of academic competence, (c) development of cognitive skills and intellectual dispositions, (e) occupational attainment, (f) preparation for adulthood and citizenship, (g) personal accomplishments, and (h) personal development. These domains reveal the multiple ways for postsecondary students to demonstrate success and suggest that if a student achieves any of these, some degree of success has been attained. Braxton's definition of student success also focused on course-based student learning as the fundamental factor in college outcomes.

Feldman, Smart, and Ethington (2008) adopted a view of student success informed by Holland's (1997) person-environment fit theory to argue for the importance of judging student success within a particular context, namely the college major. They asserted that academic environments within colleges and universities are an essential component in understanding student success. Academic environments influence student learning; however, these authors maintain that all environments can be equally successful in promoting student learning, whether students' personalities are congruent or incongruent with those environments. This finding is instructive since it is grounded in a more developmentally and futuristically oriented perspective based on the competencies and interests that students desire to develop as a result of their collegiate experiences. It suggests that student performance and ultimate success must be judged in relation to students' possession of the interests, abilities, and values that the respective academic environments seek to reinforce and reward.

Finally, Tinto and Pusser (2006) advanced an expanded persistence view of student success defined as the completion of a college degree with responsibility to enhance student persistence and degree completion, particularly of students from low-income backgrounds, resting with the institution. They argue for an institutional view and suggest that each student exists in a particular context that shapes his or her probability of succeeding in higher education. Their focus is primarily on institutional action; therefore, they outline the university conditions that are needed to promote success. They explore aspects of the institutional environment that are within the capacity of institutions to change, but they also emphasize the impact of state policies on student success.

A prominent theme across the NPEC-produced research is that the impact of collegiate experiences is conditional, as these experiences interact with each student's economic circumstances, social and cultural milieu, and attitudes and values. In addition, despite the extensive body of research on student persistence and success, it remains challenging to translate what we know about student success into forms of knowledge that institutions and states can use to direct their actions. It is also clear that no single program or well-crafted policy can increase educational success to the level that is required. It will take a systemic solution, the coordinated efforts of many educators and educational services, all focused on student success.

What Does Thriving Contribute to Student Success?

Given the strong demand from various sectors to demonstrate evidence of student success beyond completion rates, it is not surprising that multiple definitions exist and that new constructions continue to emerge. The concept of thriving offers a new vision of student success. It extends existing definitions and research by focusing on the quality of students' experiences in postsecondary education and the impact those experiences have on life outside and beyond college. It also adds to the psychosocial dimensions of success by considering the internal psychological lens through which students view the world and, hence, their experience in postsecondary education. This approach advances the identification of the psychosocial processes within students that are most predictive of their academic success and persistence, with the ultimate aim of using this perspective to design interventions to help students get the most out of their college experience. In addition, while thriving makes an obvious contribution to increasing students' abilities to maximize their college experience on an individual level, it can also have an effect on institutional outcomes by increasing overall levels of student persistence and success.

Thriving is another view of student success that encourages thinking beyond grades, retention, and graduation as the measures of success. Specifically, it offers a holistic construct that incorporates both cognitive and psychosocial components. This view is consistent with current perspectives about college outcomes that emphasize learning gains and broader societal expectations of college graduates, including civic engagement, commitment to community welfare, and lifelong learning.

The construct of thriving also moves beyond conceptions of student success that emphasize the influence of student backgrounds and experiences prior to college. Although research demonstrating the relationship between characteristics such as precollege preparation, high school grades, and socioeconomic status and college outcomes is robust, Schreiner (2010) posits that once levels of thriving are factored into the equation, students' backgrounds are not as important to understanding their success as is individual motivation and psychological processes. Her research demonstrated that students who were connected to others and were investing effort in the learning experience, regardless of their entry characteristics, were achieving higher grades and greater learning gains and were experiencing more success in college than peers of similar backgrounds. This finding is critically important, given that more students than ever before arrive at college with several of the classic predictors of premature departure from college. Even more, it suggests the potential for increasing all students' likelihood of success by designing interventions to enable them to thrive.

Thriving also expands on the popular notion of student engagement as an approach to student success. Although being engaged at high levels in educationally purposeful activities is associated with student success, thriving emphasizes the value of exploring the psychological processes that contribute to high levels of engagement and are in turn affected by that engagement. For example, information about students' psychological perspectives and attitudes, such as their sense of academic determination, positive perspective, and social connectedness, could help explain differential levels of student engagement and also help campus administrators and educators address student attitudes and perspectives that might influence their engagement in educationally purposeful activities. Combining the psychosocial elements of thriving with the behavioral and institutional aspects of student engagement creates a powerful model for understanding student success in college.

Finally, the most important aspect of all expanded definitions of student success, and particularly thriving, is the extent to which they stimulate action to enhance student learning and development in college, and ultimately, degree attainment The components of thriving are all amenable to change within students and open to intervention at the campus level rather than fixed traits with no potential for influence. As a result, knowledge of student thriving levels can help guide programming and services to increase student success. The ultimate goal of the thriving perspective is to inspire interventions that enable more students to flourish during their college years and beyond.

Conclusion

American higher education is changing dramatically as an increasingly diverse population enters college. This change provides an exciting opportunity to strengthen the potential of colleges and universities to enhance success for all students. If goals for increased college completion rates are to be reached, new models of success must address issues related to the diverse nature of students and move beyond traditional views of student success. Although it is important to attend to retention and graduation rates as measures of success, greater attention must be given to the quality of students' experience that fosters or hinders their success. New visions of success can also motivate new strategies to assist students. Visions of student success such as those represented by the thriving perspective demonstrate the potential for more students to succeed in college and suggest the campus interventions needed to support such success. Too much attention to simple measures of college completion has the potential to distract from the important work of ensuring educational quality and vibrant learning experiences that enrich students' time in college. Quite simply, there is much more to a successful college experience than earning a degree, and we must fully invest in optimizing that for all students.

References

ACT. (2010). *National collegiate retention and persistence to degree rates*. Retrieved from http://www.act.org/policymakers/pdf/retain_2010.pdf

Adelman, C. (1999). *Answers in the toolbox: Academic intensity, attendance patterns, and bachelor's degree attainment*. Washington, DC: National Center for Education Statistics.

Adelman, C. (2006). *The toolbox revisited: Paths to degree completion from high school through college*. Washington, DC: U.S. Department of Education.

Association of American Colleges & Universities (AAC&U). (2002). *Greater expectations: A new vision for learning as a nation goes to college*. Washington, DC: Author.

Association of American Colleges & Universities (AAC&U). (2005). *Liberal education outcomes: A preliminary report on student achievement in college*. Washington, DC: Author.

Astin, A. W. (1985a). *Achieving educational excellence*. San Francisco, CA: Jossey-Bass.

Astin, A. W. (1985b). Involvement: The cornerstone of excellence. *Change, 17*, 35-39.

Astin, A. W. (1993). *What matters in college? Four critical years revisited*. San Francisco, CA: Jossey-Bass.

Bandura, A. (1982). Self-efficacy mechanism in human agency. *American Psychologist, 37*, 122-147.

Bean, J. P., & Eaton, S. (2000). A psychological model of college student retention. In J. M. Braxton (Ed.), *Reworking the departure puzzle: New theory and research on college student retention* (pp. 73-89). Nashville, TN: Vanderbilt University Press.

Bensimon, E. M. (2007). The underestimated significance of practitioner knowledge in the scholarship on student success. *Review of Higher Education, 30*(4), 441-469.

Berger, J. B., & Milem, J. F. (1999). The role of student involvement and perceptions of integration in a causal model of student persistence. *Research in Higher Education, 40*(6), 641-664.

Bowen, W. G., Chingos, M. M., & McPherson, M. S. (2009). *Crossing the finish line: Completing college at America's public universities*. Princeton, NJ: Princeton University Press.

Braxton, J. M. (2008). Toward a theory of faculty professional choices that foster college student success. In J. C. Smart (Ed.), *Higher education: A handbook of theory and research* (Vol. 23, pp. 181-207). Dordrecht, The Netherlands: Springer.

Braxton, J. M. (Ed.). (2000). *Reworking the student departure puzzle*. Nashville, TN: Vanderbilt University Press.

Braxton, J. M., Hirschy, A. S., & McClendon, S. A. (2004). *Understanding and reducing college student departure* (ASHE-ERIC Higher Education Report, Vol. 30, No. 3). San Francisco, CA: Jossey-Bass.

Cabrera, A. E., Nora, A., & Castaneda, M. B. (1992). The role of finances in the persistence process: A structural model. *Research in Higher Education, 33*(5), 571-593.

Chickering, A. W. (2006). Creating conditions so every student can learn. *About Campus, 11*(2), 9-15.

Eccles, J. S. (1987). Gender roles and women's achievement-related decisions. *Psychology of Women Quarterly, 11*(2), 135-172.

Ethington, C. A. (1990). A psychological model of student persistence. *Research in Higher Education, 31*, (3), 279-293.

Feldman, K. A., Smart, J. C., & Ethington, C. A. (2008). Using Holland's theory to study patterns of college student success. In J. C. Smart (Ed.), *Higher education: Handbook of theory and research* (Vol. 23, pp. 329-380). Dordrecht, The Netherlands: Springer.

Harper, S. R., & Quaye, S. J. (Eds). (2009). *Student engagement in higher education: Theoretical perspectives and practical approaches for diverse populations*. New York, NY: Routledge.

Hauptman, A. M. (2007). *Strategies for improving student success in post-secondary education*. Boulder, CO: Western Interstate Commission for Higher Education.

Holland, J. L. (1997). *Making vocational choices: A theory of vocational personalities and work environments* (3rd ed.). Odessa, FL: Psychological Assessment Resources.

Howard, J. A. (2005). Why should we care about student expectations? In T. E. Miller, B. E. Bender, & J. H. Schuh (Eds.), *Promoting reasonable expectations: Aligning student and institutional views of the college experience* (pp. 10-33). San Francisco, CA: Jossey-Bass.

Keyes, C. M., & Haidt, J. (Eds). (2003). *Flourishing: Positive psychology and the life well-lived*. Washington DC: American Psychological Association.

Kuh, G. D. (1999). Setting the bar high to promote student learning. In G. S. Blimling, E. J. Whitt, & Associates (Eds.), *Good practice in student affairs: Principles to foster student learning* (pp. 67-90). San Francisco, CA: Jossey-Bass.

Kuh, G. D. (2001). Assessing what really matters to student learning: Inside the National Survey of Student Engagement. *Change, 33*(3), 10-17, 66.

Kuh, G. D. (2003). What we're learning about student engagement from NSSE. *Change, 35*(2), 24-32.

Kuh, G. D., Kinzie, J., Buckley, J., Bridges, B. K., & Hayek, J. C. (2007). *Piecing together the student success puzzle: Research, propositions, and recommendations* (ASHE Higher Education Report, No. 32). San Francisco, CA: Jossey-Bass.

Kuh, G., Kinzie, J., Schuh, J., Whitt, E., & Associates. (2005). *Student success in college: Creating conditions that matter.* San Francisco, CA: Jossey-Bass.

Nelson, L. (2010, March 2). 17 states pledge to increase graduation rates, joining a new national effort. *Chronicle of Higher Education.* Retrieved from http://chronicle.com/article/17-States-Pledge-to-Increase/64443/

Organization for Economic Cooperation and Development (OECD). (2010), *Education at a glance 2010: OECD indicators,* OECD Publishing. doi: 10.1787/eag-2010-en

Pace, C. R. (1982). *Achievement and the quality of student effort.* Washington, DC: National Commission on Excellence in Education.

Pascarella, P. T., & Terenzini, E. T. (1991). *How college affects students.* San Francisco, CA: Jossey-Bass.

Pascarella, P. T., & Terenzini, E. T. (2005). *How college affects students: A third decade of research.* San Francisco, CA: Jossey-Bass.

Perna, L. W., & Thomas, S. L. (2008). *Theoretical perspectives on student success: Understanding the contributions of the disciplines* (ASHE Higher Education Report 34.1). San Francisco, CA: Jossey-Bass.

Perry, R. P., Hall, N. C., & Ruthig, J. C. (2005). Perceived (academic) control and scholastic attainment in higher education. In J. C. Smart (Ed.), *Higher education: Handbook of theory and research* (Vol. 20, pp. 363-436). Norwell, MA: Springer.

Pike, G. R., & Kuh, G. D. (2005). A typology of student engagement for American colleges and universities. *Research in Higher Education, 46*(2), 185-209.

Schreiner, L. A. (2010, May/June). The "Thriving Quotient": A new vision for student success. *About Campus, 15*(2), 2-10.

Schreiner, L. A., McIntosh, E. J., Nelson, D., & Pothoven, S. (2009). *The Thriving Quotient: Advancing the assessment of student success.* Paper presented at the annual meeting of the Association for the Study of Higher Education. Vancouver, Canada.

St. John, E. R., Cabrera, A. E., Nora, A., & Asker, E. H. (2000). Economic influences on persistence reconsidered: How can finance research inform the reconceptualization of persistence models. In J. M. Braxton (Ed.), *Reworking the student departure puzzle* (pp. 29-47). Nashville, TN: Vanderbilt University Press.

St. John, E. R, Paulsen, M. B., & Starkey, J. B. (1996). The nexus between college choice and persistence. *Research in Higher Education 37*(2), 175-220.

Strauss, L. C., & Volkwein, J. F. (2002). Comparing student performance and growth in 2- and 4-year institutions. *Research in Higher Education, 43*(2), 133-161.

Tagg, J. (2003). *The learning paradigm college.* Boston, MA: Anker Publishing.

Tinto, V. (1975). Dropout from higher education: A theoretical synthesis of recent research. *Review of Educational Research, 45*, 89-125.

Tinto, V. (1993). *Leaving college: Rethinking the causes and cures of student attrition* (2nd ed.). Chicago, IL: University of Chicago Press.

Tinto, V., & Pusser, B. (2006). *Moving from theory to action: Building a model of institutional action for student success.* Washington, DC: National Postsecondary Education Cooperative, Department of Education.

Venezia, A., Callan, P. M., Finney, J. E., Kirst, M. W., & Usdan, M. D. (2005, September). *The governance divide: A report on a four-state study on improving college readiness and success.* San Jose, CA: The Institute for Educational Leadership, the National Center for Public Policy and Higher Education, and the Stanford Institute for Higher Education Research.

Weiner, B. (1985). An attribution theory of achievement motivation and emotion. *Psychological Review, 92*(4), 548-573.

Chapter 1

From Surviving to Thriving During Transitions
Laurie A. Schreiner

The college years are full of transitions. First-year students move from the structured environment of high school to the bewildering array of choices in a college or university. Sophomores transition from the visible support of the first-year experience to a year in which there is little tangible support from the institution and the academic requirements have increased significantly. Students transferring into an institution transition from the familiar processes of their former college or university into a new system with unfamiliar bureaucratic structures. Students choosing a major—or changing a major—transition from one discipline's way of viewing the world to the perspectives, expectations, and vocabulary of a new discipline. Additional transitions occur as those who have lived on campus move off campus, as each new course begins, and as responsibilities and freedoms shift with workloads and family obligations. The ultimate transition occurs as graduating seniors prepare to enter the world beyond college.

In each of these transitions, there is opportunity for growth. Times of transition can be positive experiences that involve movement toward one's full potential, but they can also be negative experiences that shatter a student's confidence or lead to disengagement from the environment (Goodman, Schlossberg, & Anderson, 2006). The pivotal force of these pervasive transitions is why they are a central focus of this book. Successful transitions are integral to a student's ability to complete and benefit from a college education, and many of the students who choose to leave college do so during transition periods. For students from high-risk backgrounds or from populations historically underserved by higher education, transition is an almost daily occurrence as they constantly move in and out of differing subcultures and environments.

1

These students in particular deserve attention, as many of the programs and services developed to help them succeed in college have not been effective (Attewell, Lavin, Domina, & Levey, 2006).

The traditional view of student success (i.e., graduation and GPA) that Kinzie outlined in the introduction has not provided higher education with an effective repertoire of interventions to enable more students to reach their educational goals. Instead, a broader vision for student success is needed, one that incorporates all the dimensions articulated by Kuh, Kinzie, Schuh, Whitt, and Associates (2005): "satisfaction, persistence, and high levels of learning and personal development" (p. xiv). The construct of *thriving* provides a new and more expansive perspective of student success by focusing not only on academic success, but also on the relationships, perspectives, and psychological well-being that allow students to gain maximum benefit from their college experience (Schreiner, 2010b). Because thriving is characterized by aspects of a student's experiences or perspectives that are amenable to change, there is enormous potential for institutions to design interventions that will enable a greater number of students to succeed.

In this chapter, the nature of transitions and why they are critical junctures for student success will be discussed in greater detail. Characteristics of successful transitions will be explored, and the construct of thriving will be described as a conceptualization of student success that holds promise for enabling more students to experience successful transitions during the college years and be prepared for the further transitions of life. Institutional efforts to intervene in ways that promote thriving will be highlighted as effective strategies for assisting students in transition.

The Nature of Transitions

All transitions involve change—change from the familiar to the unknown. As psychologists have noted for generations (Selye, 1976), anytime a person encounters change, whether minor or significant, he or she experiences a stress reaction. Thus, another aspect common to all transitions is that they produce stress in the persons experiencing them. Stress researchers have found, however, that not all people respond in the same way to the stressors in their lives; the key element is how positively or negatively the person perceives the event, which is determined by his or her cognitive appraisal of the situation (Lazarus, 1998). Schlossberg (1989), in her original conceptualization of transition theory within a higher education context, supports this view as she defines student transitions as influenced by perceptions. Each student responds differently in transitions, adjusts to the required change at varying rates, and experiences growth or decline primarily as a function of his or her perceptions and the quality of support provided during the transition.

Schlossberg (1989) originally presented her transition theory in the context of adult students returning to college, yet the principles she outlines apply to students regardless of their age or stage in life. Transition begins with an event or nonevent that is perceived as significant by the student: something occurs that was either anticipated or unexpected, or a significant event that was expected to happen does not. As a result, relationships, roles, life routines, and ways of seeing the world begin to change. The impact of such inherently stressful changes depends on the ratio of the student's assets and liabilities at the time, as well as whether there are single or multiple changes occurring simultaneously. A student with a strong repertoire of coping skills and a significant support system who perceives the changes as a necessary part of a positive new future will experience a less traumatic stress reaction than will a student who lacks adequate coping skills and sufficient support.

Although transitions begin with a single event or nonevent, dealing with a transition is a process that extends over time. Goodman et al. (2006) refer to the process as a series of phases they label *moving in, moving through,* and *moving out.* For example, first-year students transitioning from high school to college experience multiple changes in roles, routines, and relationships that continue throughout the first semester and even through the first year. How students respond to these changes depends on two aspects of what psychologists call cognitive appraisal: their primary and secondary appraisal (Lazarus & Folkman, 1984).

Primary cognitive appraisal is how one views the transition itself: Is it positive, negative, or irrelevant? When a transition is viewed as a positive opportunity, students are more likely to use what Bean and Eaton (2000) refer to as *approach* coping skills—seeking out information and assistance, engaging with support systems, and investing effort and energy in the transition activities. In contrast, those who perceive a transition as negative are more likely to engage in *avoidance* coping mechanisms—denying the need for help or information; avoiding the situation; and using alcohol, sleep, or other distracting activities to escape from the transition events.

Secondary cognitive appraisal occurs after a student has determined whether the transition is positive, negative, or irrelevant. This appraisal is a self-assessment of one's resources for coping with the change as it occurs: Does one have the information, support, and coping skills needed to handle the transition? A student's sense of control over the situation is paramount throughout the cognitive appraisal process. When students feel they have some degree of control during a transition, they are far more likely to utilize healthy coping skills and problem-solving strategies and to remain engaged with their changing circumstances in positive ways (Perry, Hall, & Ruthig, 2005).

Successful transitions thus have five hallmarks that distinguish them from unsuccessful transitions: (a) students perceive them positively as opportunities for growth; (b) students use healthy coping skills during the transition to approach the transitional activities rather than avoid them; (c) students believe they have the support they need to move through the transition successfully; (d) students access resources during the transition for relevant information, assistance, and support; and (e) students emerge from the transition having grown in personally significant ways. The construct of thriving, with its expanded perspective on student success, offers a framework for helping students move successfully through transition periods in college in ways that further their growth and enable them to benefit more fully from their college experience.

Thriving as an Expanded Vision for Student Success

The construct of thriving was developed in response to the current focus on graduation rates as the ultimate measure of student success in higher education. Although graduation is an important outcome indicative of student success, its very nature as an event that either does or does not occur conveys a survival perspective. College graduates are those who have survived the college experience. Yet there are broader qualitative outcomes of the college experience that have been overlooked in this perspective—aspects of personal growth, healthy relationships, connections to a broader community, and ways of seeing the world that enable the student to gain maximum benefit from both the college experience and life after college. Thriving implies more than just surviving in the college environment; it conveys that a student is fully engaged intellectually, socially, and emotionally, and is experiencing a sense of psychological well-being that contributes not only to his or her persistence to graduation, but also to success in life (Schreiner, Pothoven, Nelson, & McIntosh, 2009).

Thriving is conceptualized as optimal functioning in three key areas that contribute to student success and persistence: (a) academic engagement and performance, (b) interpersonal relationships, and (c) psychological well-being. Thriving students are not only succeeding academically, but they are also engaged in the learning process, investing effort to reach important educational goals, managing their time and commitments effectively, connected in healthy ways to other people, optimistic about their futures, positive about their present choices, appreciative of differences in others, and committed to enriching their community. Based on this holistic vision of college student thriving, the Thriving Quotient was developed to measure these aspects of students' academic, interpersonal, and intrapersonal engagement and well-being. Each area of thriving consists of multiple psychological constructs that combine to characterize a well-rounded, high-functioning individual (Schreiner, McIntosh, Nelson, & Pothoven, 2009).

The Thriving Quotient was derived from perspectives of psychological well-being and student success, as well as from successful students' perceptions and experiences as described through interviews and focus groups. The conceptual framework that guided the development of the instrument combines empirical research from positive psychology about what leads to optimal individual and community functioning (Keyes & Haidt, 2003; Seligman & Csikszentmihalyi, 2000) with models of student retention that emphasize students' psychosocial processes and interactions (Bean & Eaton, 2000; Braxton, Hirschy, & McClendon, 2004).

One of the key concepts to emerge within the field of positive psychology is *flourishing*, which Keyes and Haidt (2003) describe as high levels of emotional, psychological, and social well-being that lead to productive engagement with others and in society. Because flourishing is not a construct that has been studied extensively in college students and, thus, does not contain the academic component so crucial to student success, the construct is insufficient to describe the experiences of college students who are vitally and successfully engaged, both psychologically and behaviorally, in the intellectual and social demands of the college environment. The term thriving characterizes the combination of positive functioning demonstrated in flourishing with the unique perspectives and attitudes evident in highly successful college students.

The concept of thriving is not only linked to models of psychological well-being, but is also linked to models of student retention that emphasize the psychosocial nature of student success. Bean and Eaton's (2000) model highlights the psychological processes in which students engage as they experience college life, developing a sense of academic and social integration leading to institutional fit, retention, and graduation. Braxton et al. (2004) also focus on psychological processes in their persistence model that includes communal potential, proactive social adjustment, and psychosocial engagement. These models, combined with the concept of flourishing from the field of positive psychology, form the conceptual framework within which thriving was developed.

After combining these interdisciplinary perspectives on well-being and student success with descriptions derived from interviewing successful college students, the Thriving Quotient was developed to reliably measure thriving. Pilot testing, revision, and exploratory and confirmatory factor analyses resulted in a survey instrument with 25 items clustered on five factors, a model that produced an excellent fit of the data and demonstrated high reliability ($\alpha = .89$; Schreiner, Nelson, McIntosh, & Edens, 2011). The construct of thriving is represented in the Thriving Quotient with scales labeled (a) Engaged Learning, (b) Academic Determination, (c) Positive Perspective, (d) Diverse Citizenship, and (e) Social Connectedness. Each of the factors represents an element of academic, intrapersonal, or interpersonal thriving that has been empirically demonstrated to be amenable to change within students, rather than a fixed personality trait over which there is little control (Schreiner, McIntosh et al., 2009). In a national study of 14,067 students from 53 public and private four-year institutions, these aspects of thriving were found to account for an additional 11-23% of the variation in important outcomes, such as college grades and intent to graduate, over and above what was explained by institutional differences and individual student demographic characteristics (Schreiner, Nelson et al., 2011). The three major areas of thriving will be explored below, along with the specific scales that comprise each of them.

Academic Thriving

Academic thriving is characterized by two scales on the Thriving Quotient: Engaged Learning and Academic Determination. Students who are thriving academically are psychologically engaged in the learning process; they are meaningfully processing course material, making connections between what they already know or are interested in and what needs to be learned. They are focused and attentive to new learning opportunities and actively think about and discuss with others what they are learning. In short, they are energized by the learning process (Schreiner & Louis, 2011).

Thriving students also possess a strong sense of academic determination, characterized by a powerful motivation to succeed in college and the willingness to invest the necessary effort to do so. Students high in Academic Determination are able to self-regulate in order to maximize their success. They effectively manage their time and the multiple academic and personal demands of the college environment; have clear educational goals and strategies for reaching them; and when classes and assignments are difficult or boring, employ a variety of strategies to persist until they succeed (Schreiner, McIntosh et al., 2009). Students who thrive academically know that it is the investment of effort on a regular basis that will help them reach their goals.

Intrapersonal Thriving

Thriving in college requires the development of healthy attitudes toward self as well as toward the learning process. Intrapersonal thriving is reflected in the factor called Positive Perspective. Students who thrive have an optimistic way of viewing the world and their future, with the result that they tend to be more satisfied with their lives and enjoy the college experience more. This perspective is not an overly optimistic view of self that is unrealistic, however. A positive perspective is a way of viewing reality and coping with it proactively. These students are able to take more of a long-term view of events that happen to them and see those events from multiple viewpoints. As a result, they are less likely to overreact, are able to put things in perspective, and can reframe negative events to find some positive benefit or learning opportunity. Realistic optimism enables students to experience more positive emotions on a regular basis, which leads to higher levels of satisfaction with the college experience (Schreiner, McIntosh et al., 2009).

Interpersonal Thriving

Whether the research is on psychological well-being, physical health, or student success in college, most studies conclude that relationships play an important role in positive life outcomes (Bean, 2005; Diener, 2000). Two aspects of interpersonal thriving are reflected in the following factors of the Thriving Quotient: Social Connectedness and Diverse Citizenship (Schreiner, McIntosh et al., 2009). Though both of these factors describe interpersonal connections, the former captures students' beliefs about the sufficiency of their personal relationships while the latter emphasizes the attitudes and values that drive their interactions with others.

Social Connectedness is the presence of healthy relationships in students' lives. Having good friends, being in relationships with others who listen to them, and feeling connected to others so that one is not lonely all combine to form this factor. The ability to form and maintain healthy relationships is an important element in college students' growth (Chickering & Reisser, 1993). Also critical to thriving is the sense of mattering (Rayle & Chung, 2007-2008; Schlossberg, 1989), which is the belief that others care for and appreciate a person, valuing that person's contribution and taking time to understand him or her.

Diverse Citizenship is a combination of openness and valuing of differences in others, along with a desire to make a contribution to one's community and the confidence to do so. Thriving students give time to help others and respond to others with openness and curiosity, believing that the other has something important to contribute to the relationship. They want to make a difference in their community and the larger society (Schreiner, McIntosh et al., 2009).

Together, the academic, intrapersonal, and interpersonal domains of thriving represent areas of student functioning that are amenable to change. Students bring into the college environment personality predispositions, behavioral tendencies, life experiences, and ways of seeing the world that often appear to be fixed. By defining and measuring thriving with constructs that other researchers have empirically demonstrated are malleable, the Thriving Quotient provides a method for colleges and universities to measure student development holistically and suggests specific mechanisms for increasing the benefits students gain from the college experience.

Although the initial goal in creating the instrument was to develop a reliable and valid measure of positive student functioning that connects to important outcomes in higher education, the ultimate goal is to design interventions that enable a greater percentage of college students to thrive during their college years and beyond. The following section outlines specific ways that designing programs and services around the concept of thriving in transitions could enable more students to derive full benefit from the college experience during times of significant change.

Thriving in Transitions

Given that transitions occur throughout the college experience, providing students with a way of approaching these periods of change could prove useful in enabling them to successfully cope with subsequent transitions not only during college, but also throughout their lives. The construct of thriving provides a useful framework for exploring how colleges and universities might more effectively equip students for successful transitions.

Three key elements of successful transition experiences can be addressed by a focus on the components of thriving. First, a successful transition begins with a positive cognitive appraisal—the student perceives the transition as an opportunity for positive growth and believes that he or she has the ability to successfully move through the period of change and benefit from it. Second, successful transitions occur within a context of support—students are surrounded with the information, resources, feedback, and people they need to sustain their energy and motivation through the change process. Finally, successful transitions result from effective strategies employed at the appropriate time—students are equipped with proactive coping skills and ways of interacting with others and with events that occur during the transition (Schlossberg, 2007). In each element of a successful transition, an institutional focus on specific aspects of student thriving can enable students to move through the change process and emerge more confident and equipped for the future.

Positive Appraisal

Successful transitions begin with how such events are perceived. When they are perceived as positive opportunities for growth, rather than as threats to self-esteem or as challenges that are likely to result in failure, the student has the motivation and confidence to engage throughout the transition period (Schlossberg, 2007). The Positive Perspective element of thriving addresses this issue of perception, as it equips students with the ingredients for a positive primary and secondary cognitive appraisal of transition events.

Foundational to thriving in transitions is the outlook on life that students hold and the perspective they take of events that happen. Thriving college students have a positive perspective on life, what Seligman (1990) calls an *optimistic explanatory style*, which enables them to handle challenges more easily. These students' way of appraising a transitional event is to take the long view and see the bigger picture. They view the transition as necessary and tend to detect aspects of the transition events that are opportunities for them to learn and grow. As institutions attempt to equip students for successful transitions, two strategies could be helpful in bolstering a student's ability to make positive appraisals. The first approach targets all students entering a transition, while the second approach targets specific students in need.

All students about to experience a transition could benefit from intentional communication from the institution about the meaning and potential growth opportunities of the upcoming period of change well before the events begin. When an institution can frame a transition for students in terms of the positive impact it can have, the benefits to be gained from it, and the specific opportunities for learning and growth that are open to all students during the period of change, students are equipped with mechanisms for understanding what is likely to happen and how it can benefit them. Perceiving a potentially stressful time as an opportunity rather than as a threat is the first step toward a successful transition (Schlossberg, 2007).

In addition to helping students frame the upcoming transition positively, institutions could equip students to assess their own ability to handle the demands of the transition by outlining what those demands are likely to be. Secondary cognitive appraisal involves a self-assessment of one's coping skills, available resources, and potential support networks, within the context of the demands required during the transition (Lazarus & Folkman, 1984). Accordingly, a description of the expected demands, along with the types of coping skills that will be beneficial and the specific support the institution will provide, will equip students with the ability to determine their likelihood of effectively managing the transition. In particular, the way faculty communicate to students in class at the beginning of courses that occur early in a transition period is crucial. When instructors convey that there are effective strategies for success in the course—and that part of their job is to teach students those strategies—students are more likely to experience a sense of control over the demands of the course. This sense of control is vital to students' academic success and is amenable to intervention (Perry et al., 2005).

Institutions could be of further help to students by providing them with a way of measuring their current thriving and then directing them to the specific resources and support they need, based on the areas indicated in their Thriving Quotient scores. This second approach to bolstering positive cognitive appraisal of a transition thus targets specific students for intervention. Students' thriving could be measured at the beginning of the transition period, and those students whose Positive Perspective scores are significantly lower than other students of the same class level could be targeted for further intervention that would teach them an optimistic explanatory style, for example. Such interventions could be implemented in the advising relationship, in peer mentoring, or through workshops offered online or as part of student-life programming. Equipping students with an optimistic explanatory style is particularly important with first-year students who are in a new and unfamiliar environment and may be feeling they have little control. The intervention would teach students to attribute failures to controllable causes and to view them as unique to a specific event rather than global in nature (Perry et al., 2005; Seligman, 1990). As students learn about the psychological processes that impact their success, they are provided with a road map that normalizes the journey and gives them a sense of control over it.

Providing Support

The likelihood of a successful transition increases with the amount of appropriate support provided. Institutions have designed a wide array of programming for students in transition with this premise in mind. Orientation, first-year seminars, peer leadership programs, and academic support centers have all been developed as mechanisms to provide intentional support to students who are experiencing a transition period. The support is often a combination of information and emotional connections: students are connected to the information and resources they need to succeed, as well as to others who are compatriots or role models (Upcraft, Gardner, & Barefoot, 2005).

Despite this network of support created by many institutions, students are still most likely to drop out of college during a transition period (Nora, Barlow, & Crisp, 2005). Their departure may signal an appraisal of the transition resulting in the conclusion that they are not equipped to succeed, but it also could mean that the way the institution provided support was not appropriate or sufficient.

Support during transition is most effective when it meets students' emotional needs, providing assurance and generating positive emotions, but also when it meets their needs for information and feedback. Institutions provide a significant amount of information to students in transition, but students may not hear it due to the timing or method of communication (Bransford, Brown, & Cocking, 2000). Beyond midsemester warnings, it is rare for institutions to provide individual feedback to students during a transition period so that students are aware of how their effort and strategies are contributing to their experience of success or failure, yet such information can be vital to student success (Kuh, 2008).

Institutional interventions that bolster thriving as measured on the Social Connectedness and Diverse Citizenship scales can assist students in transition by providing the type of support that enables them to successfully navigate college's challenges. Social Connectedness, which involves positive interactions with others and a sense of mattering to other people, can be fostered by intentionally linking students not only to others who are experiencing the same transition but also to people who have successfully navigated that transition and to those who are part of the community to which students are transitioning. This concept is at the heart of most first-year experience programs and peer mentoring, but too many institutions end this practice in the first year. In national research with sophomores (Schreiner, 2010a), 36% reported that by the end of their second year they were still feeling lonely and wished the institution provided more opportunities for them to make friends. This finding emphasizes the importance of institutional supports that go beyond the first year. Helping students make the transition to college is an important first step, but intentional mechanisms on campus are needed to connect students to social networks after the first year. Astin's (1984) model of student involvement highlights the positive role that involvement on campus plays in students' learning and development. More specifically, Cheng's (2004) research has found that the involvement needs to be selective, intentional, and meaningfully connected to the larger campus community for students to derive the most benefit. Connecting students to other students and faculty in their major is particularly beneficial for providing the type and quality of support that is needed in an academic environment (Kuh, 2008).

Interventions designed to enhance students' Diverse Citizenship also can provide the varied types of support that are vital to a successful transition. Diverse Citizenship reflects openness to and appreciation of differences in others, a desire to make a difference in one's surrounding community and the broader society, and the confidence to do so. Interventions that enhance this aspect of thriving typically place students in regular contact with others who are different, but also provide ongoing social support and timely feedback about students' actions. For example, effective service-learning courses and living-learning communities have several key ingredients in common that contribute to their significant ability to enhance thriving during transitions, such as (a) the opportunity for sustained contact based on equal status, (b) a safe environment and structural support for providing individual feedback and managing conflict, and (c) a common goal that requires collaboration across differences (Schreiner, 2010c). Thus, when academic courses are organized to include service-learning opportunities as partnerships rather than as charity, or when living-learning communities have themes and specific goals to which all members ascribe, there is greater potential for the experience to enable successful progression through a period of transition. In both instances there is not only emotional support, but also the timely provision of contextualized information, along with feedback from faculty, classmates, and community partners about the student's growth and progress.

Effective Strategies

The final component of a successful transition involves employing effective strategies to move through the transition and experience growth. As Bean and Eaton (2000) emphasize, such strategies move the student forward toward further engagement and problem solving, rather than encourage defensive actions that lead to withdrawal and disconnection. Although positive appraisal and the perception of adequate support during a stressful transition are vital, if effective strategies for responding to the demands of the transition are not employed, the student is not likely to move successfully through the transition and be prepared for the next phase of college life.

Interventions that focus on student thriving in the classroom offer the best chance for helping students in transition develop effective strategies for success. Strategies with empirical support for their effectiveness include components of the Academic Determination aspect of thriving, such as goal-setting, effort regulation, self-regulated learning, and the development of multiple pathways to educational goals (Pintrich & Zusho, 2002; Robbins, Allen, Casillas, Peterson, & Le, 2006; Snyder et al., 2002). Classroom interventions that enhance the Engaged Learning element of thriving focus on strategies for motivating students, helping them make meaningful real-world connections to their learning, and encouraging mindful attention to new ideas (Schreiner & Louis, 2011).

Institutions that design interventions to address academic thriving focus their efforts on faculty development, advising, and curriculum design. They also work with student life professionals to normalize the help-seeking process on campus so that students feel comfortable accessing resources and learning effective strategies for success during transitions. Faculty development programs that demonstrate effective methods of engaging students in the learning process can lead more faculty to (a) utilize active learning, (b) connect with students in and out of class, and (c) teach students specific strategies for mastering the course content. The more faculty learn to "situate learning in the learners' experiences" (Baxter Magolda & King, 2004, p. 41), the more likely students are to meaningfully process course content and become academically engaged. Providing students with choices in how to demonstrate mastery of the course content also enhances students' sense of control in an unfamiliar academic environment, which can lead to greater learning (Perry et al., 2005). Faculty development programs that equip instructors with effective assessment strategies providing options to students position the institution to enhance academic thriving.

The academic advising relationship is an ideal vehicle for equipping students with effective strategies during a transition because it is a structured opportunity that all students on every college campus have for an ongoing, one-on-one interaction with a concerned faculty or staff member who is focused on the student and his or her current transition. Advising programs that teach students effective strategies for handling the demands of a transition emphasize student responsibility and initiative, teaching students specific skills for becoming engaged in their own learning and investing the necessary effort to succeed in college. Advisors can teach students coping skills that are implicit in the Positive Perspective element of thriving—that is, those that are proactive and problem-focused, rather than reactive and avoidant. They can encourage students to seek out information, reframe negative events so they see others' perspectives or can find something to be learned from the experience, use humor effectively to cope, and view failures as temporary setbacks from which they can learn (Schreiner, Hulme, Hetzel, & Lopez, 2009).

But the primary way in which academic advising can equip students with the necessary strategies for successful transitions is by building hope. Lopez and colleagues (2004) believe hope building is a skill that can be taught to students, which involves (a) clearly conceptualizing important and meaningful goals, (b) developing specific strategies for reaching those goals and breaking those strategies into steps, and (c) reframing obstacles as challenges that can be overcome. The more advisors can encourage students to brainstorm multiple pathways to their educational goals, the greater the likelihood of a smooth transition (Schreiner, Hulme et al., 2009).

The final institutional vehicle for interventions that increase academic thriving among students in transition is curriculum design. Although faculty and academic administrators may be unlikely to view curriculum design as an intervention strategy for thriving in transitions, there is research to support the power of an integrated and coherent curriculum to enhance student learning and success (Braskamp, Trautvetter, & Ward, 2006). In addition, considerable empirical support for the value of learning communities suggests that redesigning the curriculum around student cohorts, interdisciplinary content, and faculty partnerships at key points in the college years can enable more students to transition effectively through the demands of a college degree (Laufgraben, 2005; Rocconi, 2011; Tinto, 2000). Living-learning communities provide a particularly powerful means for not only providing social support and feedback, but also teaching students specific strategies for success. When students experience a sense of community within a learning environment that extends beyond the classroom into their living environment, they grow and develop intellectually, interpersonally, and emotionally (Inkelas & Weisman, 2003; Stassen, 2003).

As faculty redesign curricula and pedagogy to more effectively engage students, and advisors work with students to build hope and teach strategies for becoming self-directed learners, student life professionals join the process of helping students thrive during transitions when they normalize the help-seeking process on campus. Students in transition need to know not only the campus resources that are available and how to access them, but also that successful students seek out those resources, particularly during times of stress and change. Too often, effort is viewed as needed only by those of low ability, and help seeking is perceived as a sign of weakness (Dweck, 2006). Student-life professionals can help change the campus norms through their messages conveying that effort is a necessary ingredient in success, and through the use of peer models who emphasize help seeking as a strategy used by successful students (Schilling & Schilling, 2005; Schuh, 2005).

Conclusion

Transitions are part of every student's college experience and are pivotal times for students' decisions about their abilities and resources to succeed. By shifting the focus to thriving during transitions, institutions have a new repertoire of interventions that can enable more students to benefit from the college experience. Helping students appropriately frame transitions, providing timely information and feedback in a context of emotional support, and teaching students effective strategies to proactively cope with multiple demands during times of significant change provide a strong foundation for ensuring that students not only graduate but also establish healthy patterns for handling the many transitions of life beyond college.

References

Astin, A. W. (1984). Student involvement: A developmental theory for higher education. *Journal of College Student Personnel, 25,* 297-308.

Attewell, P. A., Lavin, D. E., Domina, T., & Levey, T. (2006). New evidence on college remediation. *Journal of Higher Education, 77*(5), 886-924.

Baxter Magolda, M., & King, P. (2004). *Learning partnerships: Theory and models of practice to educate for self-authorship.* Sterling, VA: Stylus.

Bean, J. P. (2005). Nine themes of college student retention. In A. Seidman (Ed.), *College student retention: Formula for student success* (pp. 215-244). Westport, CT: Praeger.

Bean, J. P., & Eaton, S. B. (2000). A psychological model of college student retention. In J. M. Braxton (Ed.), *Reworking the departure puzzle* (pp. 48-61). Nashville, TN: Vanderbilt University Press.

Bransford, J., Brown, A. L., & Cocking, R. R. (Eds). (2000). *How people learn: Brain, mind, experience, and school.* Washington, DC: National Research Council, Committee on Learning Research and Educational Practice, National Academy Press.

Braskamp, L. A., Trautvetter, L. C., & Ward, K. (2006). *Putting students first: How colleges develop students purposefully.* Bolton, MA: Anker Publishing.

Braxton, J. M., Hirschy, A. S., & McClendon, S. A. (2004). *Toward understanding and reducing college student departure.* (ASHE-ERIC Higher Education Research Report, No. 30). San Francisco, CA: Jossey-Bass.

Cheng, D. X. (2004). Students' sense of campus community: What it means and what to do about it. *NASPA Journal, 41,* 216-232.

Chickering, A. W., & Reisser, L. (1993). *Education and identity* (2nd ed). San Francisco, CA: Jossey-Bass.

Diener, E. (2000). Subjective well-being: The science of happiness and a proposal for a national index. *American Psychologist, 55,* 34-43.

Dweck, C. S. (2006). *Mindset: The new psychology of success.* New York, NY: Random House.

Goodman, J., Schlossberg, N., & Anderson, M. (2006). *Counseling adults in transition: Linking practice with theory.* New York, NY: Springer.

Inkelas, K. K., & Weisman, J. L. (2003). Different by design: An examination of student outcomes among participants in three types of living-learning programs. *Journal of College Student Development, 44,* 335-368.

Keyes, C. L. M, & Haidt, J. (Eds.). (2003). *Flourishing: Positive psychology and the life well-lived.* Washington, DC: American Psychological Association.

Kuh, G. D. (2008). Advising for student success. In V. N. Gordon, W. R. Habley, T. J. Grites, & Associates (Eds.), *Academic advising: A comprehensive handbook* (2nd ed., pp. 68-84). San Francisco, CA: Jossey-Bass.

Kuh, G. D., Kinzie, J., Schuh, J. H., Whitt, E. J., & Associates. (2005). *Student success in college: Creating conditions that matter.* San Francisco, CA: Jossey-Bass.

Laufgraben, J. L. (2005). Learning communities. In M. L. Upcraft, J. N. Gardner, & B. O. Barefoot (Eds.), *Challenging and supporting the first-year student: A handbook for improving the first year of college* (pp. 371-389). San Francisco, CA: Jossey-Bass.

Lazarus, R. S. (1998). *Fifty years of the research and theory of R. S. Lazarus: An analysis of historical and perennial issues.* Mahwah, NJ: Erlbaum.

Lazarus, R. S., & Folkman, S. (1984). *Stress, appraisal, and coping.* New York, NY: Springer.

Lopez, S. J., Snyder, C. R., Magyar-Moe, J. L., Edwards, L. M., Pedrotti, J. T., Janowski, K., . . . Pressgrove, C. (2004). Strategies for accentuating hope. In P. A. Linley & S. Joseph (Eds.), *Positive psychology in practice* (pp. 388-404). Hoboken, NJ: John Wiley and Sons.

Nora, A., Barlow, E., & Crisp, G. (2005). Student persistence and degree attainment beyond the first year in college. In A. Seidman (Ed.), *College student retention: Formula for student success* (pp. 129-154). Westport, CT: Praeger.

Perry, R. P., Hall, N. C., & Ruthig, J. C. (2005). Perceived (academic) control and scholastic attainment in higher education. In J. C. Smart (Ed.), *Higher education: Handbook of theory and research* (Vol. 20, pp. 363-436). Norwell, MA: Springer.

Pintrich, P. R., & Zusho, A. (2002). The development of academic self-regulation: The role of cognitive and motivational factors. In A. Wigfield & J. S. Eccles (Eds.), *Development of achievement motivation* (pp. 250-284). San Diego, CA: Academic Press.

Rayle, A. D., & Chung, K. Y. (2007-2008). Revisiting first-year college students' mattering: Social support, academic stress, and the mattering experience. *Journal of College Student Retention: Research, Theory & Practice, 9*(1), 21-37.

Robbins, S., Allen, J., Casillas, A., Peterson, C., & Le, H. (2006). Unraveling the differential effects of motivational and skills, social, and self-management measures from traditional predictors of college outcomes. *Journal of Educational Psychology, 98*(3), 598-616.

Rocconi, L. M. (2011). The impact of learning communities on first-year students' growth and development in college. *Research in Higher Education, 52,* 178-193.

Schilling, K. M., & Schilling, K. L. (2005). Expectations and performance. In M. L. Upcraft, J. N. Gardner, & B. O. Barefoot (Eds.), *Challenging and supporting the first-year student: A handbook for improving the first year of college* (pp. 108-120). San Francisco, CA: Jossey-Bass.

Schlossberg, N. K. (1989). Marginality and mattering: Key issues in building community. In D. C. Roberts (Ed.), *Designing campus activities to foster a sense of community* (New Directions for Student Services No. 48, pp. 5-15). San Francisco, CA: Jossey-Bass.

Schlossberg, N. K. (2007). *Overwhelmed: Coping with life's ups and downs* (2nd ed). Lanham, MD: Evans and Company.

Schreiner, L. (2010a). Factors that contribute to sophomore success and satisfaction. In S. Hunter, B. Tobolowsky, J. Gardner, S. Evenbeck, J. Pattengale, M. Schaller, & L. A. Schreiner, *Helping sophomores succeed: Understanding and improving the second-year experience* (pp. 43-65). San Francisco, CA: Jossey-Bass.

Schreiner, L. (2010b). The "Thriving Quotient": A new vision for student success. *About Campus, 15*(2), 2-10.

Schreiner, L. (2010c). Thriving in community. *About Campus, 15*(4), 2-11.

Schreiner, L., Hulme, E., Hetzel, R., & Lopez, S. (2009). Positive psychology on campus. In S. J. Lopez & C. R. Snyder (Eds.), *Oxford handbook of positive psychology* (2nd ed., pp. 569-578). New York, NY: Oxford University Press.

Schreiner, L., & Louis, M. (2011). The Engaged Learning Index: Implications for faculty development. *Journal of Excellence in College Teaching, 22*(1), 5-28.

Schreiner, L., McIntosh, E., Nelson, D., & Pothoven, S. (2009, November). *The Thriving Quotient: Advancing the assessment of student success.* Paper presented at the annual meeting of the Association for the Study of Higher Education, Vancouver, Canada.

Schreiner, L., Nelson, D., McIntosh, E., & Edens, D. (2011, March). *The Thriving Quotient: A new vision for student success.* Paper presented at the annual meeting of the National Association of Student Personnel Administrators, Philadelphia, PA.

Schreiner, L., Pothoven, S., Nelson, D., & McIntosh, E. (2009, November). *College student thriving: Predictors of success and retention.* Paper presented at the annual meeting of the Association for the Study of Higher Education, Vancouver, Canada.

Schuh, J. (2005). Student support services. In M. L. Upcraft, J. N. Gardner, & B. O. Barefoot (Eds.), *Challenging and supporting the first-year student: A handbook for improving the first year of college* (pp. 428-444). San Francisco, CA: Jossey-Bass.

Seligman, M. E. P. (1990). *Learned optimism.* New York, NY: Knopf.

Seligman, M. E. P., & Csikszentmihalyi, M. (2000). Positive psychology: An introduction. *American Psychologist, 55*(1), 5-14.

Selye, H. (1976). *The stress of life.* New York, NY: McGraw-Hill.

Snyder, C. R., Shorey, H. S., Cheavens, J., Pulvers, K. M., Adams, V. H., & Wiklund, C. (2002). Hope and academic success in college. *Journal of Educational Psychology, 94*(4), 820-826.

Stassen, M. L. A. (2003). Student outcomes: The impact of varying living-learning community models. *Research in Higher Education, 44*(5), 581-613.

Tinto, V. (2000). What have we learned about the impact of learning communities on students? *Assessment Update: Progress, Trends and Practices in Higher Education, 12*(2), 1-2, 12.

Upcraft, M., Gardner, J., & Barefoot, B. (Eds.). (2005). *Challenging and supporting the first-year student: A handbook for improving the first year of college.* San Francisco, CA: Jossey-Bass.

Chapter 2

Helping Students Thrive: A Strengths Development Model
Michelle C. Louis and Laurie A. Schreiner

In recent years, higher education has witnessed an unprecedented interest in creating conditions and programs designed to optimize student success, which has been defined as "satisfaction, persistence, and high levels of learning and personal development" (Kuh, Kinzie, Schuh, Whitt, & Associates, 2005, p. xiv). According to this definition, student success encompasses more than the mere completion of a course of study in that it also finds value in understanding the nature of each student's experience on campus and the quality of learning and personal development that occur within the educational context. Based on a study of highly effective postsecondary institutions, Kuh and colleagues (2005) offer support for educational environments that promote talent development, explaining that such institutions "arrange resources and learning conditions to maximize student potential" (p. 77). This emphasis on nurturing student talent has infused the ongoing dialogue about promoting student success and has led to the creation of programs and policies that build on students' strengths rather than simply remediating their deficiencies (Gardner, Upcraft, & Barefoot, 2005) and that structure learning experiences based on what students do well (Kuh, Kinzie, Buckley, Bridges, & Hayek, 2006).

These objectives are resonant with what has become known as a *strengths philosophy* or *strengths perspective* (Aspinwall & Staudinger, 2003). Grounded in the field of positive psychology that aims to understand and promote that which allows individuals and communities to thrive (Seligman & Csikszent-mihalyi, 2000), a strengths perspective seeks to leverage the positive qualities of each individual with the ultimate goal of optimizing achievement (Anderson, 2005), well-being, or character development (Peterson & Seligman, 2004). Strengths-oriented educators believe that potential exists in all students and that it is possible to develop learning opportunities to help students realize potential (Lopez & Louis, 2009). A strengths approach is characterized by "efforts to label what is right" (Buckingham, 2007, p. 6) within people and to subsequently cultivate it to bring out the best in each individual.

Some proponents of a strengths philosophy assert that capitalizing on one's areas of strength is likely to lead to greater success than would be possible by making a comparable investment of effort into overcoming personal weaknesses or deficiencies (Clifton & Harter, 2003). This paradigm highlights the importance of intentionally choosing to focus one's attention and energy on cultivating that, which will yield the most significant growth. This goal is accomplished not by ignoring weaknesses, but by seeking instead to understand and manage areas of deficiency while building on strengths (Clifton & Nelson, 1992).

At the individual level, a strengths approach encompasses the identification of positive personal qualities, along with their integration into one's view of self, resulting in behavioral changes (Clifton & Harter, 2003). Those seeking to "nurture genius" (Seligman in Keyes & Haidt, 2003, p. xv) in others have found strengths development approaches to be useful (Fox, 2008; Linley, 2008) as they enact the belief that each person has behavioral or psychological resources that can be mobilized toward desired outcomes (Anderson, 2000; Saleebey, 2006). Strengths development approaches explore empowering individuals to flourish rather than to simply survive (Liesveld & Miller, 2005) and are, therefore, an appropriate topic for a book devoted to exploring how to promote thriving during transitions.

This chapter highlights strengths development approaches as powerful strategies for promoting thriving among college students. The discussion begins by placing strengths development within the context of thriving in transitions as a precursor to summarizing the various ways that strengths are conceptualized, measured, and developed. The chapter continues with a description of how integrating a strengths perspective might inform classroom teaching efforts, advising, and student affairs work, with each of these sections offering practical strategies for adopting a strengths-oriented approach. In the conclusion, several general suggestions for educators seeking to initiate a strengths development strategy on campus will be offered.

Strengths Development and Thriving in Transitions

The focus of this book is to describe strategies that enable students to thrive during periods of transition. As noted in chapter 1, a successful transition occurs when students perceive the transition as a positive opportunity to grow and learn, when they use appropriate coping skills to engage during the transition, when they feel supported by others, and are able to access needed resources. The ability to not just survive the inevitable transitions of college life, but to thrive during these pivotal experiences, is the expanded vision for student success that is articulated throughout this book. Rather than defining success solely in terms of academic performance and persistence to graduation, a focus on thriving encourages a more holistic view of student development that includes establishing healthy relationships, making a contribution, and proactively coping with life's challenges (Schreiner, 2010).

Promoting thriving as a goal informs the strategies educators use to assist students; it requires a shift from deficit remediation to strengths development and from a focus on students' immutable pasts to their possibilities for the future. Rather than aiming to prevent failure, the goal is transformed into promoting success. This focus on strengths development is integral to thriving. As Fredrickson (2009) notes, "people who have the opportunity every day to do what they do best—to act on their strengths—are far more likely to flourish" (p. 189). Developing students' strengths holds the potential for energizing them to become engaged in the learning experience, to invest the effort necessary to succeed, and to connect with others in positive ways.

A strengths perspective appears as a recurring theme throughout this book. Chapter 5 notes that studying successful students—particularly those who were initially labeled by their institutions as academically high risk but went on to succeed—can provide models after which students can pattern themselves. This approach is echoed in chapter 8 on thriving seniors, which describes the benefits of studying the attitudes and experiences of students who are thriving as they conclude their college years. Chapter 4 emphasizes that role models of success, among both students and faculty, are particularly vital for thriving in students of color.

The concept of learning about success by studying success, and noticing what is right with people or what is working effectively, is one of the hallmarks of a strengths development approach (Buckingham, 2007; Clifton & Harter, 2003; Shushok & Hulme, 2006). Summarizing the prevalent themes that emerged from interviews with over two million successful people in a variety of professions across the world, Clifton and Harter (2003) noted three consistent characteristics of high achievers: (a) they spend most of their time in their areas of strength; (b) they focus on developing and applying their strengths while managing their weaknesses; and (c) although they do not necessarily have more talents than other people, they have developed their capabilities more fully and have learned to apply them to new situations. Teaching students to pattern their lives after such high achievers is one way of helping them thrive as they transition from the known to the unknown in each phase of college life and beyond.

Specific campus programs and practices are emphasized throughout this book and include academic advising, student-faculty interaction and engaging pedagogy, first-year experience and orientation programs, leadership development, service-learning, and living-learning communities. These practices are well established, as Kuh (2008) has termed them *high-impact educational practices* that are most likely to lead to student engagement. However, the way in which students are encouraged to become involved on campus, and the strategies for designing such programs and services, can be framed from a strengths development perspective to enable more students to gain optimal benefits from their involvement.

Various Approaches to Understanding and Building Student Strengths

To provide a context for the discussion of a strengths development perspective, we begin by summarizing the most prevalent ways that strengths are currently defined and measured in educational settings. Although different models exist regarding what constitutes strengths and how they should be cultivated, perhaps the most comprehensive understanding of personal strengths emerges from considering the valuable contribution that each perspective offers.

Conceptualizing and Measuring Strengths

Many of the strengths-oriented activities and programs on today's postsecondary campuses use one of several possible assessments to give participants individualized feedback on personal strengths, although researchers have conducted successful strengths interventions that do not utilize a specific assessment tool (e.g., Seligman, Steen, Park, & Peterson, 2005). The strengths instruments used most commonly include the Clifton StrengthsFinder (Gallup, 1999), the Values in Action Inventory of Strengths (VIA-IS; Seligman, Park, & Peterson, 2004), and the Realise2 (Centre for Applied Positive Psychology, 2010), although several others exist as well.

Each instrument offers a distinct approach to measuring strengths. These unique approaches are derived from the two main paradigms that exist regarding the definition and classification of human strengths. One approach views strengths as personal *competencies* that produce excellent performance; whereas, the other understands strengths to be elements of *character* that are the building blocks of virtue. Specifically, according to the Gallup (1999) model, strengths are cultivated when knowledge and skill are added to naturally occurring patterns of thought, feeling, or behavior (*talents*, in this model), thereby producing levels of excellence in a particular activity (Buckingham & Clifton, 2001). In contrast, the classification of strengths advanced by the Values in Action Institute conceptualizes positive individual traits as existing in several categories. The broadest category consists of the *virtues*, described as the "core characteristics [ubiquitously] valued by moral philosophers and religious thinkers" (Peterson & Seligman, 2004, p. 13). The virtues are comprised of *character strengths*, which are positive traits that are relatively stable across situations and are the "psychological ingredients—processes or mechanisms—that define the virtues" (Peterson & Seligman, p. 13). According to this paradigm, character strengths provide venues for the virtues to be displayed.

The Nature of Strengths Development Programs

Depending on the context and goals of the initiative, strengths development may assume a variety of forms and encompass a range of strategies. Some strengths development programs may simply seek to help students use their strengths more readily and with greater frequency, based upon the notion that strengths are augmented through regular use (Buckingham & Clifton, 2001). This strategy is useful in that greater strengths use has been associated with increased levels of well-being over time (Wood, Linley, Maltby, Kashdan, & Hurling, 2011). However, some students may benefit from a more complex consideration of how to modify the application of various strengths according to situational factors, a process that may actually involve learning how to reduce their use or apply them with greater insight (Kaplan & Kaiser, 2010). This approach suggests that strengths should be applied with an awareness of the impact that they have on self and others, and in alignment with personal values or desired outcomes. Strengths development initiatives may also involve evaluating how various strengths combine within an individual or a group to produce certain outcomes, contemplating which activities may be helpful in catalyzing strengths growth (Lopez & Louis, 2009) or considering how strengths can be applied in novel ways (Seligman et al., 2005).

Strengths Development Across Campus

The following sections describe how approaching teaching, advising, and student affairs practice from a strengths development perspective could enhance efforts to promote student thriving. Although the ideas presented here may prompt educators to consider new programs or initiatives that focus on cultivating student strengths, it is equally likely that the concepts described may result in a consideration of the ways in which existing programs and practices on campus could be reconceptualized using a strengths development framework.

Strengths Development in the Classroom

Two aspects of college student thriving during transitions can be directly influenced by classroom experiences. The first is engaged learning—students' abilities to meaningfully process what they are learning in class and connect it to other aspects of their life; the second is academic determination—their investment of effort to regulate their own learning, meet important educational goals, and manage multiple demands (Schreiner, 2010). A strengths development approach in the classroom may help students thrive in these important areas that lead to success. Instructors can utilize five specific strengths-oriented strategies to foster students' engaged learning and academic determination.

1. Create a sense of community in the classroom by emphasizing the strengths that each student contributes. As greater numbers of college students are commuters, the classroom becomes an increasingly important place for a sense of community to develop. Students with a strong sense of community (i.e., a feeling of belonging, contributing, connecting, and accomplishing goals with others) are more likely to engage in the learning process and experience academic success (DeNeui, 2003). A strengths development approach to teaching builds this sense of community before, during, and after class as instructors intentionally learn about their students. Knowing one's students and "their preferred learning styles, their talents, and when and where they need help" (Kuh et al., 2005, p. 301) is a key component of building a sense of community in the classroom. Such knowledge provides a foundation for connecting with those students' interests and prior learning and engaging them in the learning process.

In a strengths-based classroom, the instructor not only knows the students and how they learn but also emphasizes what each student contributes to the community. This recognition of existing talent sends a message to students that they are valued members of the academic community who are expected to contribute to mutual learning in the classroom. Throughout the term, the instructor intentionally structures the classroom experience so that students thoughtfully consider their strengths and how they can be used to master course assignments and objectives. The instructor is also transparent about his or her own strengths and how those are being applied in mastering the discipline (Anderson, Cantwell, & Schreiner, 2004). This transparency builds rapport with students and connects them not only to each other but also to the instructor and the subject matter in ways that increases students' engagement in the learning process.

2. Design active-learning experiences that are connected to students' current interests and that capitalize on students' strengths and learning styles. Learning is an active process of making meaning; it entails making connections to other learners and their different perspectives as well as to what one already knows, to meaningful goals, and to one's own strengths and ways of seeing the world (Tagg, 2003). Engaged learning reflects this meaningful processing along with the focused attention and active participation that are indicative of psychological engagement in the learning process (Schreiner & Louis, 2011). Classroom learning experiences that actively engage students with course content and with each other lead to higher levels of enjoyment as well as greater learning (Chickering & Gamson, 1987). Active learning experiences, such as learning teams, debates, lively class discussions, simulations, case studies, role playing, and jigsaw techniques engage students in their own learning, helping them derive the most out of the classroom experience (Silberman, 1996). Research indicates that these collaborative learning strategies occur more frequently on campuses where student engagement and persistence to graduation are higher than expected (Nelson Laird, Chen, & Kuh, 2008).

In a strengths development classroom, such learning experiences also tap into students' strengths and learning styles. Assignments that enable students to reflect on their strengths and how they have helped them succeed academically can equip students to use those strengths to become better learners. Intentionally creating diverse learning teams and teaching students how to work effectively together and capitalizing on the strengths each contributes to the team, helps students see others' strengths in addition to their own and to recognize and the synergy that occurs when the team harnesses its mutual strengths. Focusing on students' interests, qualities, and learning styles, as well as connecting new material to what students already know, creates a powerful dynamic in the classroom that fosters intrinsic motivation (Ryan & Deci, 2000).

3. Develop meaningful assignments in a context of clear expectations, choices, and an optimal level of challenge. Engaged learning and academic determination are more likely to develop when students are intrinsically motivated. Intrinsic motivation, or what Ryan and Deci (2000) refer to as *self-determination*, emerges when students' needs are met in three key areas: competence, autonomy, and relatedness. Carefully structured, meaningful assignments address all three needs. Competence needs are met by communicating clear expectations and structuring the assignment so that students are optimally challenged and are able to demonstrate their mastery in ways that are congruent with their strengths. Emphasizing the meaningfulness of the activity and articulating the level of effort required to master it can also equip students with an increased sense of competence. Students' needs for autonomy can be met through allowing choice in assignments, as intrinsic motivation blossoms when students see aspects of their academic tasks as chosen and relevant to their own goals and values (Ryan & Deci, 2000). When the assignments are structured so that students can work collaboratively, their needs for relatedness can be met, fostering increased engagement with learning.

Instructors committed to strengths development structure assignments to allow students to mobilize their strengths. Students are given concrete parameters and expectations for the learning objectives the assignment is to achieve, but they are also given the choice to meet those learning objectives in ways that allow them to capitalize on their strengths. For example, students whose strengths lie primarily in their verbal communication and ability to connect with an audience can demonstrate their mastery of the course objectives through podcasts or oral presentations; whereas, students whose strengths lie in their analytical thinking and carefully crafted writing skills can demonstrate course mastery through research papers or other written assignments. Choice, clarity, meaningfulness, and optimal challenge combine to create a classroom environment that engages students and unleashes their motivation to produce their best work.

4. Communicate to students that there are strategies for success and that learning is under their control. One of the hallmarks of academic determination is the investment of effort to regulate one's own learning process. Thriving during transitions is enhanced when students have learned how to monitor and regulate themselves to invest the needed energy and effort to successfully navigate the demands of the learning environment. However, it is precisely during transitions that students perceive they have the least control over their learning outcomes (Perry, 2003). Anyone in an unfamiliar environment is uncomfortable until the expectations and requirements are clear and methods for navigating the new environment become second nature. Students who are able to gain *perceived academic control* benefit most from their learning experiences. These students believe that their personal efforts will influence academic outcomes (Perry, Hall, & Ruthig, 2005).

In addition, students' beliefs about themselves and their abilities can have a pronounced effect on how they approach the learning experience. Students who have what Dweck (2006) calls a *fixed mindset* perceive their intelligence to be relatively innate and unchangeable. In contrast, students with a *growth mindset* believe that their ability is malleable with effort. These self-theories create meaning systems affecting students' goals, investment of effort, responses to failure and setbacks, and even the strategies they use to learn (Dweck & Molden, 2005). Students who are taught to approach the learning process with a growth mindset place a higher priority on their own learning and growth as a result. Rather than focusing on grades or exam performance, they focus on learning for its own sake. This focus leads them to invest more effort in learning, as they perceive effort as a natural part of the process. For them, effort is what leads to greater learning—a conclusion that Robbins, Allen, Casillas, Peterson, and Le (2006) have verified across large samples of college students. This perception of effort is in sharp contrast to those with a fixed mindset who perceive effort as an indication that a person is not naturally competent.

In a strengths-based classroom, the instructor sets the tone the first day of the course by communicating to students the specific strategies for success in the class. He or she also makes a commitment to teach students those strategies. A strengths-oriented instructor places the control of the learning process in students' hands by reminding them that they have strengths that can be applied to succeed in the class. The instructor also communicates, however, that it is the quality of the effort students invest in learning that will determine their academic outcome. Encouraging a growth mindset focuses on learning as the goal; thus, it promotes the acquisition of effective strategies rather than specific content. By teaching students to have a growth mindset, instructors can affect students' feelings of control, which in turn increases their motivation to learn, level of effort invested, and persistence in the face of setbacks (Perry et al., 2005).

5. Provide feedback that is timely, frequent, and constructive. Students who perceive themselves as capable of accomplishing academic tasks are not only more likely to achieve but also to persist and experience greater levels of personal adjustment (Chemers, Hu, & Garcia, 2001). Frequent feedback provides information specific to the task and enhances students' perceived competence because it targets specific actions they can take to attain to higher levels of excellence (Ryan & Deci, 2000). When feedback is constructive rather than simply critical, it also builds a sense of relatedness between the professor and student (Kuh et al., 2005). Students who receive this type of feedback are more likely to perceive themselves as capable of accomplishing academic tasks. Throughout a course, feedback to students that acknowledges the actions they took to be successful, rather than praising personal attributes such as their intelligence or writing ability, will continue to cultivate a growth mindset that leads students to invest the effort necessary to succeed.

In a strengths development classroom, instructors take this feedback one step further by tying students' successful outcomes to the effective application of their strengths. Instructors note the strengths they see in students' work, and they also note the skills, knowledge, and strategies that were utilized to be successful. Areas in need of improvement are noted as well, with suggestions for specific skills or strategies to be employed that capitalize on the strengths seen in the work. The process of offering timely, constructive, and specific feedback occurs in the context of the relationship that the instructor has built within the classroom, leading students to engage more fully in their learning experiences.

Advising From a Strengths Development Perspective

During transition periods, the provision of timely information and feedback in the context of an ongoing relationship can be particularly helpful to students (Schlossberg, 2008). The advising relationship is the one opportunity all students have for an ongoing relationship with someone who knows both the institution and the student; thus, it is the ideal vehicle for helping students through transitions. It is also an excellent venue for teaching students how to develop their strengths (Schreiner & Anderson, 2005).

Yet, as chapter 6 notes, although advising is pivotal to students during times of uncertainty and change, it is an often-neglected aspect of their experience. Light (2001) concludes that the impact of advising is underestimated and too often unexamined. If the institutional advising strategy tends to emphasize course selection rather than helping the student envision his or her future and make plans toward reaching those goals, then there is unfulfilled potential in campus advising practices.

Advising that focuses on strengths development approaches the advisor-student relationship and the entire college experience from a different perspective. Rather than focusing on problems the student is encountering, this approach emphasizes possibilities. Instead of assessing the areas in which the student is deficient and in need of remediation, strengths-based advising assesses the personal assets or qualities that the student brings into the college environment and considers how they can be multiplied by gaining the necessary knowledge and skills to develop them into strengths. In short, advising from a strengths perspective represents a paradigm shift for higher education from failure prevention and a survival mentality to success promotion and a thriving perspective (Schreiner & Anderson, 2005).

The literature describes two similar approaches to advising that integrate a strengths perspective: *strengths-based advising* and *appreciative advising*. Strengths-based advising is derived from an interdisciplinary approach grounded in the fields of social work, positive psychology, and positive organizational scholarship (Schreiner & Anderson, 2005). Appreciative advising emerges from positive psychology and the organizational development theory of appreciative inquiry (Cooperrider & Whitney, 1999), and is described in chapter 8 as a helpful approach in the senior transition to life beyond college. Both advising models have as their goal "building rapport with students, discovering their strengths, unleashing their hopes and dreams, and devising plans to make those hopes and dreams come true" (Hutson & Bloom, 2007, p. 7). The two approaches will be combined in this chapter into one *strengths development* approach to advising that is believed to capture the best of both perspectives.

The Steps of Strengths Development Advising

Step 1: Identifying and affirming students' strengths. This process of discovery builds rapport with students as advisors focus on who the student is and what he or she can contribute to the learning environment. Advisors can ask open-ended questions about students' previous successes, or they can provide students with access to instruments that measure their talents and strengths. As previously noted, the Clifton StrengthsFinder (Gallup, 1999) measures strengths of competence; whereas, the Values in Action Inventory of Strengths (Seligman et al., 2004) assesses strengths of character. Regardless of which tool is used, these types of assessments offer students positive feedback about themselves in concrete language that not only identifies their strengths but also provides external affirmation and increased self-awareness.

This phase of strengths development advising builds positive emotions in students as they learn about aspects of themselves that can equip them for success and psychological well-being. These positive emotions, in turn, enhance students' problem-solving skills and capacity for creativity, as Fredrickson (2001, 2009) notes in her broaden-and-build theory. Particularly during times of transition, these positive emotions and enhanced creative problem-solving skills equip students with the realistic optimism that is foundational to thriving.

Step 2: Helping students envision their future. Discussing their dreams and aspirations naturally leads students to set goals. Picturing a desired future self starts the process, and learning how their strengths are pathways to that future self provides students with both the motivation and specific strategies for reaching that goal (Schreiner & Anderson, 2005).

In this envisioning phase of strengths development advising, self-efficacy and intrinsic motivation are generated by the process of articulating what Markus and Nurius (1986) call *possible selves*—those aspects of oneself that one most wants to embody in the future. For some students, particularly those from disadvantaged backgrounds, a highly motivating possible self may be a negative vision of the future they wish to avoid—their most feared version of themselves that they do not want to become. Whether positive or negative, a concrete and vivid depiction of one's possible selves can serve to motivate students to take specific steps in the present to create (or avoid) those future selves.

Step 3: Designing a plan for reaching the student's goals. Helping students connect their passions and their strengths to their future selves often opens possibilities for academic majors and careers that the student had not previously considered (Bloom, Hutson, & He, 2008). In this step of advising, the focus is on creating a concrete plan that students can implement, with both short- and long-term goals that are important to the student and congruent with his or her values and strengths.

This step of strengths development advising utilizes strategies that Lopez and colleagues (2004) have labeled *hope building*. Research on college students has indicated that, after controlling for entrance exam scores and other demographic characteristics, levels of hope are significantly predictive of college outcomes such as GPA and persistence to graduation (Snyder et al., 2002). Building hope in the academic advising process involves helping students (a) identify an educational goal that is meaningful and realistically attainable for them, (b) develop multiple pathways for reaching the goal, and (c) brainstorm how to handle obstacles and remain motivated along the way. The strengths that students have identified through instruments and dialogue throughout the advising process become pathways for reaching their goals. Advisors can help students reframe potential obstacles to success as challenges that can be overcome with effort, providing the essential encouragement and support that can sustain the motivation necessary for reaching their goals (Schreiner, Hulme, Hetzel, & Lopez, 2009).

The final phase of strengths development advising is teaching students to apply their strengths to the challenges they face in college. Rather than communicating that there is one strategy for success, this approach to advising suggests the secret to success lies in capitalizing on one's strengths by using them as the foundation for addressing and overcoming challenges. Teaching students to transfer strengths from one setting to another, such as from the playing field or the theatre stage to the classroom, is a critical component of a strengths-based approach to advising (Schreiner & Anderson, 2005). Yet, the emphasis on skill transfer is often missing in traditional advising practices.

Taken together, these phases of strengths-based advising address key issues that are salient during important transitions in college students' lives, such as (a) their ability to accurately and positively appraise the situations they face, (b) the provision of support and challenge that sustains students' energy and motivation through the change process, and (c) the use of effective strategies at the appropriate time. As students learn how to develop their strengths and apply them to meet challenges and reach important goals, they experience a level of self-efficacy that can sustain them through difficult times. They also develop a wider repertoire of success strategies and proactive coping skills because they learn to use their strengths as pathways to their goals and as the foundation for addressing the inevitable challenges of college life (Schreiner & Anderson, 2005). These skills are developed within a context that is affirming and supportive, teaching students that they are valued members of the college community (Bloom et al., 2008).

Strengths Development in Student Affairs Programs

Mather (2010) describes possible ways that the emerging research in positive psychology might be applied within the context of student affairs work on today's college campuses. This author notes that positive psychologists and student affairs professionals have the mutual goal of actualizing human potential, and he suggests that a strengths approach could make a valuable contribution to that objective within the domain of student affairs by providing clues to effective intervention strategies that build upon what students do well.

Chapter 3 on first-year students describes how campus involvement is a strong predictor of thriving for this population, yet the authors note that the multitude of cocurricular activities and organizations available on campus may cause some students to feel overwhelmed, and therefore, shrink away from these opportunities to engage. A strengths development perspective may benefit students in this category, as well as all students who readily seek involvement but have difficulty discerning where to best focus their energies. Specifically, encouraging students to invest in curricular and cocurricular opportunities that will help them draw upon and intentionally cultivate their strengths may be useful in helping students determine the activities in which to engage. Indeed, one of the characteristics of the thriving college seniors highlighted in chapter 8 is that these students engage in self-evaluation, helping them discover and pursue their passions as undergraduates and use the results of that evaluation as criteria for decision making regarding optimal involvement avenues on campus and beyond. It is clear that thriving seniors who possess enough self-awareness to have insight into their own uniqueness are able to tap into intrinsic sources of motivation by engaging in activities that match their passions and strengths. Programs that emphasize strengths development may be a notable contributor to this kind of self-knowledge and informed action.

Chapter 4 describing strategies for promoting thriving among students of color on predominantly White campuses notes that a strong predictor of thriving across racial groups is a sense of community. Students' sense of belonging on campus may be a significant contributor to thriving because it increases the likelihood that students will become engaged in their own learning and in the campus community as a whole (DeNeui, 2003). In an increasingly individualized and fragmented society (Putnam, 2000), integrating a strengths approach into community-building efforts offers a platform for underscoring the value of community and interdependence by highlighting the unique contributions brought to the collective group by people with different strengths constellations. Strengths-oriented initiatives not only help students gain confidence through understanding what they bring of value to the community, but these programs also highlight the benefits inherent in building relationships with people whose strengths are different than one's own and partnering with others who have complementary strengths.

Integrating a strengths perspective into areas of student life programming can provide a venue for students to be mindful of their similarities, as opposed to merely their differences. This awareness can facilitate the building of relationships by laying the groundwork for students to connect with each other in a positive way that acknowledges the value of each contributor to an interdependent community. For example, student orientation programs might include an assessment that helps students identify their strengths, offers a shared positive language among incoming students, and reminds them of the capabilities they possess to navigate the transition into college. Diversity programming might be enhanced through the use of a strengths perspective because this approach provides insight into another dimension of individual uniqueness and can help students celebrate their own positive qualities and appreciate those of others. Team-building efforts in areas such as residence life, athletics, or student leadership could include a strengths perspective to help students understand the behavioral tendencies of their team and recognize the contribution that each member makes. When students understand the best of what each individual brings to a group effort and then learn to interpret others' behaviors accordingly, a climate of respect develops and relationships are enhanced.

Strengths development works most effectively when educators conceptualize strengths as dynamic qualities and adopt a developmental perspective in their approach to cultivating them (Louis, 2011). These principles align with the aims of many leadership development programs that exist on today's campuses. Instead of understanding leadership ability in narrow, dichotomous ways that frame it as something one either has or lacks, a strengths approach offers a more generous, nuanced foundation for leadership development by asserting that each individual has strengths of character or competence that could contribute to effective leadership if leveraged with insight and proficiency. This perspective emphasizes the acquisition of skills and the nurturing of character over the mere presence of certain traits as being primary contributors to leadership excellence and suggests the importance of a collaborative mindset in leadership endeavors. In this sense, a strengths-oriented leader has at least two central objectives: (a) to understand his or her own strengths and assume responsibility for developing them and (b) to recognize and cultivate the strengths of others. These dual foci are resonant with recent literature on leadership theory and practice, which has witnessed a shift in the past two decades from hierarchical, individualistic models to understandings of leadership that emphasize collaboration, collegiality, and empowerment (Kezar, Carducci, & Contreras-McGavin, 2006; Rost, 1991).

Guidelines for Implementing a Strengths Development Initiative on Campus

For campuses seeking to initiate new opportunities for students to explore and develop their strengths in the ways described in this chapter, the following suggestions are offered to provide a context for the successful launch of such a program. Some of the ideas noted here refer to macro-level decisions that may initiate a climate of readiness for the addition of strengths-oriented curriculum; whereas, others offer remarks on how to design the program so that it will be most effective.

Connect Efforts to Institutional Mission and Seek Broad-Based Input and Participation

As is the case with any educational reform, it is critical to consider how a strengths initiative might address current priorities on campus (such as the desire to promote student success, increase retention, or encourage appreciation for diverse perspectives) and how it aligns with the institutional mission. Clarity of perspective on these issues provides a foundation for communicating how a strengths perspective might contribute to the attainment of institutional goals and increases the likelihood of engendering support for the program from high-level institutional leaders.

The formation and implementation of a successful strengths initiative can be facilitated when the planning efforts include representation from multiple departments or arenas of campus, such as student affairs, academic affairs, and the student body. One of the many benefits of such a group is that it is well-positioned to consider how a strengths approach might be infused into various areas of the curricular or cocurricular experience, thereby reinforcing key learning objectives and providing a more seamless approach to helping students develop their strengths.

Specify Meaningful and Measurable Learning Outcomes

When planning for the implementation of a strengths program, it is important to establish a clear sense of the specific objectives or learning outcomes that it is designed to facilitate, as this information will determine the nature and content of the curriculum. Forming measurable and attainable learning objectives, which encompass the "knowledge, skills, attitudes, and habits of mind that students take with them from a learning experience" (Suskie, 2004, p. 75), provides guidance during the initial formation of a strengths initiative and is essential for assessing its effectiveness. Strengths-oriented programs have been used successfully to heighten learning and engagement in the classroom (Cantwell, 2005), increase students' sense of control over their academic outcomes (Louis, 2008), and cultivate leadership qualities (Lehnert, 2009), among many other possibilities. Although strengths-oriented initiatives on various campuses may share a common philosophical core, they will likely vary greatly in form as they are tailored to the specific goals of the setting or population for which they are developed.

Provide Adequate Support

Program administrators should consider ways to provide practical support to those charged with leading or implementing any aspect of a strengths initiative, whether through resources, training, or opportunities for collaboration. Once a strengths program has been successfully launched, the support required to sustain it may be in the form of outcomes assessment results that provide valuable feedback on the program's effectiveness and offer insight into what is working well and what needs to be reconsidered. Ongoing professional development for strengths program leaders may entail formal educational experiences or may be more informal in nature, such as the opportunity to participate in occasional discussion forums to share questions, insights, and success strategies with others on campus who are involved in the strengths initiative.

Engage Students in a Developmental Process and Conceptualizing Strengths as Dynamic

Regardless of one's approach to defining and measuring strengths, research suggests that merely offering students affirming labels to help them categorize their positive personal qualities is an incomplete strengths intervention strategy. Instead, it is critical for educators leading strengths-oriented programs to describe strengths as characteristics that are malleable and provide activities that encourage their development. Specifically, research indicates that creating strengths initiatives that exclusively seek to help students identify personal strengths may unintentionally send the message that individual success is dependent primarily on the presence of certain attributes rather than on the work required to cultivate and use them skillfully (Louis, 2011). It is therefore essential for campuses integrating strengths programs into their student success strategy to adopt a developmental perspective in their approach, helping students understand the importance of personal effort in developing and mobilizing strengths in optimal ways.

In a practical sense, this charge may have implications for the way in which educators describe the nature of strengths to their students and the approach they use to help students make meaning of any strengths assessment results included in the program. Specifically, it may be more beneficial to frame strengths as personal tendencies that can be developed as opposed to innate characteristics that are either present or absent. In addition, a developmental approach emphasizes the importance of finding ways to cultivate strengths and offers students tangible support in exploring strategies to do so by making them aware of resources and opportunities available on and off campus that may be useful in their ongoing learning.

Conclusion

In chapter 1, successful transition experiences were characterized as embodying three vital components: (a) an individual's positive cognitive appraisal of the transition, (b) the use of helpful strategies for navigating the transition, and (c) the presence of the kind of support—whether informational or interpersonal—that facilitates effective coping. A strengths development approach stimulates thriving during transitions because it is able to foster all three of these elements that contribute to a smooth transition. Specifically, strengths development approaches may encourage positive cognitive appraisal by increasing students' awareness of the personal strengths and resources they have at their disposal when facing the challenges inherent in the college experience. Such a stance may support the development of confidence and self-efficacy, thereby helping students view transitions as opportunities for growth as opposed to threats. When students are encouraged to develop their strengths, they discover and build the very strategies that will help them navigate the transitions they will encounter throughout their college years and beyond. In the process of cultivating their strengths, students learn vital information about themselves and their surroundings and are also equipped to view others through an appreciative lens, a stance that provides a foundation for building supportive relationships. These outcomes contribute to the creation of a climate of support, the third factor that is present in successful transition experiences.

As described in this chapter, strengths development may adopt a variety of forms and can be tailored to address the unique goals of the institution or individuals for which it is designed. This chapter provides a rationale for using a strengths development strategy to promote thriving and offers practical ideas for implementing this framework effectively on postsecondary campuses. The ideas presented here can provide a springboard for educators to consider how strengths development might be integrated into the campus ethos to help students realize their personal potential, derive maximum benefit from the educational experiences offered on campus, and thrive throughout college and beyond.

References

Anderson, E. C. (2000, February). *Affirming students' strengths in the critical years.* Paper presented at the Annual Conference on The First-Year Experience, Columbia, SC.

Anderson, E. C. (2005). Strengths-based educating: A concrete way to bring out the best in students—and yourself. *Educational Horizons, 83*(3), 180-189.

Anderson, E. C., Cantwell, L., & Schreiner, L. A. (2004). *Strengths-based teaching.* Retrieved from www.apu.edu/strengthsacademy

Aspinwall, L. G., & Staudinger, U. M. (Eds.). (2003). *A psychology of human strengths: Fundamental questions and future directions for a positive psychology.* Washington, DC: American Psychological Association.

Bloom, J., Hutson, B., & He, Y. (2008). *The appreciative advising revolution.* Champaign, IL: Stipes Publishing.

Buckingham, M. (2007). *Go put your strengths to work.* New York, NY: The Free Press.

Buckingham, M., & Clifton, D. O. (2001). *Now, discover your strengths.* New York, NY: The Free Press.

Cantwell, L. (2005). A comparative analysis of strengths-based versus traditional teaching methods in a freshman public speaking course: Impacts on student learning and engagement. *Dissertation Abstracts International, 67*(02A), 478-700. (UMI No. AAT3207574)

Centre for Applied Positive Psychology (CAPP). (2010). *Realise2.* Retrieved from http://www.cappeu.com/realise2.htm

Chemers, M. M., Hu, L., & Garcia, B. F. (2001). Academic self-efficacy and first-year college student performance and adjustment. *Journal of Educational Psychology, 93*(1), 55-64.

Chickering, A. W., & Gamson, Z. F. (1987). Seven principles for good practice in undergraduate education. *AAHE Bulletin, 39*(7), 3-7.

Clifton, D. O., & Harter, J. K. (2003). Investing in strengths. In K. S. Cameron, J. E. Dutton, & R. E. Quinn (Eds.), *Positive organizational scholarship* (pp. 111-121). San Francisco, CA: Berrett-Koehler.

Clifton, D. O., & Nelson, P. (1992). *Soar with your strengths.* New York, NY: Dell.

Cooperrider, D. L., & Whitney, D. (1999). *Appreciative inquiry.* San Francisco, CA: Berrett-Koehler.

DeNeui, D. L. C. (2003). An investigation of first-year college students' psychological sense of community on campus. *College Student Journal, 37*(2), 224-234.

Dweck, C. S. (2006). *Mindset: The new psychology of success.* New York, NY: Random House.

Dweck, C. S., & Molden, D. C. (2005). Self-theories: Their impact on competence motivation and acquisition. In A. J. Elliot & C. S. Dweck (Eds.), *Handbook of competence and motivation* (pp. 122-140). New York, NY: The Guilford Press.

Fox, J. (2008). *Your child's strengths: Discover them, develop them, use them.* New York, NY: Viking.

Fredrickson, B. L. (2001). The role of positive emotions in positive psychology: The broaden-and-build theory of positive emotions. *American Psychologist, 56*(3), 218–26.

Fredrickson, B. L. (2009). *Positivity.* New York, NY: Crown Publishers.

Gallup. (1999). *Clifton StrengthsFinder.* Washington, DC: Author.

Gardner, J. N., Upcraft, M. L., & Barefoot, B. O. (2005). Principles of good practice for the first college year and summary of recommendations. In M. L. Upcraft, J. N. Gardner, & B. O. Barefoot (Eds.), *Challenging and supporting the first-year student: A handbook for improving the first year of college* (pp. 515-524). San Francisco, CA: Jossey-Bass.

Hutson, B., & Bloom, J. (2007). The impact of appreciative advising on student success. *E-Source for College Transitions, 5*(1), 1, 7.

Kaplan, R. E., & Kaiser, R. B. (2010). Toward a positive psychology for leaders. In P. A. Linley, S. Harrington, & N. Garcea (Eds.), *Oxford handbook of positive psychology and work* (pp. 107-117). New York, NY: Oxford University Press.

Keyes, C. L. M., & Haidt, J. (Eds.) (2003). *Flourishing: Positive psychology and the life well-lived.* Washington, DC: American Psychological Association.

Kezar, A. J., Carducci, R., & Contreras-McGavin, M. (2006). *Rethinking the "L" word in higher education: The revolution of research on leadership* (ASHE Higher Education Report, No. 31). San Francisco, CA: Jossey-Bass.

Kuh, G. D. (2008). *High impact educational practices: What they are, who has access to them, and why they matter.* Washington, DC: Association of American Colleges and Universities.

Kuh, G. D., Kinzie, J., Buckley, J. A., Bridges, B., & Hayek, J. C. (2006, July). *What matters to student success: A review of the literature.* Paper presented at the National Symposium on Postsecondary Student Success, Washington, DC.

Kuh, G. D., Kinzie, J., Schuh, J. H., Whitt, E. J., & Associates. (2005). *Student success in college: Creating conditions that matter.* San Francisco, CA: Jossey-Bass.

Lehnert, A. B. (2009). *The influence of strengths-based development on leadership practices among undergraduate college students.* Unpublished doctoral dissertation, Regent University, Virginia Beach, VA.

Liesveld, R., & Miller, J. A. (2005). *Teach with your strengths: How great teachers inspire their students.* New York, NY: Gallup Press.

Light, R. J. (2001). *Making the most of college: Students speak their minds.* Cambridge, MA: Harvard University Press.

Linley, P. A. (2008). *Average to A+: Realising strengths in yourself and others.* Coventry, UK: CAPP Press.

Lopez, S. J., & Louis, M. C. (2009). The principles of strengths-based education. *Journal of College and Character, 10*(4), 1-8.

Lopez, S. J., Snyder, C. R., Magyar-Moe, J. L., Edwards, L. M., Pedrotti, J. T., Janowski, K., . . . Pressgrove, C. (2004). Strategies for accentuating hope. In P. A. Linley & S. Joseph (Eds.), *Positive psychology in practice* (pp. 388-404). Hoboken, NJ: John Wiley and Sons.

Louis, M. C. (2008). A comparative analysis of the effectiveness of strengths-based curricula in promoting first-year college student success. *Dissertation Abstracts International, 69*(06A). (UMI No. AAT 3321378)

Louis, M. C. (2011). Strengths interventions in higher education: The effect of identification versus development approaches on implicit self-theory. *The Journal of Positive Psychology, 6*(3), 204-215.

Markus, H., & Nurius, P. (1986). Possible selves. *American Psychologist, 41*, 954-969.

Mather, P. (2010). Positive psychology and student affairs practice: A framework of possibility. *Journal of Student Affairs Research and Practice, 42*(7), 157-173.

Nelson Laird, T. F., Chen, D., & Kuh, G. D. (2008). Classroom practices at institutions with higher-than-expected persistence rates: What student engagement data tell us. In J. M. Braxton (Ed.), *The role of the classroom in college student persistence* (New Directions for Teaching and Learning No. 115, pp. 85-100). San Francisco, CA: Jossey-Bass

Perry, R. P. (2003). Perceived (academic) control and causal thinking in achievement settings. *Canadian Psychology, 44*(4), 312-331.

Perry, R. P., Hall, N. C., & Ruthig, J. C. (2005). Perceived (academic) control and scholastic attainment in higher education. In J. C. Smart (Ed.), *Higher education: Handbook of theory and research* (Vol. 20, pp. 363-436). Norwell, MA: Springer.

Peterson, C., & Seligman, M. (2004). *Character strengths and virtues: A handbook and classification.* New York: Oxford University Press; Washington, DC: American Psychological Association.

Putnam, R. (2000). *Bowling alone: The collapse and revival of American community.* New York, NY: Simon & Schuster.

Robbins, S., Allen, J., Casillas, A., Peterson, C., & Le, H. (2006). Unraveling the differential effects of motivational and skills, social, and self-management measures from traditional predictors of college outcomes. *Journal of Educational Psychology, 98*(3), 598-616.

Rost, J. C. (1991). *Leadership for the twenty-first century.* Westport, CT: Praeger.

Ryan, R. M., & Deci, E. L. (2000). Self-determination theory and the facilitation of intrinsic motivation, social development, and well-being. *American Psychologist, 55*(1), 68-78.

Saleebey, D. (2006). Introduction: Power in the people. In D. Saleebey (Ed.), *The strengths perspective in social work practice* (4th ed., pp. 1-24). Boston, MA: Pearson.

Schlossberg, N. K. (2008). *Overwhelmed: Coping with life's ups and downs.* Lanham, MD: M. Evans.

Schreiner, L. A. (2010). Thriving in the classroom. *About Campus, 15*(3), 2-10.

Schreiner, L. A., & Anderson, E. C. (2005). Strengths-based advising: A new lens for higher education. *NACADA Journal, 25*(2), 20-29.

Schreiner, L., Hulme, E., Hetzel, R., & Lopez, S. J.(2009). Positive psychology on campus. In S. J. Lopez & C. R. Snyder (Eds.), *Oxford handbook of positive psychology* (2nd ed., pp. 569-578). New York, NY: Oxford University Press.

Schreiner, L., & Louis, M. C. (2011). The Engaged Learning Index: Implications for faculty development. *Journal of Excellence in College Teaching, 22*(1), 5-28.

Seligman, M .E. P., & Csikszentmihalyi, M. (2000). Positive psychology: An introduction. *American Psychologist, 55*, 51-82.

Seligman, M. E. P., Park, N., & Peterson, C. (2004). The Values in Action (VIA) classification of character strengths. *Ricerche di Psicologia, 27*(1), 63-78.

Seligman, M. E. P., Steen, T. A., Park, N., & Peterson, C. (2005). Positive psychology progress: Empirical validation of interventions. *American Psychologist, 60*(5), 410-421.

Shushok, F., & Hulme, E. (2006). What's right with you: Helping students find and use their personal strengths. *About Campus, 11*(4), 2-8.

Silberman, M. (1996). *Active learning: 101 strategies to teach any subject.* New York, NY: Pearson, Allyn, & Bacon.

Snyder, C., Shorey, H., Cheavens, J., Pulvers, K., Adams, V., & Wiklund, C. (2002). Hope and academic success in college. *Journal of Educational Psychology, 94*(4), 820-826.

Suskie, L. (2004). *Assessing student learning: A common sense guide.* Bolton, MA: Anker.

Tagg, J. (2003). *The learning paradigm college.* Bolton, MA: Anker Publishing.

Wood, A. M., Linley, P. A., Maltby, J., Kashdan, T. B., & Hurling, R. (2011). Using personal and psychological strengths leads to increases in well-being over time: A longitudinal study and the development of the strengths use questionnaire. *Personality and Individual Differences, 50*(1), 15-19.

Chapter 3

Thriving in the First College Year
Denise D. Nelson and Deb Vetter

Transitioning from high school to college poses an enormous opportunity for success or failure in the lives of young people. Rising levels of federal and philanthropic funding available for first-year initiatives (Upcraft, Gardner, & Barefoot, 2005) demonstrate the ubiquity of concern regarding students' successful transition into the college setting and through the first year, yet first-to-second-year persistence rates have plateaued or even declined slightly over the last three decades (Mortenson, 2005). Moreover, the fact that well over 30% of first-year college students do not persist to the second year (ACT, 2010) suggests that concerns regarding student success and retention are well founded. Retention of these new students is not only financially beneficial to the institution (Bean, 1990), but it also helps colleges and universities fulfill their responsibilities to the students they have admitted.

The transitional nature of the first year of college makes it "the most critical in shaping persistence decisions" (Trotter & Roberts, 2006, p. 372) and forming students' attitudes about learning throughout their academic careers (Astin, 1993b; Pascarella & Terenzini, 2005). For that reason, this window of opportunity should draw institutions' focused attention and intense efforts; it is the point at which supportive initiatives may have the most powerful long-term effects. Students who perceive strong institutional commitment to their success are more likely to persist (Braxton & Mundy, 2001-2002). The more fully colleges and universities understand the hurdles encountered by first-year students and the tools required to navigate those obstacles successfully, the more effectively institutions can construct curricular and cocurricular support structures on behalf of entering students. Consequently, much of the chapter is devoted to discussing the role students' degree goals, campus involvements, and sense of belonging play in regard to their overall success. The chapter offers thriving as a framework for structuring efforts to support students in the first college year and describes how common curricular and cocurricular initiatives fit within this framework.

First-Year Success

Upcraft and colleagues (2005) suggest that the acceptance of "overwhelming evidence that student success is largely determined by student experiences in the first year" (p. 1) has triggered nearly three decades of creating and expanding initiatives aimed at first-year students. Such intentional programmatic support of new students intensifies the frustration caused by first-to second-year retention rates that have remained unchanged for decades (Mortenson, 2005) and indicates that the mere existence of such programs is insufficient to address the challenges of the transition to college. Supporting first-year success requires a new perspective that not only has persistence as its goal but also emphasizes individual student thriving and seeks to understand the forces that enable it. Astin's (1993a) Inputs-Environment-Outcomes (I-E-O) model provides a useful framework for studying the transition to college and the conditions that lead to a successful transition.

Incoming Characteristics

Prior to students' arrival at their chosen institutions of higher learning, admissions offices and student development teams create profiles of the newly enrolled learners—both as individuals and as a cohort. Precollege characteristics are widely accepted as factors in persistence and attrition behaviors (Astin & Oseguera, 2005), and a clear understanding of incoming students helps colleges and universities craft programs to support the new class or specific subgroups of the class. Such programs demonstrate the reasonable inclination to intervene on behalf of students who enter college with known risk factors.

For first-year students, characteristics such as family financial resources (Bozick, 2007), educational aspiration levels (Lohfink & Paulsen, 2005; Pike & Kuh, 2005), prior academic performance (Miller & Herreid, 2008), and parents' levels of education—particularly in terms of exposure to higher education (Fike & Fike, 2008; Lohfink & Paulsen, 2005)—have been identified as predictive of retention. Colleges can investigate these factors prior to students' arrivals and plan transition programs accordingly.

The College Environment

The established power of new students' pre-existing characteristics is insufficient to adequately predict or prevent attrition (Swing & Skipper, 2007). Some students whose entering characteristics seem to predispose them to success adjust poorly and fail to persist. In contrast, many students experience profound success despite profiles that seem predictive of academic failure or dropout.

Not surprisingly, research confirms that students' experiences once they arrive at college influence first-to-second-year persistence in several ways. Although academic and social integration, foundational concepts in Tinto's (1975) original theory of student departure, are traditionally discussed as discrete concepts, subsequent iterations of that theory have acknowledged that they are "mutually interdependent" (Tinto, 1987, p. 118). A more recent qualitative study (Wilcox, Winn, & Fyvie-Gauld, 2005) demonstrates that many first-year students, particularly those living in campus residences, blur the lines imposed between the academic and social domains of student life. This lack of distinction between domains accentuates the importance of acknowledging the interactive influences of academic goals and achievement, relationships with others, and satisfaction with one's life generally. Despite the inherent overlaps among these categories, some distinctly academic and social factors are known to predict retention in first-year students.

Academic integration. Tinto's (1975) seminal theory of student departure posits that integration into the academic life of one's institution indicates alignment of personal academic goals with the school's perceived ability to support their fulfillment. This integration is evident in three areas: (a) institutional commitment, (b) academic progress, and (c) engaged learning. Institutional commitment—the ongoing desire to graduate from one's current institution—understandably predicts first-year students' intent to reenroll the following year (Hausmann, Schofield, & Woods, 2007). Commitment to full-time study has also been correlated with persistence, based on the number of units or hours first-year students attempt (Fike & Fike, 2008) and successfully earn (Kiser & Price, 2007-2008), indicating that students who remain strongly aligned with their college choice and who attend full-time are more likely to graduate.

Further evidence of academic integration resides in the level of students' engaged learning, represented by the attitudes and behaviors that indicate an investment of psychological energy in the learning process (Schreiner & Louis, 2006). Mattick and Knight (2007) describe this engagement in "educationally purposeful activities" (Kuh, Cruce, Shoup, Kinzie, & Gonyea, 2008, p. 541) as "learning through interest with the intention of understanding" (Mattick & Knight, p. 638). Kuh et al. (2008) confirm that an engaged approach to college's academic demands predicts not only first-year grades but also persistence to the second year.

Social integration. Social integration and perceptions of social support are also important for the success of first-year students (Tinto, 1975, 1993). Social support includes relationships with compatible friends, social connections that can provide academic support, and the perception that one's living situation (specifically for those who reside in shared accommodations on campus) is acceptable (Wilcox et al., 2005). Students who enroll expecting to participate in social organizations associated with the college are more likely to be retained (Miller & Herreid, 2008), suggesting that the intention to form social relationships may facilitate their persistence. These positive connections likely support a sense of belonging within the college community, which is itself predictive of retention to the second year (Hausmann et al., 2007). *Psychological sense of community* (PSC), a construct originally described by Sarason in 1974, also captures the extent to which individuals feel they belong within a community, have a voice, and can connect meaningfully with other people.

Institutional experiences extend beyond academic and social integration to encompass the broader environment in which students experience higher education. Support structures within the institution often provide the means for students to persist when they might otherwise be unable to do so. Though neither academic nor social, these structures provide for students' needs. For first-year students, receiving financial aid and formal student support services from the institution (Fike & Fike, 2008) positively predicts retention. In contrast, demanding work commitments (Bozick, 2007; Miller & Herreid, 2008) and off-campus living arrangements (Bozick, 2007) correlate with a diminished likelihood to persist beyond the first year, possibly because they distance students from campus life and may inhibit a student's freedom to access these helpful services.

Toward New Perspectives

Experienced practitioners realize that a student's characteristics upon enrollment and levels of integration into the academic and social environments of the college provide insight into his or her success, but that additional forces shape experiences and decisions. To help explain this complex phenomenon, Bean and Eaton (2000) contend, "leaving college is a behavior, and that behavior is psychologically motivated" (p. 49). Similarly, Tinto (1987) noted that personal motivations inform students' decisions to stay or leave, calling departure "a highly idiosyncratic event" (p. 39). The same holds true for engagement in the learning process, connection with faculty and other students, and for other indicators of holistic success in college. Students are individual decision makers whose attitudes and perspectives encompass a wide variety of influences. For this reason, researchers (Bean & Eaton, 2000; DeBerard, Spielmans, & Julka, 2004; Pascarella & Terenzini, 2005) encourage the consideration of psychological, rather than strictly sociological, factors to more fully understand the components of retention and attrition. Student thriving, described as optimal functioning in academic, interpersonal, and intrapersonal domains of the college experience (Schreiner, McIntosh, Nelson, & Pothoven, 2009), is one such model. On the whole, thriving students report higher college grades, stronger intentions to graduate from their current institution, greater feelings of institutional fit, and a higher likelihood of selecting the same school again if given a chance to revisit their college enrollment choice (Schreiner, Pothoven, Nelson, & McIntosh, 2009).

Students who function well academically and interpersonally, view their circumstances optimistically, and experience a sense of well-being are able to approach the demands of college well-equipped for success. However, students who lack these essential characteristics are unable to fully enjoy the breadth of positive experiences offered by the postsecondary living and learning environment and may struggle to persist. Such students can be said to *languish* (Keyes, 2002) in the higher education environment. Because both thriving and languishing are likely to gain momentum throughout the transitional experience of the first year, colleges and universities must gather information about the predictors of thriving in first-year students. Armed with such data, institutions will be appropriately equipped for supporting new students as they succeed and for intervening on their behalf before a lack of success leads to dissatisfaction, poor performance, or departure.

Predicting Thriving in the First Year

In order to identify the precursors of thriving in first-year students, hierarchical multiple regression was conducted on the Thriving Quotient scores of a subset of 908 first-year students whose data were collected in association with a larger thriving study that included students across the full range of class levels at 21 four-year institutions, 12 private and 9 public, representing several regions across the United States. Sampling procedures differed by institution; most schools delivered the thriving questionnaire online via an e-mail invitation distributed to all students or to a random sample of the student population.

Of the students included in the first-year sample, nearly three quarters (74.2%; $n = 673$) were female, and close to 78% ($n = 690$) identified themselves as Caucasian or White. The second largest ethnic group was African American/Black students (6.6%), followed by Latino/Latina (5.5%), Multiracial (3.4%), and Asian/Pacific Islander students (3.3%). Nearly one quarter of the participants (24.3%) indicated that they were the first in their immediate families to attend college. Table 3.1 depicts several characteristics of the study sample.

The Thriving Quotient is a valid and reliable instrument described in chapter 1 of this book that assesses students' well-being and positive functioning via five scales: Academic Determination, Engaged Learning, Positive Perspective, Social Connectedness, and Diverse Citizenship. In addition to the 25 items reflecting student thriving, the survey administered to students contains questions regarding their demographic characteristics, participation in various campus experiences, student-faculty interaction, and psychological sense of community.

Among the many outcomes investigated by the study were overall satisfaction with college, satisfaction with several specific components of the college experience, students' intention to remain at their chosen institution through graduation, and the extent to which they deemed their tuition well spent. At the heart of the study was the desire to better understand the relationships among student characteristics, college involvement, thriving, and other positive outcomes of the college experience.

Data analysis followed recommendations in the literature, controlling for student input characteristics and prior academic performance in blocks 1 and 2, respectively, using the direct method to enter variables at each stage. The variables included in block 1 were *first-generation* (yes or no), *gender, income,* and *race.* Although data for race initially included several categories as described above, small samples for a number of ethnic groups indicated that it was advisable to collapse all groups comprising students of color into a single category for this analysis, effectively creating a dichotomous variable. Block 2 included two variables, high school grades and degree goal, to control for prior academic performance and educational aspiration. Involvement entered the analysis in block 3 as a scale score reflecting the extent of students' participation in given aspects of

Table 3.1
Characteristics of the First-Year Student Sample (N = 908)

Characteristic	N	%
Gender		
Male	234	25.8
Female	673	74.2
Race/Ethnicity		
White/Caucasian	690	77.5
African American/Black	59	6.6
Latino/a	49	5.5
Multiracial	30	3.4
Asian/Pacific Islander	29	3.2
International student	8	0.9
Native American	6	0.7
Decline to respond	19	2.1
Generational Status		
First-generation	219	24.3
Not first-generation	682	75.7
Residence		
On campus	785	86.9
Off campus	118	13.1

the college environment; finally PSC, also a scale score, entered the regression in block 4. Measures of student-faculty interaction were not significantly correlated with thriving scales in this student sample, and thus were not included in the multiple regression analysis.

Six separate regression analyses were conducted—one in which thriving was the criterion variable, along with one for each its five component factors. Although student success depends on a combination of forces and experiences that are not yet fully understood, the variables measured in this analysis could account for nearly one quarter (24%) of the variance in students' Engaged Learning scores and well over half (57%) of the variation in overall thriving scores. In essence, then, knowing students' demographic characteristics, high school grades and degree aspirations, level of involvement in campus organizations and activities, and their sense of community on campus enables us to predict with some confidence the extent to which they are thriving. A summary of the analyses is presented in Table 3.2. Three important predictors of thriving in first-year students emerged: (a) degree goal, (b) campus involvement, and (c) psychological sense of community.

Degree Goal

Previous research (Lohfink & Paulsen, 2005; Pike & Kuh, 2005) has found that the level of education to which students aspire is powerfully associated with their likelihood of persisting to the second year of college. Admittedly, persisting and thriving are not synonymous; still, the established connection between thriving and reenrollment (Schreiner, Pothoven et al., 2009) suggests that such a relationship between educational aspiration and thriving likely exists. For this reason, the current study used degree goal as one control variable to take into account the influence of students' aspirations and then proceeded to examine the usefulness of additional factors in explaining the differences among students' levels of thriving. The results confirmed that degree goal is indeed predictive of overall thriving as well as both of the factors that comprise academic thriving.

Astin's (1993a) I-E-O model would likely place educational aspiration with input variables because students arrive at college with such aspirations already established. Unlike characteristics such as race or first-generation status, however, students' degree goals are not indelibly fixed. Some students may enter college never having been exposed to the opportunities afforded by graduate education. Others may be unaware of financial aid options that could decrease the fiscal burden associated with advanced degrees. Despite an absence of intervention studies seeking to raise students' educational goals, it is reasonable to believe that some learners who begin their first year of college aspiring to earn only a bachelor's degree may adjust their degree goals as they gain confidence academically, interact with highly educated faculty, and learn about potential courses of study or funding for graduate programs.

Table 3.2

Summary of Hierarchical Regression Analyses for Variables Predicting Five Thriving Factors and Overall Thriving (N = 908)

Variable	Academic determination β	Engaged learning β	Positive perspective β	Social connectedness β	Diverse citizenship β	Overall thriving β
Step 1						
First-generation (no)	.066	.038	.050	.044	.089*	.079
Gender (male)	-.137***	-.103**	-.050	.023	-.125**	-.109**
Income	.061	-.007	.103*	.123**	.055	.092*
Student of color	-.002	-.029	.011	.055	-.053	-.003
Adj. R²	**.023**	**.006**	**.013**	**.020**	**.023**	**.025**
Step 2						
HS grades	.203***	.082*	.108**	.097*	.056	.153***
Degree goal	.091*	.135**	.035	.002	.079*	.092*
R² Change	**.051**	**.027**	**.013**	**.009**	**.010**	**.034**
Step 3						
Involvement	.131**	.124**	.296***	.167***	.400***	.308***
R² Change	**.016**	**.015**	**.084**	**.027**	**.153**	**.091**
Step 4						
PSC	.423***	.467***	.510***	.578***	.526***	.684***
R² Change	**.161**	**.197**	**.235**	**.301**	**.250**	**.422**
Total R²	**.249**	**.242**	**.343**	**.355**	**.435**	**.571**

* $p < .05$. ** $p < .01$. *** $p < .001$.

Students' degree aspirations must be considered valid personal decisions that are neither inherently good nor bad. Different career goals require varying levels of education, and pushing all students toward advanced degrees would almost certainly prove detrimental. At the same time, some students may artificially limit their goals due to fear of failure, lack of highly educated role models, underestimation of the education required for their desired profession, or simply never having considered graduate education. For these students, programming that provides information about career requirements and advanced educational opportunities and that helps them set suitable educational goals may prove highly beneficial. Not only does increased degree aspiration correspond to higher levels of overall thriving, but expectancy-value motivation theory (Eccles & Wigfield, 2002) suggests that appropriately high degree goals should engender persistence in pursuing those goals.

Campus Involvement

Campus involvement is the second noteworthy predictor of thriving among first-year college students. Although the higher education literature often uses the terms involvement and engagement interchangeably (Wolf-Wendel, Ward, & Kinzie, 2009), for the purposes of this study, campus involvement is measured as a scale score of students' responses regarding the frequency of their participation in five areas: (a) student organizations on campus, (b) leadership roles in such organizations, (c) student activities or events, (d) fraternities or sororities, and (e) community service. Astin (1984) underscores the importance of involvement in his foundational theory of student development, demonstrating that investment in the learning process, interaction with other students individually and through organizations, and interaction with faculty outside the classroom increase students' learning and development. Thriving's emphasis on the academic, relational, and personal aspects of students' lives explains the natural relationship between involvement and thriving.

Involvement in campus activities and organizations is an essential component of the environment portion of Astin's (1993a) I-E-O model. Some student experiences during the first year are passively received; for example, enrollment in a first-year seminar may be required of all students, and the campus climate may already be well established. Other experiences, however, are undertaken at the student's discretion. These voluntary experiences, including participation in selected organizations and activities, comprise the campus involvement variable that proves predictive of thriving in the current study.

The behavioral nature of involvement makes it particularly amenable to change. Students need not gain new skills or academic knowledge to expand their involvement. In many cases, first-year students may simply lack an awareness of the breadth of opportunities afforded by their institutions for activities, organizations, or events. In other circumstances, the highly stimulating postsecondary environment may overwhelm some students who, not knowing how best to become involved, simply shrink from cocurricular involvement altogether. For both the uninformed and the reluctant, universities may be wise to create incentives that spur students to participate in college events or activities in new ways.

Psychological Sense of Community

The final predictor, PSC (Sarason, 1974), proved to be the single variable that significantly predicted overall thriving as well as all five of the factors that comprise thriving. These relationships are evident after controlling for input characteristics, prior academic performance, and degree aspiration. DeNeui (2003), who surmised that student expectations may influence the development of PSC over time, found significant positive correlations between PSC and extroversion, which correlates with participation in campus activities.

Not only are involvement and sense of community both predictive of thriving, but their connection to one another, while not examined in depth in the current study, seems apparent. One pertinent finding drawn from the study is that involvement is predictive of Social Connectedness only until sense of community enters the regression equation. At that point, the influence of sense of community drowns out involvement, suggesting that involvement predicts Social Connectedness only to the extent that the activities in which a student participates result in a sense of community. The college or university campus environment is inarguably a community, and the extent to which students positively identify with the institution's educational and social structures informs their success, both individually and collectively. Previously, levels of PSC among college students have been correlated primarily with demographic variables, including gender, class standing, and residential versus commuter status, among other categorical data (Bohus, Woods, & Chan, 2005; DeNeui, 2003; Lounsbury & DeNeui, 1995); however, the relationship between sense of community and thriving in first-year students is newly established.

Although only recently identified, the correlation between sense of community and thriving should not be surprising. Students who score high on the

PSC scale have indicated strong agreement that they belong at the institution, students at their chosen institution have a meaningful voice in the life of the school, help is available on campus in times of need, they are proud of the school they have chosen to attend, and forming friendships is not difficult. These students are conveying a sense of assurance that they are valued and supported by their institution, sufficient personal relationships are available, and they have chosen well in their college search.

Programming for Thriving

The transition from high school to college, from the familiar to the unknown, can be a daunting experience. Most students begin college with little knowledge of what to expect and few strategies for engaging successfully. Colleges that understand the importance of educational aspiration, campus involvement, and sense of community as predictors of first-year thriving can implement specific practices with potential to enrich the college experience of these new students in ways that encourage their success. Based on the findings of this study, college faculty and staff need to focus on initiatives and interventions that provide first-year students with opportunities to examine and expand their degree goals, encourage involvement in campus activities or organizations, and facilitate a psychological sense of community.

Beneficial Structures

In their examination of college impact, Pascarella and Terenzini (2005) contend that when first-year students are part of a supportive community that facilitates genuine relationships with peers and creates opportunities for greater interaction with faculty, they are likely to develop a positive perspective about themselves as learners and as members of the community. This positive perspective is indicated by the quality and diversity of their relationships and their clear sense of purpose in pursing an education as demonstrated by the psychological energy they devote to the learning process. This section identifies first-year programs or structures that may facilitate such a positive perspective while actively addressing the predictors of thriving identified by this study: degree aspiration, campus involvement, and psychological sense of community.

New student orientation. At the outset of the school year, new student orientation sessions and activities can be valuable mechanisms for communicating a supportive campus environment to first-year students. Welcome Week events and other orientation programs offer practical help in adjusting to college, articulate the values and culture of the institution, and provide opportunities for interpersonal connections through social activities. The most educationally effective schools (Kuh, Kinzie, Schuh, Whitt, & Associates, 2005) use introductory programs to demonstrate "what is valued and how things are done" (p. 113) at the institution, helping first-year students acclimate to their new environment and begin to feel as though they belong to the community. Students learn about the ethos and culture of the institution as well as what services and resources are available to assist them academically and personally.

Although they provide a pragmatic welcome to first-year students' new environment, short-term orientation programs like Welcome Week activities are, by nature, limited in scope by their emphasis on the early days of students' transition to the first year of college. For orientation programs to enhance first-year student thriving, they need to extend beyond the first few days or weeks of a semester, so that orientation is not perceived as an event but rather an ongoing process for students throughout their first year. The best orientation programs reflect the mission and values of the institution and balance students' academic and social needs during this time of transition. They also connect students to faculty throughout the process, introduce senior administrators, and involve the students' families appropriately, in an effort to not only build community and communicate the institution's commitment to student welfare, but also to facilitate the academic engagement that is crucial to student thriving and success. Orientation is viewed as an ongoing partnership of academic and student affairs professionals, so that students experience a seamless learning experience in their first year. Finally, orientation programs that most effectively position the first-year student to thrive find alternatives to the barrage of testing that too often communicates to students all the ways they are deficient as they begin the college journey (Mullendore & Banahan, 2005). Carefully chosen assessments and appropriate timing and feedback from those assessments can make the difference between a student who survives and one who thrives.

First-year seminars and courses. Orientation programs help ease students' initial transition to a new environment and acquaint them with campus services and personnel, yet they typically lack the ongoing academic and social structures required to most effectively support new students throughout their first year. In contrast, first-year seminars and courses that extend throughout the first semester or the entire first year provide students a point of regular contact with a cohort of peers and at least one faculty member as they adjust to life and learning in college. At the outset of the new millennium, Barefoot

(2002) reported that nearly all campuses (94.1%) had some type of first-year course. The ubiquity of first-year seminars suggests that they offer a prime venue for delivering interventions that enable thriving across the class of newly enrolled students.

Research on first-year seminars has proliferated over the last 30 years, with Pascarella and Terenzini (2005) reporting that first-year seminars "produce uniformly consistent evidence of positive and statistically significant advantages to students who take the courses" (p. 400). Their review emphasizes the benefits of first-year seminars in regard to persistence, graduation rates, and academic performance. The wide array of positive outcomes associated with participation in first-year seminars should drive those schools that have not yet initiated such courses to do so. Further, the benefits that accrue to first-year seminar participants demonstrate that the resources assigned to staffing these classes are meaningfully invested.

First-year seminars intentionally designed to enhance student thriving have a number of key features. In addition to the smaller class sizes, discussion focus, and emphasis on creating community and navigating university systems that currently characterizes such courses (Upcraft et al., 2005), a seminar with thriving as its goal would employ instructors who also serve as academic advisors for the students in their courses for the first year (Schreiner, 2010). Such an approach would provide learners with concrete assistance in connecting course content to their broader academic and life goals. This structure would encourage the development of a more substantive relationship with the advisor, as well.

Linking the course thematically within a learning community, using peer instructors who coteach with the faculty in these classes, and focusing the course intentionally on learning how to learn would foster students' academic determination and engaged learning, setting them on a trajectory for success as they transition to college (Schreiner, 2010). The learning community context helps students view their academic experience holistically and from an interdisciplinary perspective, encouraging greater engagement in the learning process. The use of peer instructors not only offers the support that is integral to developing a psychological sense of community, but also provides student role models for self-regulated and engaged learning. Additionally, focusing the course content on learning how to learn is a research-based strategy that encourages students to move away from the rote memory typical of high school toward the inquiry-based learning that leads to engagement (Heiman, 2010).

Learning communities. Learning communities deserve special attention in the discussion regarding student success in the first year of college because they "attempt to move collaborative learning beyond the classroom and into broader aspects of a college student's life" (Pascarella & Terenzini, 2005, p. 109). Kuh et al. (2005) identify learning communities as an especially useful approach to this sort of expansive learning environment, suggesting that students in learning communities engage more actively with academic material and with their peers. Rocconi (2011) confirms this assertion in his findings that "learning community students exert more effort in their coursework and in their interactions with faculty members and other students" (p. 188). Laufgraben's (2005) emphasis on the educational and developmental benefits of learning communities demonstrates that the extent of students' integration into shared academic and social experiences corresponds to their overall success within the college environment.

Learning communities likely include first-year seminars and other introductory or general education courses, and they also build upon those course experiences with activities and, in some cases, shared on-campus living arrangements. As noted earlier in the chapter, the power of any first-year seminar to improve levels of thriving for student participants increases appreciably when the lead professor serves as the students' advisor and the seminar group is collectively enrolled in one or more additional courses to create a cohort of learners with strong ties to a small team of faculty members (Schreiner, 2010). By offering blocks of thematically linked courses in conjunction with social activities, out-of-class academic activities, and other learning or service opportunities, colleges create environments that encompass both academic and social aspects of students' development (Kuh et al., 2005; Pascarella & Terenzini, 2005), thereby fueling their ability to thrive.

Strategies for Facilitating Thriving Within These Structures

Educational aspirations. Effective orientation or first-year transition programs should provide opportunities for students to interact both formally and informally with institutional faculty. Although such interaction is beneficial for several reasons, one important consideration is that contact with highly educated individuals may help broaden the educational aspirations of first-year students whose prior exposure to graduate education is limited. In formal first-year courses, guest faculty may be included as participants in panels or as assigned presenters. Excellent opportunities for faculty to initiate quality interaction with students outside the classroom lie in serving as mentors for orientation groups, hosting gatherings of first-year students in their homes, eating meals in campus dining areas during the first weeks of the semester, and participating in social events or service activities. Learning communities offer even more extensive opportunities for students to interact with faculty by creating an environment within which professors and students share academic, social, and advising relationships over an extended period.

In an effort to spur conversations within first-year students regarding educational aspiration, institutions should consider scheduling an alma mater day on which faculty and staff wear or display paraphernalia associated with the institution from which they earned their highest degree. Special programming associated with the day could include presentations where faculty describe the circumstances that propelled them toward an advanced degree and the obstacles they overcame in the course of their postbaccalaureate education. Similarly, staff from various offices could discuss the ways in which their academic experiences prepared them for their roles at the institution. Within learning communities, students should be given opportunities for informal one-on-one interactions with their faculty to discuss the possibilities of post-baccalaureate education and to explore their dreams or concerns about the options available to them. More formal activities for students could involve goal-setting exercises that map a path from the first year of college to the student's ultimate career goal, acknowledging the level of education required to enter the chosen profession competitively.

Involvement. In addition to evaluating their long-term educational goals, first-year students must examine their level of involvement in their immediate living and learning environment. Campus involvement gives students a sense that they belong to the community. It helps them become more aware of the campus services and resources available to help them succeed; increases the frequency of encounters with peers, staff, and faculty; offers practical experience in leadership; and provides a voice in the decisions and policies that impact what happens on campus.

Students should be provided a wide variety of high-quality, diverse opportunities for involvement through academic and social organizations, formal student activities, and volunteer opportunities. First-year courses offer an ideal venue for promoting these options by introducing students to institutional opportunities for involvement and encouraging participation through grading incentives. Small-group assignments can connect pairs or trios of students with particular campus organizations for a designated period. Not only does this association introduce the assigned group to a given organization, but reporting back to fellow students about the organization's purpose and activities increases the familiarity of the entire class with campus offerings.

In learning communities, faculty and cocurricular staff from student development offices can collaborate to identify involvement opportunities that build on the themes explored in class. Together, they can provide students with directed activities and with evaluative tools to discern whether additional clubs or activities will suit their interests and fit their schedules. Service-learning activities provide another beneficial opportunity for involvement. Working alongside classmates and members of the larger community provides students with a valuable opportunity to create new relationships and deepen existing connections while contributing meaningfully to enrich the lives or circumstances of others. When this work is undertaken collaboratively by a group of students in an established learning community, expanding relationships with faculty and peers, connecting service experiences with course material, and reflecting meaningfully about social justice and other relevant issues are just a few of the opportunities that accompany the endeavor.

Sense of community. Sarason (1974) and McMillan and Chavis (1986) describe the components of a sense of belonging: membership, influence, integration and fulfillment, and shared emotional connection. First and foremost, students must feel that they belong at their chosen institution. In order to help students visualize their membership within the institutional learning community, first-year seminar instructors might ask students to work in groups to identify several concise descriptions of the school, of groups within it, or of the values it represents. These descriptions should be posted throughout the classroom. Students can then brainstorm several words or phrases that describe themselves or their values. The students are given several minutes to move throughout the classroom, posting descriptions of themselves or their values under corresponding categories that describe the school. Either in discussion or in a written assignment, students reflect on the areas in which they were able to connect their own values with those of the institution and are encouraged to speculate on ways to use their unique attributes to benefit their fellow students. Facilitated well, this activity can demonstrate students' existing points of connection to the larger community and frame their uniqueness as a tool for contributing to their living and learning environments. This learning experience could also take place outside the classroom. For example, the activity could be facilitated by hall directors, resident assistants, peer leaders, or other student life staff as part of a student development seminar within residence halls, relating students' values to those of the residential environment and to the institution at large.

Influence, the second component of sense of community, reflects the extent to which students believe their input is respected in decision-making processes at the institution. For colleges and universities with a student government or a similar student-led policy group, representatives could be invited to address first-year seminar classes. Their presentations should include specific examples of the initiatives accomplished by the group and clear invitations for the new students to participate in every appropriate way.

In addition to understanding the ways in which students can contribute to the institution, first-year students also need to feel that the institution provides resources to safeguard their individual well-being. Integration into the institution's structures and community requires that students have access to help when they need it. One way to help a first-year students learn about the resources available to them is to create a case study project in which small groups are each assigned a fictitious student with a well-described set of needs. To fulfill the assignment, groups are required to identify appropriate campus resources for each of the given needs and visit the office responsible for the designated service to obtain a description of the resources provided. Each group should make a presentation to the class that describes the needs of their assigned individual and explains how the case study student could pursue assistance.

The framework of a psychological sense of community suggests not only that students' needs are met but also that they experience positive psychological consequences as a result of their association with the institution. Fulfilled students are proud of their college or university and believe that their student role fills an important need in their lives. The first-year seminar can engender this sense of fulfillment by featuring successful alumni as guest speakers and asking those individuals to describe how the institution prepared them for their current success. Following this panel or special presentation, students may be asked to identify two or three of their personal goals for life after college and then explain how their current learning experiences support the accomplishment of those goals. Similar events could be hosted in first-year residence halls or by the campus career center.

Finally, a psychological sense of community requires that students feel a shared emotional connection with others in the community. Particularly within the college environment, these connections are expressed as friendships. The first-year seminar can help initiate and enrich friendships by providing nonacademic social gatherings for seminar members. A combination of voluntary and required activities gives participants freedom to form connections in a variety of settings. Activities, such as scavenger hunts or group games, allow students to work together in friendly competition with one another, while less-structured events, such as picnics, bonfires, or local sightseeing outings, encourage informal interaction with peers. These types of activities traditionally fall within the cocurricular realm, so institutions that offer first-year seminars should consider partnering with student life professionals who may already be delivering these programs. At institutions where these activities tend to involve only residential students, the first-year seminar may be one way of connecting commuting students with valuable opportunities for social interaction. Learning communities offer the most robust form of community building, as faculty and cocurricular staff mentor students through the challenges of coursework, the ups and downs of interpersonal relationships, and the numerous stages of envisioning their possible futures.

Conclusion

For many institutions, first-year programming already exists—at least at a rudimentary level. Within the context of these initiatives, colleges and universities can equip new students to thrive through their initial year of college and beyond. First-year seminars provide an expansive venue for institutional programming that reaches large groups of new students. Yet, learning communities—in which students can explore common themes, learn both collectively and collaboratively, and interact extensively with peers and faculty—potentially offer the greatest exposure to institutional structures and opportunities that fuel thriving. As colleges and universities learn about the predictors of thriving for new college students, they should eagerly pursue initiatives that provide opportunities for first-year students to examine their degree goals, expand their involvement in campus organizations and activities, and bolster their psychological sense of community.

If the successful transition to college hinges to a great extent on students' inner resources as exemplified by the concept of thriving, the persistent challenge for colleges is the creation of living and learning environments within which such resources may be maximized to a student's benefit. Clearly conveying institutional expectations within these supportive settings empowers students to take responsibility for themselves and their learning throughout their postsecondary experience. By creating programs that serve all first-year students, colleges and universities increase a student's likelihood of persistence and success, even for learners whose needs may not have been apparent upon enrollment. This essential notion should prompt researchers, practitioners, and institutions of higher education to take action in the interest of supporting higher comprehensive levels of healthy functioning for all students.

References

ACT. (2010). *National collegiate retention and persistence to degree rates.* Retrieved from http://www.act.org/policymakers/pdf/retain_2010.pdf

Astin, A. W. (1984). Student involvement: A developmental theory for higher education. *Journal of College Student Personnel, 25,* 297-308.

Astin, A. W. (1993a). *Assessment for excellence: The philosophy and practice of assessment and evaluation in higher education.* Westport, CT: The American Council on Education/Oryx Press.

Astin, A. W. (1993b). *What matters in college: Four critical years revisited.* San Francisco, CA: Jossey-Bass.

Astin, A. W., & Oseguera, L. (2005). Pre-college and institutional influences on degree attainment. In A. Seidman (Ed.), *College student retention: Formula for student success* (pp. 245-276). Bolton, MA: Anker Publishing.

Barefoot, B. (2002). *Second National Survey of First-Year Academic Practices.* Brevard, NC: Policy Center on the First Year of College.

Bean, J. P. (1990). Why students leave: Insights from research. In D. Hossler & J. P. Bean (Eds.), *The strategic management of college enrollments* (pp. 147-169). San Francisco, CA: Jossey-Bass.

Bean, J. P., & Eaton, S. B. (2000). A psychological model of college student retention. In J. M. Braxton (Ed.), *Reworking the student departure puzzle: New theory and research on college student retention* (pp. 48-61). Nashville, TN: Vanderbilt University Press.

Bohus, S., Woods, R. H., & Chan, K. C. (2005). Psychological sense of community among students on religious collegiate campuses in the Christian evangelical tradition. *Christian Higher Education, 4,* 19-40.

Bozick, R. (2007). Making it through the first year of college: The role of students' economic resources, employment, and living arrangements. *Sociology of Education, 80*(3), 261-284.

Braxton, J. M., & Mundy, M. E. (2001-2002). Powerful institutional levers to reduce college student departure. *Journal of College Student Retention, 3*(1), 91-118.

DeBerard, M. S., Spielmans, G. I., & Julka, D. L. (2004). Predictors of academic achievement and retention among college freshmen: A longitudinal study. *College Student Journal, 38*(1), 66-80.

DeNeui, D. (2003). An investigation of first-year college students' psychological sense of community on campus. *College Student Journal, 37*(2), 224-234.

Eccles, J. S., & Wigfield, A. (2002). Motivational beliefs, values, and goals. *Annual Review of Psychology, 53*, 109-132.

Fike, D. S., & Fike, R. (2008). Predictors of first-year student retention in the community college. *Community College Review, 36*(2), 68-88.

Heiman, M. (2010). Solving the problem: Improving retention in higher education. *Academic Leadership, 8*(1). Retrieved from http://www.academicleadership. org/406/solving_the_problem_improving_retention_in_higher_education/

Hausmann, L. R. M., Schofield, J. W., & Woods, R. L. (2007). Sense of belonging as a predictor of intentions to persist among African American and White first-year college students. *Research in Higher Education, 48*(7), 803-839.

Keyes, C. L. M. (2002). The mental health continuum: From languishing to flourishing in life. *Journal of Health and Social Behavior, 43*(2), 207-222.

Kiser, A. I. T., & Price, L. (2007-2008). The persistence of college students from their freshman to sophomore year. *Journal of College Student Retention, 9*(4), 421-436.

Kuh, G. D., Cruce, T. M., Shoup, R., Kinzie, J., & Gonyea, R. M. (2008). Unmasking the effects of student engagement on first-year college grades and persistence. *Journal of Higher Education, 79*(5), 540-563.

Kuh, G. D., Kinzie, J., Schuh, J. H., Whitt, E. J., & Associates, (2005). *Student success in college: Creating conditions that matter.* San Francisco, CA: Jossey-Bass.

Laufgraben, J. L. (2005). Learning communities. In M. L. Upcraft, J. N. Gardner, & B. O. Barefoot (Eds.), *Challenging and supporting the first-year student: A handbook for improving the first year of college* (pp. 371-389). San Francisco, CA: Jossey-Bass.

Lohfink, M. M., & Paulsen, M. B. (2005). Comparing the determinants of persistence for first-generation and continuing-generation students. *Journal of College Student Development, 46*(4), 409-428.

Lounsbury, J. W., & DeNeui, D. (1995). Psychological sense of community on campus. *College Student Journal, 29*, 270-277.

Mattick, K., & Knight, L. (2007). High-quality learning: Harder to achieve than we think? *Medical Education, 41*, 638-644.

McMillan, D. W., & Chavis, D. M. (1986). Sense of community: A definition and theory. *Journal of Community Psychology, 14*, 6-23.

Miller, T. E., & Herreid, C. H. (2008). Analysis of variables to predict first-year persistence using logistic regression analysis at the University of South Florida. *College & University, 83*(3), 2-11.

Mortenson, T. G. (2005). Measurements of persistence. In A. Seidman (Ed.), *College student retention: Formula for student success* (pp. 31-60). Westport, CT: Praeger.

Mullendore, R. H., & Banahan, L. A. (2005). Designing orientation programs. In M. L. Upcraft, J. N. Gardner, & B. O. Barefoot (Eds.), *Challenging and supporting the first-year student: A handbook for improving the first year of college* (pp. 391-409). San Francisco, CA: Jossey-Bass.

Pascarella, E. T., & Terenzini, P. T. (2005). *How college affects students: A third decade of research*. San Francisco, CA: Jossey-Bass.

Pike, G. R., & Kuh, G. D. (2005). First- and second-generation college students: A comparison of their engagement and intellectual development. *Journal of Higher Education, 76*(3), 276-300.

Rocconi, L. M. (2011). The impact of learning communities on first-year students' growth and development in college. *Research in Higher Education, 52,* 178-193.

Sarason, S. B. (1974). *The psychological sense of community: Prospects for a community psychology*. San Francisco, CA: Jossey-Bass.

Schreiner, L. A. (2010). Thriving in the classroom. *About Campus, 15*(3), 2-10.

Schreiner, L. A., & Louis, M. (2006, November). *Measuring engaged learning in college students: Beyond the borders of NSSE*. Paper presented at the annual meeting of the Association for the Study of Higher Education, Anaheim, CA.

Schreiner, L. A., McIntosh, E. J., Nelson, D., & Pothoven, S. (2009). *The Thriving Quotient: Advancing the assessment of student success*. Paper presented at the annual meeting of the Association for the Study of Higher Education, Vancouver, Canada.

Schreiner, L. A., Pothoven, S., Nelson, D., & McIntosh, E. J. (2009). *College student thriving: Predictors of success and retention*. Paper presented at the annual meeting of the Association for the Study of Higher Education, Vancouver, Canada.

Swing, R. L., & Skipper, T. L. (2007). Achieving student success in the first year of college. In G. L. Kramer & Associates (Eds.), *Fostering student success in the campus community* (pp. 369-391). San Francisco, CA: Jossey-Bass.

Tinto, V. (1975). Dropout from higher education: A theoretical synthesis of recent research. *Review of Educational Research, 45*(1), 89-125.

Tinto, V. (1987). *Leaving college: Rethinking the causes and cures of student attrition*. Chicago, IL: University of Chicago.

Tinto, V. (1993). *Leaving college: Rethinking the causes and cures of student attrition* (2nd ed.). Chicago, IL: University of Chicago.

Trotter, E., & Roberts, C. (2006). Enhancing the early student experience. *Higher Education Research and Development, 25*(4), 371-386.

Upcraft, M. L., Gardner, J. N., & Barefoot, B. O. (2005). *Challenging and supporting the first-year student: A handbook for improving the first year*. San Francisco, CA: Jossey-Bass.

Wilcox, P., Winn, S., & Fyvie-Gauld, M. (2005). "It was nothing to do with the university, it was just the people": The role of social support in the first-year experience of higher education. *Studies in Higher Education, 30*(6), 707-722.

Wolf-Wendel, L., Ward, K., & Kinzie, J. (2009). A tangled web of terms: The overlap and unique contribution of involvement, engagement, and integration to understanding college student success. *Journal of College Student Development, 50*(4), 407-428.

Chapter 4

Thriving in Students of Color on Predominantly White Campuses: A Divergent Path?

Kristin Paredes-Collins

When asked to describe her first-year transition to college, Katrina, a Black student in her third year at a small, private, predominantly White institution (PWI) on the West Coast, used words such as "unbearable" and recalled feelings of invisibility among her peers. When Katrina was interviewed as a part of a broad study on campus climate for diversity[1], she gave in-depth descriptions of her experience as a Black woman in the classroom, her overall cultural transition, and the difficulty she encountered as she attempted to forge real relationships with White students:

> I didn't fit in. I wore Jordan's, Timberlands, I listened to hip-hop, and I was loud. I just, I was honest, and I met this kind of façade in a way. Everyone wants you to think that they are your friend and you really believe that you're really their friend, but after the first semester…it started to become really cliquey.

Katrina continued, describing some of the struggles she experienced as she tried to fit in during her first year.

> I really became conscious of watching what I said, and simple things like smell. I don't wash my hair every day; they do. The people I lived with in my dorm, they are all White, they wash their hair every single day. So I became conscious of the smell of hair and whether mine smelled different or not. What we ate [was also different]: tofu, what is that? I had never

---

[1] The author collected Katrina's statements in a qualitative case study that explored multiple perspectives of the campus climate for diversity at a private university with a strong commitment to diversity.

heard of that. Okay, sushi—yes, it is an Asian cuisine, but why are all the people here eating it? Coffee? I don't drink coffee. Who drinks coffee? My grandparents drink coffee. Tea? That is for when you are sick. Stuff like that just did not register. I did not fit in, and I had to become okay with not fitting in.

Beyond the more visible differences between Katrina and her college peers, she also expressed how difficult it was to be seen. To Katrina, it seemed that her White peers could not see past the color of her skin.

Sometimes, people can get lost in how you're saying it and never hear you and never see you for who you are. That hurts. So in that way, yes I feel judged, I feel discriminated against. Has anyone ever outright called me the N-word? No. Has anyone ever made motions or said, "You can't sit at this table"? No. But I feel it, and I shouldn't have to.

Although Katrina's skin color seemed to separate her from the majority of students on campus, she was very drawn to those who looked like her.

When people of color come here, particularly Black people, I am so excited; I just want to go meet them. Part of me is, I don't want them to feel like, "Oh my gosh, the only reason they are saying hello is because we look alike." But at the same time, when I came, it was awesome to have someone reach out to me and say, "I'm happy you are here."

Three years later, when asked if she fits in now, Katrina responded, "Oh, I still don't fit in. But I learned the culture, I learned the society." Katrina's feelings are shared by an unfortunate proportion of students of color at PWIs (Feagin & Sikes, 1995; Fries-Britt & Turner, 2001; Rankin & Reason, 2005; Solberg & Villareal, 1997; Winkle-Wagner, 2009). Her lived experience serves as an example of the daily transitions from one culture to another experienced by students of color on traditionally White campuses.

This chapter provides a brief overview of the transitions that students of color like Katrina tend to experience at predominantly White institutions. Most notably, the campus climate for diversity contributes to the experience for students of color at PWIs (Harper & Hurtado, 2007). In light of the unique challenges associated with being a student of color at a PWI, the various paths to thriving for this important population of students are explored. The concept of thriving extends beyond survival in college, as it includes factors that contribute to academic success and retention. Thriving students are fully engaged intellectually, socially, and emotionally, and they experience a sense of community and psychological well-being, all of which contribute to overall student success (Schreiner, McIntosh, Nelson, & Pothoven, 2009). As many students of color at predominantly White institutions struggle socially and emotionally (Guiffrida & Douthit, 2010), the concept of thriving is of particular value to this population of students. Drawing on data from a national quantitative study using the Thriving Quotient (Schreiner, Pothoven, Nelson, & McIntosh, 2009), this chapter also highlights the characteristics that are predictive of thriving in students of color (Schreiner, Seppett, & Kitomary, 2010). In conclusion, specific recommendations to enhance the opportunity for students of color to thrive in college will be provided.

Students of Color in Transition

Bennett and Okinaka (1990) conceptualized the phenomenon of positive college adjustment as the "opposite of transitional trauma," which they define as the "level of alienation a student experiences when unfamiliar with the norms, values, and expectations that predominate" (p. 35). The transition from high school to college can be challenging for any student, but is particularly challenging for students of color (Guiffrida & Douthit, 2010; Hurtado, Carter, & Spuler, 1996). In addition to the host of transitional experiences typical to the first college year, students of color at predominantly White institutions must navigate additional challenges (Allen, 1992; Bourke, 2010; Fries-Britt & Turner, 2001; Hurtado & Carter, 1997). These challenges can encompass the social struggles related to fitting in with peers or roommates (Rankin & Reason, 2005; Winkle-Wagner, 2009) and transitioning from their home culture to a predominantly White culture (Yosso, 2005). In the academic environment, students of color might be expected to speak on behalf of their entire race or ethnicity (Bourke, 2010), or their scholarly abilities might be doubted (Fries-Britt & Turner, 2001; Guiffrida & Douthit, 2010). These subtle racial attitudes, also called racial microaggressions, further impact the academic and social environment for students of color (Solorzano & Yosso, 2000). Although such insults are often unconsciously made, they negatively contribute to students' perceptions of the campus climate and enhance feelings of self-doubt, frustration, and isolation (Solorzano & Yosso, 2000).

Allen (1992) found that Black students at PWIs experience feelings of alienation and lack of integration, and they sense hostility and racial discrimination. Nearly two decades after Allen's research, students of color at PWIs still reported such feelings (Hurtado & Carter, 1997). As compositional diversity continues to increase, student bodies will have a progressively wider range of educational and social needs during the transitional years and beyond. For example, students who are the first in their family to attend college are more likely to struggle with a lack of confidence about their academic performance (Ramos-Sanchez & Nichols, 2007), experience anxiety about financial resources, and may find themselves alienated from family and friends who are unfamiliar with the demands of higher education (Allen, 1992; Maldonado & Willie, 1995).

Many students' first experiences on campus are characterized by stereotypes held by their peers (Bourke, 2010; Fries-Britt & Turner, 2001; Newman, Keough, & Lee, 2009; Tatum, 1999). For example, Bourke (2010) found that Black students experienced peer expectations that they grew up in an urban area, that they had to triumph over insurmountable odds to enroll, and that affirmative action or athletic talent might have played a role in their acceptance. In many cases, these first experiences can influence future success. Peer stereotypes can negatively shape Black students' understanding of what it means to be a Black student, where "doing well in school becomes identified as trying to be White" (Tatum, 1999, p. 63). Newman and colleagues (2009) found that when students are stereotyped as poor academic performers, they withdraw effort in order to protect self-esteem, to the detriment of their academic performance. Any negative stereotype can adversely impact performance if the individual internalizes the stereotype.

In another example of how early experiences can impact the future, Hurtado and Carter (1997) found that positive transition experiences of Latina/o students were significant predictors of sense of belonging during the junior year in college, and early negative perceptions of the campus climate for diversity contributed to lower levels of sense of belonging. Further, perceptions of racial tension were negatively associated with personal-emotional adjustment, institutional attachment, and academic and social adjustment (Hurtado, et al., 1996). According to Hurtado and Carter, "the easier the transition to college, the less likely students are to perceive a hostile climate in the second year" (p. 337).

Campus Climate for Diversity

When institutions succeed in expanding compositional diversity, yet engage in a passive role regarding race relations on campus, negative interactions and misunderstandings among students are likely to occur (Allen, Bonous-Hammarth, & Teranishi, 2006; Chang, 2000; Steele, 1995). As Steele notes, "All that remains unresolved between Blacks and Whites, all the old wounds and shames that have never been addressed, present themselves for attention—and present our youth with pressures they cannot always handle" (p. 177). Research on students' perceptions of the college environment has demonstrated that campus climate for diversity can have a significant impact on students both academically and socially (Hurtado et al., 1996; Hurtado, Milem, Clayton-Pederson, & Allen, 1998). For example,

> Even the most talented Latinos are likely to have difficulty adjusting if they perceive a climate where majority students think all minorities are special admits, Hispanics feel like they do not "fit in," groups lack good communication, there is group conflict, and there is a lack of trust between minority students and the administration. (Hurtado et al., 1996, p. 152)

Campus climate for diversity is an essential component of feelings of belonging for students of color; accordingly, faculty and staff must facilitate an environment of respect, understanding, interaction, and openness where all students can thrive (Bok, 2006).

When considering the manifold challenges experienced by students of color at predominantly White institutions, it is critical to understand how the overall campus climate for diversity might impact the transition for these students. The campus climate for diversity is a comprehensive reflection and demonstration of diversity (Hurtado, 2007) that includes the experiences and quality of interactions between individuals and groups on a campus (University of California, Diversity Work Team, 2007). Although research has demonstrated the link between climate and educational outcomes for all students, understanding how the campus climate for diversity impacts students of color is of particular importance (Milem, Chang, & Antonio, 2005). For example, research highlights the benefits associated with meaningful cross-racial engagement (Chang, 1999; Gurin, Dey, Hurtado, & Gurin, 2002; Pike & Kuh, 2006) while also persistently demonstrating that students of different races have different perceptions of campus climate (Ancis, Sedlacek, & Mohr, 2000; D'Augelli & Hershberger, 1993; Nora & Cabrera, 1996; Rankin & Reason, 2005). Majority students may underestimate the antagonism experienced by students of color even while underrepresented students widely report prejudicial treatment and racist campus environments (D'Augelli & Hershberger, 1993; Hurtado & Carter, 1997; Rankin & Reason, 2005). For example, Harper and Hurtado (2007) found that White and Asian students reported the highest levels of satisfaction with the campus environment, Latino and Native American students were satisfied to a lesser degree, and Black students were the least satisfied. Further, White students overestimated the satisfaction of students of color. Although White students noticed that students of color participated in campus events at a lower rate than White students, they assumed students of color had identical levels of satisfaction. Solberg and Villareal (1997) and Feagin and Sikes (1995) had similar findings; students of color at highly selective PWIs reported greater levels of stress associated with their racial and ethnic group status. Because there is great variance in perceptions of campus climate for diversity among different groups of students, and students of color note the challenges associated with their race, this exploration is of particular importance.

Elements Influencing the Campus Climate for Diversity

A variety of elements contribute to the campus climate for diversity. Adapted from Hurtado, Milem et al. (1998), Hurtado, Milem, Clayton-Pederson, and Allen (1999), and Milem et al.'s (2005) frameworks to address the numerous forces, policies, perceptions, attitudes, and behaviors that affect campus climate for diversity, the following three interrelated components within the institutional context contribute to the climate for diversity: (a) compositional diversity, (b) the behavioral dimension, and (c) the psychological dimension. The combination of these factors relate to the transition to predominantly White campuses for students of color. For example, as was the case for Katrina, the lack of compositional diversity on campus impacted her ability to fit in. She felt particularly drawn to reach out to any new students of color on campus in order to offset the lack of diversity. Although Katrina remarked that she had never been called a derogatory name, she felt judged and discriminated against when people did not see her for who she was. These feelings reflect the psychological dimension of the climate for diversity. In terms of the behavioral dimension, Katrina noted that it was particularly difficult to establish real friendships with White students, and in order to do so, she had to adapt to the culture of the campus community.

Compositional diversity. Compositional diversity refers to the actual diversity demonstrated within the student body, faculty, and staff. Park (2009) found that satisfaction with compositional diversity was positively associated with greater sense of community, racial heterogeneity of the student body, and higher satisfaction with peer interactions and the overall college experience for all students. Park also found that Black students were the least satisfied with the diversity of the student body. As satisfaction with compositional diversity is associated with overall college satisfaction for Black students (Einarson & Matier, 2005), this finding indicates a distinct disadvantage for Black students. However, as diversity is not "an end in itself" (Chang, 2005, p. 10), institutions must move beyond the primary focus on compositional diversity, as a stronger educational impact is garnered when diversity is paired with student engagement and involvement through institutional support, intervention, and programming.

Behavioral dimension. The behavioral dimension of campus climate for diversity refers to the informal and formal cross-racial interactions between peers, the level of diversity in the curriculum and the cocurriculum, and the level of participation in diversity-related activities, both socially and academically (Allen, 2006; Bok, 2006; Chang, 1999; Hurtado, 2007; Hurtado, Milem et al., 1998). Institutions across the country have devoted resources and staff to facilitate diversity interactions, which include racial awareness programs, group discussions about social and race issues, diversity-related courses, mentoring programs, and historical curricula based on non-Western cultures (Bok, 2006; Delgado Bernal, Alemán, & Garavito, 2009; Hurtado, 2006). The number of schools requiring courses on diversity is increasing yearly; by 2003, nearly two thirds of all institutions of higher education had implemented a diversity-related course in their required curriculum (Bok, 2006). Although these programs have certainly not fully mitigated racial tension on campuses, they have had an impact on student awareness and understanding. As Bok notes, "Rather than merely assimilating minority students into White society, colleges are creating greater understanding among the races while enhancing respect and appreciation for America's different cultures among undergraduates" (p. 199). Nonetheless, Tatum (1999) described society as being thick with "the cultural images and messages that affirm the assumed superiority of Whites and the assumed inferiority of people of color" (p. 6). This cultural racism is "like smog in the air. Sometimes it is so thick that it is visible, other times it is less apparent, but always, day in and day out, we are breathing it in" (p. 6). Although progress has been made, the cultural images that Tatum describes continue to impact the behavioral dimension of campus climate for diversity today.

Psychological dimension. The psychological climate refers to perceptions of and encounters with racial tension, conflict, or discrimination on campus (Hurtado, 1992; Hurtado, Milem et al., 1998, 1999). Two broad themes have emerged from studies that have observed this dimension of the climate for diversity. First, individuals experience the campus climate very differently (Ancis et al., 2000; Chavous, 2005; Hurtado et al., 1999; Johnson et al., 2007; Rankin & Reason, 2005). According to Ancis et al. (2000) and Chavous (2005), the lived experience on campus is very different for underrepresented students than for White students. Johnson et al. (2007) found that White students reported a significantly higher sense of belonging than all underrepresented student groups, and Black students were the least likely to report positive racial climates. Ancis and colleagues also found that White students had a more positive perception of the campus racial climate, and Black students perceived more racial tension on campus and felt they received unequal treatment from faculty. Chavous found that White students reported a significantly higher sense of community than Black students. Similar findings emerged from Rankin and Reason's (2005) comprehensive, 10-campus study. They found that students of color were much more likely to report the campus as being unfriendly, racist, and disrespectful; whereas, White students perceived the climate to be exactly the opposite. This finding was surprising, as nearly 40% of White students acknowledged that race-based harassment occurred on campus.

The second theme that has emerged from research on the psychological dimension of the campus climate for diversity is that perceptions of a hostile climate can negatively impact various outcomes for all students, and especially for students of color (D'Augelli & Hershberger, 1993; Hurtado & Carter, 1997; Johnson et al., 2007; Nora & Cabrera, 1996). Johnson et al. (2007) found that smooth college transition processes, positive perceptions of campus racial climate, and socially supportive residence halls were significant predictors of students' sense of belonging. In a small single-institution study at a predominantly White institution, D'Augelli and Hershberger (1993) found that nearly every Black student reported having been the subject of a racist comment, harassment, or discrimination from a White peer or professor, and Black students overall exhibited lower general well-being scores than their White peers. In Rankin and Reason's (2005) study, one third of students of color reported experiencing race-based harassment from peers. Locks, Hurtado, Bowman, and Oseguera (2008) found that a perception of racial tension was negatively associated with sense of belonging for White students and for students of color. According to Hurtado, Griffin, Arellano, and Cuellar (2008), "Subtle perceptions of a hostile climate had more of an impact on all areas of adjustment to college (social, academic, personal-emotional, and attachment to the institution) than actual behaviors" (p. 209). Further, the behavioral dimension of campus climate for diversity is linked to the psychological climate for diversity. Frequent positive interactions with diverse peers, a behavioral component, are positively associated with psychological components such as higher sense of belonging (Locks et al., 2008), enhanced critical thinking and social cognitive skills (Hurtado, 2006; Hu & Kuh, 2003), cultural and social awareness, and civic engagement (Hurtado, 2007).

Predictors of Thriving in Students of Color

Research conducted over the past two decades has clearly demonstrated that students of color at predominantly White colleges and universities experience a variety of unique challenges during their transitional years and beyond. In response to such evidence, a few researchers have explored the various paths to thriving in students of color (Schreiner, Nelson, McIntosh, & Edens, 2011; Schreiner, Seppelt, & Kitomary, 2010). Students who are thriving in college surpass simple survival; they are fully engaged intellectually, socially, and emotionally. Further, they experience an overall sense of community and psychological well-being, all of which contribute to student success (Schreiner, Pothoven et al., 2009).

In a national quantitative study using the Thriving Quotient (Schreiner et al., 2011; Schreiner et al., 2010), the authors sought to identify the activities, practices, or involvements that are predictive of thriving in students of color. The Thriving Quotient is comprised of five distinct factors that measure students' academic, intrapersonal, and interpersonal engagement and well-being (Schreiner, McIntosh et al., 2009): Positive Perspective, Engaged Learning, Academic Determination, Social Connectedness, and Diverse Citizenship.

Predictors

For most student groups, sense of belonging, spirituality, and faculty interaction emerged as significant predictors of thriving. Background variables (i.e., gender, high school grades, and first choice of institution) only emerged as significant predictors of thriving for White students. Campus involvement, including participation in campus activities, student organizations, Greek life, on-campus living, community service, and athletics, was only predictive for White students, as well. Twice as many predictors of thriving emerged for White students as compared to students of color. Each of the significant predictors for students of color is discussed below.

Sense of belonging refers to psychological identification and affiliation with the campus community (Hausmann, Ye, Schofield, & Woods, 2009; Hurtado & Carter, 1997; Locks et al., 2008). Also termed *perceived social cohesion* by Bollen and Hoyle (1990), "sense of belonging is fundamental to a member's identification with a group and has numerous consequences for behavior" (p. 484). According to Hausmann et al. (2009), social and academic integration leads to a psychological sense of belonging, "which is an important precursor to desirable outcomes such as increased commitment and persistence" (p. 650). Further, a lack of student community is negatively associated with satisfaction with the overall college experience and student life, and with desire to re-enroll (Astin, 1993).

Among college students, spirituality is associated with college engagement (Kuh & Gonyea, 2005), service involvement (Astin, 2004; Chickering, Dalton, & Stamm, 2006; Kuh & Gonyea, 2005), leadership (Yasuno, 2004), and purpose in life (Greenway, 2005). Spirituality involves an internal pursuit for the sacred (e.g., the divine, concepts of God, things that are transcendent), a search that usually occurs within a larger religious context, whether traditional or nontraditional in format (Hill & Pargament, 2008). As defined by Astin, Astin, and Lindholm (2011) spirituality is a complex quality that

> involves an active quest for answers to life's "big questions," a global worldview that transcends ethnocentrism and egocentrism, a sense of caring and compassion for others coupled with a lifestyle that includes service to others, and a capacity to maintain one's sense of calm and centeredness, especially in times of stress. (p. 4)

Gender (being female), spirituality, and sense of community significantly predict thriving among Black students. Student-faculty interaction, a significant predictor for all other students of color as well as for White students, was not predictive of thriving among Black students. This finding is particularly troubling. It leads to the question, Is there something different about faculty interactions with Black students as compared to other students? Research does suggest that the academic environment is particularly difficult for Black students, as they are expected to speak on behalf of their entire race or ethnicity (Bourke, 2010) and people are often skeptical about their scholarly abilities (Fries-Britt & Turner, 2001; Guiffrida & Douthit, 2010). Katrina's experience in the classroom mirrored this research:

> I felt like I had to bust my butt harder than the [White students] to prove myself more than they did because my professors were judging me, they were thinking these things at me, and that is how I thought of myself, but that is because I was surrounded by what you see on TV. I had to learn, how to feel okay...Adapt or die...When I did not understand [something], I had to get past the thoughts of, "Oh, of course I will not understand, because I am the only Black girl in class. Of course, I was the dumb one."

In Katrina's own words, "It is a tough role to play, and there is a lot on your shoulders." Lundberg and Schreiner (2004) found that Black students interacted the most with faculty, yet benefited the least in terms of their learning gains, and were least satisfied with those interactions. Cole (2007) postulated that the increased critique and negative feedback from faculty reported by Black students was a factor in the lack of positive impact on their intellectual self-concept.

Among Asian students, spirituality, faculty interaction, and sense of community emerged as significant predictors of thriving. Of these predictors, sense of community was the most powerful. For Hispanic students, spirituality, faculty interaction, and sense of community emerged as significant predictors. Spirituality was more important for Hispanic students than any other group. It is particularly interesting to note that campus involvement did not contribute to thriving for students of color, although it did for White students. This finding raises concerns about the actual involvement of students of color in campus activities, student organizations, Greek life, on-campus living, community service, and athletics. If negative perceptions of campus climate can lead to a lack of involvement, perhaps students of color might be more involved if the campus climate for diversity were to improve. If this were the case, then campus involvement might also emerge as a predictor of thriving for students of color as it does for White students.

Overall, these studies demonstrated that there are indeed different paths to thriving for students of color, with sense of belonging emerging as a particularly important predictor of thriving. Emphasizing an element that would have positively contributed to her own transition and the success of other students of color on her campus, Katrina also acknowledged the importance of sense of belonging:

> There should be a place with couches and movies and magazines, all kinds of things, where you can just come and be. A place where you can plug in, a place where you have nowhere else to go and you could sit down and plug in. I think we should have a directory [of the students of color]. Not to say that this is teaching separation, but it is just different; there is something about being around people who look like you that make you feel comfortable and welcome, and I think that we need to be intentional about that feeling. Giving people the space and the opportunity to have that feeling, which helps them when they move into this place that is all White, pretty much predominantly White university, and be encouraged to feel comfortable in their own skin. With that comfort, they feel strengthened enough to venture out and get outside their bubble. At any time when you need to plug in and you need to feel like, I am not the oddball, you have somewhere to do that.

Although Katrina's words are those of only one student, her voice mirrors the significant quantitative research that demonstrates the difficulties facing students of color as they transition into college.

Implications for Institutions

Campus climate for diversity is not static, and patterns of belief and behaviors can shift with intentional efforts to change or improve (Hurtado, Carter, & Kardia, 1998). According to Bensimon (2007),

> The challenge is how to change practitioners' ways of thinking and interpreting the problem of inequality. In particular, in what ways could research encourage practitioners to reflect on how practices—their own and the institution's—are implicated in producing unequal educational outcomes. (p. 456)

Much of the research on campus climate for diversity shows that institutional action is an important factor in the success of all campus community members; to ensure a healthy campus climate, the institution must clearly and tangibly communicate support of diversity (Milem et al., 2005; Williams & Clowney, 2007). Educators, administrators, and staff must be willing to share the responsibility in facilitating an environment where students of color can thrive. Assessing the climate for diversity is vital for institutions that desire to create healthy, diverse learning environments where students of color can thrive during and beyond their transition to college. The recommendations in this section draw upon the various themes presented in this chapter in order to provide faculty, staff, administrators, and decision makers with changes that can be implemented on their own campuses. The suggestions for change fit within two broad categories: (a) tangible programmatic changes and (b) more comprehensive institutional change.

Programmatic Change

These tangible recommendations correspond with the significant predictors of thriving in most students of color (i.e., sense of community, faculty engagement, and spirituality), in conjunction with the various elements that make their transition more challenging. Opportunities for campus involvement are also included. Although campus involvement is not a significant predictor of thriving for students of color, institutions should examine how to enhance the involvement experiences for this important population of students. Faculty and staff may enhance the learning environment for all students by considering these recommendations.

- Establish educational and/or emotional small groups for first-year students that are led by successful students of color who are farther along in the educational journey. The older students can share success stories, study techniques, and methods to reduce the stressors of college life (Ramos-Sanchez & Nichols, 2007).
- Identify students of color who are thriving and encourage them to mentor first-year students during the transition process (Winkle-Wagner, 2009).
- Connect students with subcultures (e.g., ethnic organizations) early on in their college career to provide opportunities to share experiences, offer support, and work toward common goals together (Museus, 2008) to foster a sense of community and group membership within the larger campus community.

- When students first arrive on campus, facilitate programming that addresses how to balance family life at home with expectations of academic success in college, and engage parents of students of color in discussions on the college experience (Winkle-Wagner, 2009).

- Implement early academic advising programs to enhance confidence in academic abilities (Ramos-Sanchez & Nichols, 2007).

- Create spaces and opportunities for critical discourse and individual expression on issues of race and the experiences of students of color (Delgado Bernal et al., 2009; Museus, 2008). For example, establish a participatory art exhibit where students can anonymously write their stories, ask questions, and read about other people's experiences at the school.

- Because students of color bring much more to campus than their race, be mindful of the type of participation that is sought. For example, students of color should be called on to participate in things other than celebrating diversity, and the achievements of students of color that expand beyond athletics should be highlighted (Bourke, 2010).

- Educate faculty and students about the harmful effects of asking and/or expecting students of color to speak on behalf of their race, in or out of the classroom (Bourke, 2010).

- Acknowledge, validate, and learn about the experiences of students of color (Bourke, 2010) through focus groups, panels, surveys, and classroom conversations. Respond to the issues raised in these conversations. For example, find out why students of color are not participating in particular campus activities.

- Be cognizant of the unseen benefits associated with being White on campus, and work to expose such privilege in order to equalize the student experience (Wildman & Davis, 2008). For example, White students typically do not worry about being harassed by campus security officers after dark, whereas Black men might not have that luxury.

- Promote service-learning programs and provide spaces for critical self-reflection, in conjunction with opportunities to deconstruct the experiences (Delgado Bernal et al., 2009; Winkle-Wagner, 2009).

- Provide opportunities for expressions of faith and spirituality. For example, facilitate transportation or attendance to local multicultural churches or churches that minister to specific ethnic congregations.

- Integrate discussions of calling and vocation within the context of faith and spirituality into classroom, mentorship, or small-group settings.

These are only a few of the ways that faculty and staff can encourage thriving among students of color on predominantly White campuses. Although programmatic changes will likely improve the experience of students of color, the greater concern of campus climate for diversity must be addressed at an institutional level.

Institutional Change

The campus climate for diversity plays a significant role in the experiences of students of color on predominantly White campuses. Accordingly, improving the climate for diversity is both a substantial and important undertaking. Movement toward change must be grounded in an institutional commitment to integrate diversity into the campus community, with senior leadership (e.g., the president and provost) at the forefront (Milem et al., 2005; Williams & Clowney, 2007). Further, in order to achieve a paradigm and value shift on behalf of the institution, the president must be willing to commit to a long-term change process that leads to institutionalization. In terms of diversity, institutionalization means that leaders have made a commitment to integrate diversity into all aspects of the campus community, stretching beyond the creation of an inclusive environment for people of varied backgrounds to include a change in resources, policies, practices, climate, and culture (Kezar, 2007). Such change alters the way an organization conducts daily practices, essentially "revisit[ing] and redefin[ing] their public purpose in light of the new change forces" (Fullan & Scott, 2009, p. 21).

These recommendations for change are directed toward administrators, institutional stakeholders, and policy makers.

- Create a multistep strategic diversity platform that is driven by educational, social, cultural, and business rationales for change (Williams & Clowney, 2007). At first, understanding the importance of integrating diversity into the academic community will be minimal, and conversations around the topic might be tense. The focus will initially revolve around issues of access, and little effort will be directed toward retention and persistence to graduation. Perhaps one of the most important elements of this phase includes the president's willingness and commitment to help people understand why it is important to create a diversity agenda. The rationale for diversity "needs to be simple and straightforward" (Kezar, 2007, p. 424).

- Modify the existing institutional culture by engaging the campus community in the change process. For example, conduct both quantitative and qualitative research on the campus climate for diversity among faculty, staff, and students; develop faculty, staff, and administrators as diversity leaders on campus; and report progress over time to the campus community (Williams & Clowney, 2007).

- Establish infrastructure by garnering support from the institution's board or governing body, integrating the commitment into the strategic plan, establishing mechanisms to measure change, and allocating financial resources. In an extensive study of university presidents who have made considerable progress toward diversity, one president asserted, "No matter how limited your budget is, it can be used to support change" (Kezar, 2007, p. 427).

- Identify individuals who are committed to enhancing the diversity initiatives on campus and hire new faculty and staff with a demonstrated commitment. Hiring faculty and staff of color should be a high priority.

- Develop safe havens for students of color on campus, and establish opportunities for all students to engage in a broad and multicultural living and learning environment.

- Continually engage the community in the discussion of diversity, stimulating the community to identify growth areas and create opportunities for continued progress (Kezar, 2007).

- Integrate diversity into the curriculum, which includes implementing alternative pedagogical strategies that will reach students with different learning styles.

Once institutions have fully implemented monitoring practices and measurement mechanisms so that progress can be assessed and areas in need of improvement can be identified, it will be possible to address the needs of more specific subpopulations of students. Further, the conversation regarding access, equity, and retention will shift to concentrate on student success and outcomes. In this final phase, institutions can more adequately facilitate and measure thriving in students of color.

Although these recommendations are grounded in best practices and case studies in organizational change, it is important to recognize the unique nature of every institution. There is no single reliable way to ensure that change occurs; however, institutional strategies that take a multifaceted approach are more likely to be successful. For example, Kezar (2007) points heavily to presidential leadership as a catalyst. However, consider institutions where a key issue in creating a better campus climate for diversity requires hiring faculty of color. If the established faculty are resistant to the idea, then the goal of hiring more diverse faculty members is unlikely to be reached even if the president supports the initiative. Individual institutions will be best served by developing a multifaceted strategy that focuses on cultural change. Identifying champions or opinion leaders in all sectors, including faculty, administration, staff, board members, students, and alumni, is an initial step to developing a cohesive strategy. Strategies in each area should evolve as information is collected about the climate for racial diversity in each sector of the institution. It is essential for universities and colleges to move beyond equating demographic diversity with a healthy climate for diversity. Strategic goals and measures of climate should be incorporated into an institution-wide plan and led by a diversity council or a designated group with a task force mentality for advancing the learning environment for students and the work environment for employees.

Conclusion

Research has repeatedly shown that diverse learning environments produce benefits for all students (Chang, 1999; Gurin et al., 2002; Pike & Kuh, 2006). Furthermore, compositional diversity is only an initial step toward a healthy climate for racial and ethnic diversity and a robust learning environment. In other words, the achievement of compositional diversity alone will not create the necessary environment to help students of color thrive, especially in times of transition. The Thriving Quotient is a tool that can yield important results for institutions that are trying to progress through the phases of creating a healthy and diverse learning environment. Findings from thriving studies show that White students have twice as many predictors as students of color, meaning that many more campus experiences contribute to their thriving than is the case for students of color. This indicates that interventions and strategies to promote thriving require a distinct strategy to elevate the higher education experience for students of color beyond survival to thriving. Although institutional resources are increasingly limited at colleges and universities, if higher education is not able to equip students from all backgrounds with the intended learning outcomes, a college degree will function more as a symbol of stratification and inequality than as evidence of learning. Creating a healthy and diverse learning environment is not only valuable, but also necessary for institutions to maximize the student experience. The strategies outlined in this chapter will help to advance a thriving college experience for all students.

References

Allen, W. (1992). The color of success: African-American college student outcomes at predominantly White and historically Black public colleges and universities. *Harvard Educational Review, 62*(1), 26-44.

Allen, W. (2006). Sticks, stones, and broken bones: Rhetoric and reality in the University of Michigan affirmative action cases. In W. Allen, M. Bonous-Hammarth, & R. Teranishi (Eds.), *Higher education in a global society; Achieving diversity, equity and excellence: Advances in education in diverse communities: Research, policy and praxis* (Vol. 5, pp. 203-226). San Diego, CA: Elsevier.

Allen, W., Bonous-Hammarth, M., & Teranishi, R. (2006). Innovation and diversity: New horizons in higher education. In W. Allen, M. Bonous-Hammarth, & R. Teranishi (Eds.), *Higher education in a global society; Achieving diversity, equity and excellence: Advances in education in diverse communities: Research, policy and praxis* (Vol. 5, pp. 345-347). San Diego, CA: Elsevier.

Ancis, J. R., Sedlacek, W. E., & Mohr, J. (2000). Student perceptions of campus cultural climate by race. *Journal of Counseling & Development, 78*(2), 180-85.

Astin, A. W. (1993). *What matters in college? Four critical years revisited.* San Francisco, CA: Jossey-Bass.

Astin, A. W. (2004, Spring). Why spirituality deserves a central place in liberal education. *Liberal Education,* 34-41.

Astin, A. W., Astin, H., & Lindholm, J. (2011). *Cultivating the spirit: How college can enhance students' inner lives.* San Francisco, CA: Jossey-Bass.

Bennett, C., & Okinaka, A. M. (1990). Factors related to persistence among Asian, Black, Hispanic, and White undergraduates at a predominantly White university: Comparison between first and fourth year cohorts. *Urban Review, 22,* 33-60.

Bensimon, E. M. (2007). The underestimated significance of practitioner knowledge in the scholarship on student success. *The Review of Higher Education, 30*(4), 441-469.

Bok, D. C. (2006). *Our underachieving colleges: A candid look at how much students learn and why they should be learning more.* Princeton, NJ: Princeton University Press.

Bollen, K. A., & Hoyle, R. H. (1990). Perceived cohesion: A conceptual and empirical examination. *Social Forces, 69,* 479-504.

Bourke, B. (2010). Experiences of Black students in multiple cultural spaces at a predominantly White institution. *Journal of Diversity in Higher Education, 3*(2), 126-135.

Chang, M. (1999). Does racial diversity matter? The educational impact of a racially diverse undergraduate population. *Journal of College Student Development, 40*(4), 377-395.

Chang, M. (2000). Improving campus racial dynamics: A balancing act among competing interests. *The Review of Higher Education, 23*(2), 153-175.

Chang, M. (2005). Reconsidering the diversity rationale. *Liberal Education, 91*, 6-13.

Chavous, T. M. (2005). An intergroup contact-theory framework for evaluating racial climate on predominantly White college campuses. *American Journal of Community Psychology, 36*(3-4), 239-257.

Chickering, A., Dalton, J., & Stamm, L. (2006). *Encouraging authenticity and spirituality in higher education.* San Francisco, CA: Jossey-Bass.

Cole, D. (2007). Do interracial interactions matter? An examination of student-faculty contact and intellectual self-concept. *The Journal of Higher Education, 78*(3), 249-281.

D'Augelli, A. R., & Hershberger, S. L. (1993). African American undergraduates on a predominantly White campus: Academic factors, social networks, and campus climate. *The Journal of Negro Education, 62*(1), 67-81.

Delgado Bernal, D., Alemán, E., & Garavito, A. (2009). Latina/o undergraduate students mentoring Latina/o elementary students: A borderlands analysis of shifting identities and first-year experiences. *Harvard Educational Review, 79*(4), 560-585.

Einarson, M. K., & Matier, M. W. (2005). Exploring race differences in correlates of seniors' satisfaction with undergraduate education. *Research in Higher Education, 46*(6), 641-676.

Feagin, J. R., & Sikes, M. P. (1995). How Black students cope with racism on White campuses. *Journal of Blacks in Higher Education, 8*, 91-97.

Fries-Britt, S. L., & Turner, B. (2001). Facing stereotypes: A case study of Black students on a White campus. *Journal of College Student Development, 42*(5), 420-29.

Fullan, M., & Scott, G. (2009). *Turnaround leadership for higher education.* San Francisco, CA: Jossey-Bass.

Greenway, K. (2005). Purpose in life: A pathway to academic engagement and success. *Dissertation Abstracts International, 66*(04A), 1292-1487. (UMI No. 3171374)

Guiffrida, D. A., & Douthit, K. Z. (2010). The Black student experience at predominantly White colleges: Implications for school and college counselors. *Journal of Counseling & Development, 88*, 311-318.

Gurin, P., Dey, E. L., Hurtado, S., & Gurin, G. (2002). Diversity and higher education: Theory and impact on educational outcomes. *Harvard Educational Review, 72*(3), 330–366.

Harper, S. R., & Hurtado, S. (2007). Nine themes in campus racial climates and implications for institutional transformation. In S. R. Harper & L. D. Patton (Eds.), *Responding to the realities of race on campus* (New Directions for Student Services No. 120, pp. 7-24). San Francisco, CA: Jossey-Bass.

Hausmann, L., Ye, F., Schofield, J. W., & Woods, R. L. (2009). Sense of belonging and persistence in White and African American first-year students. *Research in Higher Education, 50,* 649-669.

Hill, P. C., & Pargament, K. I. (2008). Advances in the conceptualization and measurement of religion and spirituality: Implications for physical and mental health research. *American Psychologist, 58*(1), 64-74.

Hu, L., & Kuh, G. D. (2003) Diversity experiences and college student learning and personal development. *Journal of College Student Development, 44,* 320-344.

Hurtado, S. (1992). The campus racial climate: Contexts of conflict. *The Journal of Higher Education, 63*(5), 539-569.

Hurtado, S. (2006). Diversity and learning for a pluralistic democracy. In W. Allen, M. Bonous-Hammarth, & R. Teranishi (Eds.), *Higher education in a global society; Achieving diversity, equity and excellence: Advances in education in diverse communities: Research, policy and praxis* (Vol. 5, pp. 249-268). San Diego, CA: Elsevier.

Hurtado, S. (2007). Linking diversity with the educational and civic missions of higher education. *Review of Higher Education, 30*(2), 185-196.

Hurtado, S., & Carter, D. F. (1997). Effects of college transition and perceptions of the campus racial climate on Latino college students' sense of belonging. *Sociology of Education, 70*(4), 324-345.

Hurtado, S., Carter, D. F., & Kardia, D. (1998). The climate for diversity: Key issues for institutional self-study. In K. W. Bauer (Ed.), *Campus climate: Understanding the critical components of today's colleges and universities* (New Directions for Institutional Research No. 98, pp. 53-63). San Francisco, CA: Jossey-Bass.

Hurtado, S., Carter, D., & Spuler, A. (1996). Latina/o student transition to college: Assessing difficulties and factors in successful college adjustment. *Research in Higher Education, 37*(2), 135-157.

Hurtado, S., Griffin, K. A., Arellano, L., & Cuellar, M. (2008). Assessing the value of climate assessments: Progress and future directions. *Journal of Diversity in Higher Education, 1*(4), 204-221.

Hurtado, S., Milem, J., Clayton-Pederson, A., & Allen, W. (1998). Enhancing campus climates for racial/ethnic diversity: Educational policy and practice. *The Review of Higher Education, 21*(3), 279-302.

Hurtado, S., Milem, J., Clayton-Pedersen, A., & Allen, W. (1999). Enacting diverse learning environments: Improving the climate for racial/ethnic diversity in higher education. *ASHE-ERIC Higher Education Reports, 26,* 1-50.

Johnson, D. R., Soldner, M., Leonard, J. B., Alvarez, P., Inkelas, K. K., Rowan-Kenyon, H. T., & Longerbeam, S. D. (2007). Examining sense of belonging among first-year undergraduates from different racial/ethnic groups. *Journal of College Student Development, 48*(5), 525-542.

Kezar, A. (2007). Tools for a time and a place: Phased leadership strategies to institutionalize a diversity agenda. *The Review of Higher Education, 30*(4), 413-439.

Kuh, G. D., & Gonyea, R. M. (2005). *Exploring the relationships between spirituality, liberal learning, and college student engagement. A special report prepared for the Teagle Foundation.* Bloomington, IN: Center for Postsecondary Research, Indiana University. Retrieved from http://www.teaglefoundation.org/learning/pdf/20050711_kuh_gonyea.pdf

Locks, A. M., Hurtado, S., Bowman, N. A., & Oseguera, L. (2008). Extending notions of campus climate and diversity to students' transition to college. *The Review of Higher Education, 31*(3), 257-285.

Lundberg, C., & Schreiner, L. A. (2004). Quality and frequency of faculty-student interaction as predictors of learning: An analysis by student race/ethnicity. *Journal of College Student Development, 45*(5), 549-565.

Maldonado, L., & Willie, C. (1995). Developing a "pipeline" recruitment program for minority faculty. In L. Rendón & R. Hope (Eds.), *Educating a new majority* (pp. 309-329). San Francisco, CA: Jossey-Bass.

Milem, J. F., Chang, M. J., & Antonio, A. L. (2005). *Making diversity work on campus: A research-based perspective.* Washington, DC: American Association of Colleges and Universities.

Museus, S. D. (2008). The role of ethnic student organizations in fostering African American and Asian American students' cultural adjustment and membership at predominantly White institutions. *Journal of College Student Development, 49*(6), 568-586.

Newman, M. L., Keough, K. A., & Lee, R. M. (2009). Group identification and college adjustment: The experience of encountering a novel stereotype. *The Journal of Social Psychology, 149*(6), 694-708

Nora, A., & Cabrera, A. F. (1996). The role of perceptions of prejudice and discrimination on the adjustment of minority students to college. *The Journal of Higher Education, 67*(2), 119-148.

Park, J. J. (2009). Are we satisfied? A look at student satisfaction with diversity at traditional White institutions. *The Review of Higher Education, 32*(3), 291-320.

Pike, G., & Kuh, G. (2006). Relationship among structural diversity, informal peer interactions and perceptions of campus environment. *The Review of Higher Education, 29*(4), 425-450.

Ramos-Sanchez, L., & Nichols, L. (2007). Self-efficacy of first-generation and non-first-generation college students: The relationship with academic performance and college adjustment. *Journal of College Counseling, 10*, 6-18.

Rankin, S. R., & Reason, R. D. (2005). Differing perceptions: How students of color and White students perceive campus climate for underrepresented groups. *Journal of College Student Development, 46*(1), 43-61.

Schreiner, L. A., McIntosh. E. J., Nelson, D., & Pothoven, S. (2009). *The Thriving Quotient: Advancing the assessment of student success.* Paper presented at the annual meeting of the Association for the Study of Higher Education, Vancouver, Canada.

Schreiner, L., Nelson, D., McIntosh, E., & Edens, D. (2011, March). *The Thriving Quotient: A new vision for student success.* Paper presented at the annual meeting of the National Association of Student Personnel Administrators, Philadelphia, PA.

Schreiner, L., Pothoven, S., Nelson, D., & McIntosh, E. (2009, November). *College student thriving: Predictors of success and retention.* Paper presented at the annual meeting of the Association for the Study of Higher Education, Vancouver, Canada.

Schreiner, L. A., Seppelt, T., & Kitomary, A. (2010). *Predictors of thriving among first-year students of color.* Paper presented at the 29th Annual Conference on The First-Year Experience, Denver, CO.

Solberg, V. S., & Villareal, P. (1997). Examination of self-efficacy, social support, and stress as predictors of psychological and physical distress among Hispanic college students. *Hispanic Journal of Behavioral Sciences, 19*(2), 182-201.

Solorzano, D., & Yosso, T. (2000). Critical race theory, racial microaggressions, and campus racial climate: The experiences of African American college students. *Journal of Negro Education, 69*(1-2), 60-73.

Steele, S. (1995). The recoloring of campus life: Student racism, academic pluralism, and the end of a dream. In J. Arthur & A. Shapiro (Eds.), *Campus wars: Multiculturalism and the politics of difference* (pp. 176-187). Boulder, CO: Westview Press.

Tatum, B. D. (1999). *Why are all the Black kids sitting together in the cafeteria? And other conversations about race.* New York, NY: Basic Books.

University of California, Diversity Work Team. (2007). *Campus climate report.* Retrieved from http://www.universityofcalifornia.edu/diversity/documents/07-campus_report.pdf

Wildman, S. M., & Davis, A. D. (2008). Making systems of privilege visible. In P. S. Rothenberg (Ed.), *White privilege: Essential readings on the other side of racism* (3rd ed., pp. 109-116). New York, NY: Worth Publishers.

Williams, D., & Clowney, C. (2007). Strategic planning for diversity and organizational change: A primer for higher-education leadership. *Effective Practices for Academic Leaders, 2*(3), 1-16.

Winkle-Wagner, R. (2009). The perpetual homelessness of college experiences: Tensions between home and campus for African American women. *The Review of Higher Education, 33*(1), 1-36.

Yasuno, M. (2004). *Spirituality into action: Exploring the spiritual dimensions of college student activists and their leadership for social change* (Doctoral dissertation, University of California, Los Angeles).

Yosso, T. J. (2005). Whose culture has capital? A critical race theory discussion of community cultural wealth. *Race Ethnicity Education, 8*(1), 69-91.

Chapter 5

Thriving in High-Risk Students
Rishi Sriram and Deb Vetter

Helping college students thrive is perhaps of greatest concern for those students who are most at risk to depart before obtaining a degree. Higher education institutions consider students high risk if their academic backgrounds or personal characteristics, such as status as a first-generation student, increase their potential for academic failure (Pizzolato, 2004). Current efforts in higher education to promote academic persistence and success among high-risk students are not generally effective, especially at four-year institutions (Attewell, Lavin, Domina, & Levey, 2006; Calcagno & Long, 2008; Martorell & McFarlin, 2007). Therefore, colleges need new and better methods for intervening with these students, and thriving offers an alternative conceptual framework with promising results. For the student group examined in this chapter, the academic component of thriving and its two contributing factors, engaged learning and academic determination, likely present the areas most in need of enrichment. Two recent studies highlight the importance of thriving for high-risk students. The first study employed a qualitative research methodology in order to explore the experiences of academically successful graduating seniors who were labeled high risk when admitted to the institution as first-year students. The second study utilized an experimental design with quantitative analyses to demonstrate how a thriving intervention can positively impact the success of high-risk students. The results of both studies, when combined with the existing literature on college student success, have numerous implications for higher education scholars and practitioners.

Academically High-Risk Students

To convey risk for withdrawal on a continuum (as opposed to a dichotomous characteristic a student does or does not possess), research suggests that scholars and practitioners use the term *high risk* instead of *at risk*. Because the label high risk is relative to other students in the same institution, high-risk students have always existed as a portion of the college student body. However, the population that comprises the college student body has changed due to historic events, such as the GI Bill, the Civil Rights Act of 1964, and the Higher Education Act of 1965. Although these policies diversified the student population, they also increased the variance in academic knowledge and skills for students transitioning into their first year of college (Arendale, 2002). High-risk students must compensate for their lack of academic preparation relative to their peers in addition to negotiating the transitional challenges of most college students.

First-Generation Students

Certain demographics are often related to academically high-risk students. For instance, many academically high-risk students are also first-generation students—those who do not have a parent who enrolled in any kind of post-secondary education. As Pascarella, Pierson, Wolniak, and Terenzini (2004) note, "The evidence is reasonably clear that first-generation students as a group have a more difficult transition from secondary school to college than their peers" (p. 250). First-generation students are more likely to leave college than their counterparts (Ishitani, 2006), and those who do graduate are less likely to enroll in graduate school. They also possess less cultural and social capital, which negatively affects their ability to make decisions that could promote degree attainment (Pascarella et al., 2004).

Pascarella et al. (2004) analyzed longitudinal data on first-generation students from 18 four-year colleges. They found the level of parental education significantly influences college selection, academic and nonacademic college experiences, and cognitive and noncognitive college outcomes. First-generation students tend to choose less prestigious institutions even after controlling for academic qualifications and, once enrolled, take less advantage of the in- and out-of-class opportunities a college experience offers. Moreover, these students are less engaged in college and have lower educational aspirations than their peers (Pike & Kuh, 2005).

Remedial Education and High-Risk Students

In order to help high-risk students achieve desired academic outcomes, colleges provide these students with special developmental education programs, also known as remedial education. The modern form of remedial programming is an offspring of academic and social forces present as long ago as the late 1600s. Perhaps surprisingly, the earliest forms of developmental education appear at some of the most prestigious colleges in the United States, such as Harvard, Yale, and Princeton (Arendale, 2002). Coinciding with changes in the landscape of the college student population, remedial programs continued to evolve and eventually became part of the mainstream services provided by colleges and universities in the United States. These programs are intended to help high-risk students gain the knowledge and skills necessary to perform successfully in college and may comprise advisement, special courses, and other forms of academic support (Bettinger & Long, 2008; Calcagno & Long, 2008; Martorell & McFarlin, 2007). The number of students requiring developmental education has steadily increased, and current estimated percentages of students in these programs range from 29% to 40% (Attewell et al., 2006).

Despite the prominent and controversial role remedial programs have in higher education, there is a surprising paucity of research concerning them (Bettinger & Long, 2008; Calcagno & Long, 2008). Bettinger and Long (2008) note that "little is known about their effects on subsequent student performance in college" (p. 2), and most postsecondary institutions neither possess exit standards for these courses nor systematically evaluate them. Additionally, scholars who have reviewed the literature find that the majority of previous research on remedial education has serious methodological flaws (Boylan & Saxon, 1999). Many studies simply compare students placed in remedial programs to those who are not in such programs without accounting for inherent differences between the two groups of students (Bettinger & Long, 2008; Calcagno & Long, 2008; Martorell & McFarlin, 2007).

Recent and more robust research studies provide mixed results on the effectiveness of remedial programs. Researchers find that remedial education has a neutral impact at best and perhaps may even hurt the academic achievement of high-risk students. Calcagno and Long (2008) studied the effect of remedial programming on 100,000 college students in the state of Florida. Although they found that developmental education does have some short-term benefits, it was not a significant predictor of students earning a degree. They conclude that, considering how colleges currently design and implement remedial programs, it is questionable whether the effect of these programs on degree completion justifies their cost. Attewell et al. (2006) determined that remedial coursework might have a negative effect on students enrolled in four-year institutions. Utilizing a sample of 6,879 that represented a single nationwide cohort of students who went on to college within eight years of graduating from high school, they conducted research in which the treatment and control groups had similar background characteristics, thereby reducing potentially biasing factors. After controlling for academic preparation and other characteristics, they found that remedial education reduced the likelihood a student would graduate by approximately 7%. Also, Attewell and colleagues did not find any evidence that developmental education increased graduation rates in alternative models explored in their study.

Additional research further raise concern about whether college remediation works. Martorell and McFarlin (2007) conducted a longitudinal study of the effect of remediation using a large data set of college students in Texas. Their results provide little indication that remedial programming benefits high-risk students. Even though Martorell and McFarlin found evidence that students who participated in developmental education had better grades in math courses, the "estimated effects of remediation are small in magnitude and statistically insignificant" (p. 3). In fact, some of their results indicate a small negative effect of remedial programming on the number of academic credits attempted and the probability of completing at least one year of postsecondary education. Overall, Martorell and McFarlin conclude that "remediation does little to improve students' marketable human capital" (p. 25). Said differently, current remedial education does not help students thrive.

Thriving and Remediation

Considered collectively, the most recent and robust studies on remedial education indicate that current programs are not especially effective at helping academically high-risk students succeed. They do not meaningfully influence the two factors within the domain of academic thriving: engaged learning and academic determination. Therefore, a tension exists among colleges and universities between the desire to preserve access and the evidence from current empirical studies indicating that the benefits of remedial programming may not justify their cost. In response to this tension, Arendale (2002) calls for a significant shift in how developmental education is delivered:

> The challenge for learning assistance and developmental educators is to reinvent themselves as part of the new wave of "talent developers" on their campus. When policy makers begin to see the role [as]... developing the

talent of all students, then postsecondary education will take another major step in achieving two of the noble goals of American higher education: higher levels of personal and academic success with broader access to more students. (p. 10)

Scholars suggest that future research on remedial education should emphasize new practices, policies, and strategies in order to explore institutional and program delivery differences in the effects of remediation (Calcagno & Long, 2008). As Arendale suggests, remedial programming needs to shift away from trying to help students avoid failing and toward developing factors such as active participation, self-regulation, and the investment of effort.

Unfortunately, current cultural views surrounding the role of effort may be major obstacles to providing effective interventions. Scholars conducting research on how various countries perceive effort have found that effort is credited as the primary factor for achievement in Japan, but receives relatively less emphasis in the United States (Heine et al., 2001). In other words, Americans tend to identify innate ability as the primary determinant for success. Consequently, because they are perceived as having less ability than their peers, high-risk students may have little motivation or confidence for success.

Research on remediation also indicates a negative stereotype often associated with such programs. This stereotype creates additional obstacles for high-risk students that further impede academic thriving. Bettinger and Long (2004) describe this phenomenon:

> First, being placed into remediation may produce a stigma, or "Scarlet Letter" effect, as perceived by other students and faculty. In this way, remediation could exact a psychological burden that negatively affects outcomes. If remedial students feel that their colleges are singling them out as poor performers, this may discourage additional effort. Previous research in education suggests that stigmas attached to underprepared students are real and can impact students negatively. (p. 23)

Therefore, these students question their own abilities and feel a loss of control over their academic performance (Aronson & Steele, 2005). Such research suggests that high-risk students' perceptions of their basic abilities contribute to less academic effort and environmental mastery, two key components of academic determination. However, influencing their self-perceptions could subsequently reverse these effects and help high-risk students thrive in college.

There is great need in higher education to discover innovative approaches that improve the success of high-risk students and to evaluate those approaches with rigorous research designs. Scholars and practitioners can significantly contribute to student success by helping students thrive, thereby increasing the engagement and academic determination of students. Yet, helping academically high-risk students thrive has two prerequisites. First, scholar-practitioners must examine high-risk students who have succeeded in college in order to understand what promoted their ability to thrive. Second, scholar-practitioners must create interventions that help to foster this kind of thriving in other high-risk students. Two recent studies conducted on separate campuses represent steps toward achieving these goals.

Transitioning to Success

In a phenomenological study, meaning was ascribed to the lived experiences of academically successful senior students who had been conditionally admitted on academic probation as high-risk due to high school GPA and/or standardized college entrance test scores below the institutional admittance requirement. Specifically, the study sought to discover what successful seniors experienced throughout their four years that contributed to their successful transition, academic and social integration, and persistence at a private, faith-based, liberal and applied arts university. The study pursued several questions: What resources did these successful students utilize? With whom did they interact at the institution and to what extent? In what activities, organizations, and programs did they participate? How did family members influence their experience? In other words, how did the collegiate experience of the identified group impact their beliefs, attitudes, educational goals, and ambition to obtain a degree?

Methodology

Phenomenological research depends on the extent to which the research question is answered through lived experiences rather than theoretical explanations (Moustakas, 1994). As such, what was seen, heard, and thought by the students in the target group was intentionally sought in order to elicit descriptive data that could create a picture of their underlying experience. Using purposeful sampling, a narrowing strategy was employed to select three academically successful seniors who had been conditionally admitted on academic probation and who could inform the researcher about the question under examination (Creswell, 2007).

Participants in the study were selected from the 33 first-year students conditionally admitted to the university on academic probation in fall 2006. Senior students were classified as academically successful if they achieved a cumulative grade point average by the end of their junior year that was equivalent to or higher than the average earned by the combined first-year cohort with whom they entered the institution. Participants also had high school grade point averages and entrance test scores lower than the 2006 overall peer group conditionally admitted to the university on academic probation. The three students in the final purposeful criterion sample, two female students and one male student, agreed to join in an open-ended investigation of their experience. The students had a mean cumulative grade point average of 3.37 the spring semester of their junior year and had remained enrolled full-time since entering the university. All of the students were White and 21 or 22 years of age. Over a one-week period, 90-minute, semistructured, individual interviews were conducted with each student. The student participants were sent a copy of their interview transcripts and invited to make corrections and/ or submit additional information. The transcribed interviews of the student participants were studied, and statements that provided relevant descriptions of the experience of academically successful senior students conditionally admitted on academic probation were highlighted and recorded. Related significant statements were clustered into larger units of information identified as themes.

Findings

From the three individual verbatim transcripts, more than 600 significant statements were extracted. Four themes emerged from arranging the formulated meanings into clusters: (a) success mindset, (b) academic strategies, (c) supportive relationships, and (d) meaningful involvement. All four themes connect to the three domains of thriving: academic, intrapersonal, and interpersonal. For each theme, qualitative data for each student were synthesized into descriptions that depicted what the collegiate experience was like for the group as a whole. Analysis sought to understand how the students viewed and evaluated what they had experienced. Finally, the descriptions were integrated to provide a composite description and to capture the overarching meaning and essence of the collegiate experience for academically successful students who had been conditionally admitted on academic probation.

Theme 1: Success mindset. The academically successful senior students in the study believed they would achieve success in college and were focused firmly on the positive, thereby exhibiting the positive perspective factor of intrapersonal thriving. As one student stated,

> I really honestly wasn't worried about the probation because I knew I could do well. I knew I was going to succeed. When I knew I was on [academic] probation I kind of just said, well I'm going to work hard and I am going to do well, and I did.

Four strategies essential to this positive mindset were identified. Negative information confronting the student participants was met by refusal to dwell on it and by quickly postulating positive outcomes based on their high level of confidence in their own ability and determination to work hard. In addition, two positive motivating factors held by the student participants were identified: (a) the belief that their family deserved them to be successful and (b) a driving need to prove to everyone that they could achieve success in college. The connection to family exhibits the interpersonal relationships component of thriving, while the drive to succeed demonstrates the intrapersonal well-being found in students who thrive.

Theme 2: Academic strategies. Within the domain of academic thriving, the engagement of academic strategies was identified by the student participants as a major part of their lived experiences, which contributed to retention and a successful collegiate experience. For example, Matthew stated,

> I started out [at college]...I would just read through the notes once...but when I started reading through the notes...[more], then I did far better. And with papers, that took about a semester or so until I realized, Matthew, you can't wait until a few days before; you need to start working on it at least two weeks beforehand or it's just not going to come together.

Five such strategies emerged and appeared to be hierarchical in that, when the first one was utilized by the student participants, it positively influenced the second strategy, and so on. The first strategy was to establish either an academic program or graduation goal or both. The second strategy, the use of academic resources, overlaid the first strategy. The third strategy, adapting learning techniques, was then added, resulting in each strategy becoming a step to help achieve goals. An internalized determination and perceived ability to work hard—academic determination—was recognized by the student participants as necessary to ensure their success with the first three strategies. However, the last strategy was seen as permeating all those previously used. The fifth academic strategy, and capstone for the set, was for students to learn about themselves and, with that knowledge, to engage in their learning.

Theme 3: Supportive relationships. Participants described four types of meaningful and supportive relationships that they all believed contributed to the success of their collegiate experience and retention. These four types illustrate how interpersonal thriving positively influences college student success. Possessing a supportive relationship with a parent was the first and most frequently identified type. Support from extended family and siblings for the student's endeavors were also noted, as was support from specific faculty members; as one student stated, "Harold [faculty] is just amazing…he takes a positive interest in me and is very caring. I know he wants the best for me. It was important that I had someone to go to…that can understand me." Although support by faculty members, staff members, and peers was noted with appreciation, the student participants also credited God, upon whom they relied for personal strength, as their greatest support to successfully persist in college.

Theme 4: Meaningful involvement. The student participants all reported that they became involved, on and off campus, in cocurricular activities that had a considerable impact on their personal growth and academic success. One such student who became involved with the equestrian club reported,

> I got involved with the horse barn and then the horse vaulting team…it helps a lot with confidence and your riding skills…it is very challenging [requiring] a lot of physical work and mental work. I love the people, and it is a wonderful sport because you end up doing things you never thought you were able to do.

Such active participation highlights both interpersonal and intrapersonal thriving as students interacted with their peers and increased their feelings of confidence and well-being. Leadership positions were sought on the students' own initiative in some of the organizations. Campus involvement was credited by the participants as having helped them develop confidence in their abilities; increase self-awareness and self-esteem; increase their knowledge of leadership skills, such as time management; and facilitate social connections with other students. These involvements enhanced their sense of being in and of the community, thus easing the transition to college.

Developing a Success Mindset

The qualitative study reviewed above highlights a success mindset, academic strategies, supportive relationships, and meaningful involvement as key elements of success for academically high-risk students. Understanding these four concepts and their subsequent impact on college students provides a foundation for improving academic performance. However, such understanding leads to limited long-term benefit unless colleges develop interventions for supporting these elements of success and facilitating their role in student thriving. To address this need, an experimental intervention was conducted at a large private research university in order to determine whether the development of a particular mindset in academically high-risk students leads to academic thriving, such as increased use of academic strategies and improved academic effort.

A necessary step toward increasing academic effort in high-risk students, and thereby improving their academic achievement, is to help these students see that they possess the potential to thrive. In her research on self-theories, Dweck (2006) described how the beliefs individuals have about themselves create different psychological paradigms that lead to various feelings and behaviors. These influences can be fundamental to whether a student thrives because they can determine what a student believes to be within his or her control. Much of this research has focused on how implicit views of the malleability of intelligence affect subsequent behavior, including the level of effort exerted. These implicit theories are known as mindsets and could be applicable for improving the academic success of high-risk college students.

The Role of Mindset in Student Success

A critical aspect of understanding achievement motivation is knowledge of an individual's competence self-theory. The belief that intelligence is an innate entity that cannot change, otherwise known as a *fixed mindset*, can lead students to purposefully withhold effort when they think they might fail in order to protect their confidence and self-esteem. If they do not try, any failure they experience can be excused as lack of effort rather than a commentary on their ability. However, a focus on the malleable nature of intelligence and the potential to increase it—a *growth mindset*—fosters positive self-regulation of motivation, self-esteem, and attention (Dweck & Molden, 2005). Thus, mindset has a central role in motivation, particularly in response to emotional events, such as successes or failures. Individuals who conceive of their own intelligence as a fixed entity adopt performance goals, while people with a growth mindset possess learning goals. The former focuses on securing positive judgments of current competence, while the latter emphasizes increasing competence. In addition, a fixed mindset draws on extrinsic motivation, while a growth mindset relies upon intrinsic motivation. Students' theories about intelligence influence the goals that they pursue, and these goals subsequently generate mastery-oriented or helpless response patterns. A student's mindset shapes the core of a whole system of meaning, creating a framework for understanding and interpreting achievement and effort (Dweck, 1999, 2006). If a growth mindset promotes positive responses, while a fixed mindset is associated with destructive reactions, then an emphasis on fostering a growth mindset within high-risk students could alter their behavior in foundational ways, leading to desired outcomes such as active participation, self-regulation, and investment of effort.

People with a growth mindset do not deny differences in talent or ability among individuals, but they emphasize that these present levels can be improved. Therefore, growth mindset students want to learn, and they possess a desire to engage in challenging tasks. They focus on long-term outcomes, effort, and strategies that will result in learning and achievement (Dweck, 2002). This mindset helps people thrive even during the most difficult situations they encounter (Dweck, 2006). Rather than being overly concerned with appearing intelligent, these students work hard to become smarter. Effort and progress are more important than achievement and appearance of competence. Of course, these students still care about goal-directed thinking, but they will forego opportunities to appear intelligent in order to stretch their current knowledge and skills. Thus, individuals with a growth mindset thrive on challenges (Dweck, 1999). Research suggests that mindset can play a key role in college student success and can be altered through interventions with this population (Aronson, Fried, & Good, 2002; Robins & Pals, 2002).

Methodology

The purpose of this study was to determine whether helping academically high-risk, first-year college students form a growth mindset of intelligence resulted in significant differences in their academic effort and grade point averages when compared to students in a control condition. Using a sample of 105 high-risk, first-year students enrolled in a remedial course at a private research university in the Southwest (Table 5.1), a pre-posttest control group design was employed to determine the effect of a web-based mindset intervention on outcomes critical to student success: mindset, academic effort, and grade point average.

Table 5.1

Characteristics of the High-Risk, First-Year Student Sample (N = 105)

Variable	Percent of sample
Gender	
Men	33.3
Women	66.7
Race/Ethnicity	
European American	58.1
Hispanic	21.9
African American	12.4
Asian	2.9
Native American	0.9
Other	3.8
Experimental group	
Treatment group	57.1
Control group	42.9

The study randomly assigned students to a treatment or control group and then measured the mindset of students before and after the interventions. The treatment group (*n* = 45) was taught that intelligence is malleable and can be improved. The control group (*n* = 60), on the other hand, was taught additional study skills and strategies. The purpose of using a study skills curriculum as the control intervention was to compare the effects of promoting a growth mindset to what is typically done in remedial programming in higher education.

For the growth mindset intervention, the four sessions were each comprised of these basic components: (a) a quote from a famous person in history emphasizing a malleable view of intelligence; (b) teaser questions before showing a particular portion of a movie; (c) a movie clip portraying the positive effects of a growth mindset or the negative effects of a fixed mindset; (d) reflection questions about the movie clip; (e) a video lecture about intelligence, the brain, and its malleability; (f) a summary of research pertaining to mindset and college students; and (g) teaser questions for the next session. This growth mindset intervention was based on previous mindset interventions (Aronson et al., 2002; Blackwell, Trzesniewski, & Dweck, 2007; Chiu, Dweck, Tong, & Fu, 1997). The studies used elements of neuroscience and psychology to teach about the anatomy and function of the brain; employed videos and articles to promote a growth mindset of intelligence; and taught participants that, like exercise does for muscles, the brain can be intentionally strengthened.

The study compared group means of the treatment and control groups on the dependent variables of academic effort and achievement, while controlling for pretest levels of academic effort, high school class rank, and college entrance exam scores. Academic effort was measured through the six separate but related dependent variables of academic discipline, academic self-confidence, commitment to college, general determination, goal striving, and study skills. Each of these variables represents a scale on the Student Readiness Inventory (Le, Casillas, Robbins, & Langley, 2005), published by the American College Testing (ACT) program as a measure of psychosocial factors that are predictive of college retention and academic success (Peterson, Casillas, & Robbins, 2006). Academic achievement was measured by the cumulative grade point average at the end of the first semester of the first year. The primary independent variable in this study was the mindset intervention designed to promote a malleable view of intelligence. The three-item Implicit Theory of Intelligence Scale (Dweck, Chiu, & Hong, 1995) was used to determine the extent to which a student holds a growth or fixed mindset of intelligence.

Findings

Statistical analyses were performed to evaluate treatment fidelity (whether the mindset intervention actually changed the students' perceptions of intelligence) and to compare the scores of high-risk, first-year students in the treatment and control conditions on the dependent variables of academic effort and achievement. Differences within each group on the mindset variable were evaluated using paired sample t-tests. Significant differences between the two groups on effort and achievement were determined via Multivariate Analysis of Covariance (MANCOVA) and Analysis of Covariance (ANCOVA), respectively.

Results demonstrated that students in the mindset intervention significantly increased their growth mindset, while students in the study skills control group did not experience a change in mindset. These initial findings confirmed the fidelity of the growth mindset intervention. The findings also suggest that students' perceptions of intelligence do not change without direct intervention.

The primary question of the study was whether a growth mindset intervention would significantly increase the academic effort of high-risk students in a remedial course. As stated above, academic effort was defined as a multivariate variable comprised of six separate and related variables. Tables 5.2, 5.3, and 5.4 demonstrate that academic effort differed significantly between the two groups with a moderately large effect size (Wilks' Lambda = .787, $F(6, 89) = 4.02$, $p < .01$, partial $\eta^2 = .213$), with the growth mindset group displaying higher levels of effort than the study skills group.

Both mindset and academic effort were demonstrated to be amenable to positive change as a result of the growth mindset intervention; however, further statistical analyses were conducted to examine if there were significant differences in academic achievement between the two groups. Findings indicated that there was no significant difference between the two groups in terms of cumulative semester grade point average or grades for the remedial course.

Exploring the Studies

Most traditional-aged students transitioning from high school to college encounter many unknowns and uncertainties; being conditionally admitted on academic probation was an additional uncertainty for the students in both of these studies. Yet, these two studies offer important insights into how certain high-risk students not only survive but thrive in the face of such uncertainties.

Academically Successful Seniors

In the qualitative study, it had been suggested to the students that they would likely struggle academically due to their low standardized college admissions tests scores and enrollment status. Nevertheless, these students engaged academically, held a positive perspective, and maintained supportive relationships. In other words, they thrived.

On an intrapersonal basis, academically successful seniors who were conditionally admitted had a positive perspective that predisposed them to eschew the negative; they maintained a can-do attitude. Academically, they exerted a high level of determination. The students in this study set academic goals, employed academic strategies to facilitate their success, and worked hard to be engaged learners. They adapted and adopted effective academic practices and

Table 5.2

Multivariate Analysis of Covariance of Posttest Academic Effort as a Function of Academic Discipline, Academic Self-Confidence, and Commitment to College

Source	Multivariate		Univariate					
			Academic discipline		Academic self-confidence		Commitment to college	
	$F(6, 89)$	η^2	$F(1, 94)$	η^2	$F(1, 94)$	η^2	$(1, 94)$	η^2
Condition	4.02**	.213	1.23	.431	3.85	.039	.089	.001
Pretest academic discipline (covariate)	15.08***	.504	71.07***	.431	.228	.002	.084	.001
Pretest academic self-confidence (covariate)	33.34***	.692	.838	.009	159.55***	.629	.102	.001
Pretest commitment to college (covariate)	45.98***	.756	1.21	.013	2.02	.021	186.42***	.665
Pretest general determination (covariate)	10.95***	.425	1.48	.015	1.53	.016	.589	.006
Pretest goal striving (covariate)	12.09***	.449	.361	.004	7.33**	.072	.002	.000
Pretest study skills (covariate)	17.55***	.542	3.03**	.031	.799	.008	.268	.003

Note. Multivariate *F* ratios were generated from the Wilks' Lambda statistic.

*p < .05. **p < .01. ***p < .001.

Table 5.3
Multivariate Analysis of Covariance of Posttest Academic Effort as a Function of General Determination, Goal Striving, and Study Skills

Source	Multivariate		Univariate					
			General determination		Goal striving		Study skills	
	$F_{(6, 89)}$	η^2	$F_{(1, 94)}$	η^2	$F_{(1, 94)}$	η^2	$F_{(1, 94)}$	η^2
Condition	4.02**	.213	.382	.004	.059	.001	14.33***	.132
Pretest academic discipline (covariate)	15.08***	.504	8.09**	.079	.326	.003	.080	.001
Pretest academic self-confidence (covariate)	33.34***	.692	.682	.007	2.44	.025	.223	.002
Pretest commitment to college (covariate)	45.98***	.756	.003	.000	1.66	.017	.030	.000
Pretest general determination (covariate)	10.95***	.425	43.53***	.316	4.18*	.043	1.12	.012
Pretest goal striving (covariate)	12.09***	.449	.040	.000	31.83***	.253	.178	.002
Pretest study skills (covariate)	17.55***	.542	1.91	.020	2.84**	.029	92.01***	.495

Note. Multivariate *F* ratios were generated from the Wilks' Lambda statistic.

*$p < .05$. **$p < .01$. ***$p < .001$.

Table 5.4

Adjusted Posttest Mean Scores and Standard Errors as a Function of Treatment Condition

Intervention Variable	Pretest				Posttest			
	Growth mindset (treatment)		Study skills (control)		Growth mindset (treatment)		Study skills (control)	
	M	SD	M	SD	M	SE	M	SE
Academic discipline	46.78	8.73	48.88	8.77	45.45	.64	46.58	.77
Academic self-confidence	48.37	9.40	49.90	9.16	49.88	.64	47.89	.77
Commitment to college	54.90	5.63	56.76	5.42	55.11	.47	54.89	.56
General determination	58.10	7.16	59.57	5.61	58.32	.43	57.90	.51
Goal striving	49.83	7.60	52.62	5.59	50.91	.45	50.73	.55
Study skills	52.55	10.27	54.79	10.51	55.50	.75	50.98	.90

utilized campus resources. Interpersonally, they recognized the importance of supportive relationships with family members, faculty and staff members, and peers in college, in addition to their relationship with God, to provide them with the encouragement, support, and the direction they needed to persist. Meaningful involvement in student groups and leadership roles augmented their academic endeavors.

Our conclusion from this study was that academically successful senior students who have been conditionally admitted may realize academic success and persist to graduation when they (a) possess a mindset focused on success, (b) acquire and execute good academic practices, (c) sustain supportive relationships, and (d) maintain group and leadership involvement. How a student approaches conditional admittance to college and what action the student takes to implement that approach determine whether or not the student will achieve academic success and persist to graduation.

A Growth Mindset

An important factor in increasing academic thriving is improving the amount of effort students invest in their academic experiences. The results of the second study are important and relevant for faculty, staff, and campus leaders in higher education, providing another avenue to increase the academic effort of students, especially those who are most at risk for failure. They further reveal the potential of a growth mindset to shape academic skills. The implications for practice are especially pertinent to remedial programs, which are often assigned the task of helping college students succeed who are academically underprepared and may lack proper motivation for success.

The findings of the second study provide a framework for understanding how institutions can increase the motivation and energy students exert toward their academic experiences by intervening with how students view themselves. In particular, the high-risk student's concept of intelligence as something that can be increased can help boost factors of academic thriving, but such an increase must be sustained.

Although the six variables that comprised academic effort were significantly higher for the growth mindset group than the control group, most of the difference was powered by the study skills variable. In other words, the study skills variable changed so much that it had a ripple effect for the other five variables that were used to define academic effort. Therefore, a mindset intervention may be best suited as one component of a broader academic intervention designed to increase academic determination in college students.

These findings present a certain level of irony, however. The results indicated that students who were encouraged to view intelligence as malleable reported employing study skills significantly more than the students who were directly taught more study skills. Although it did not significantly change all of the variables comprising academic effort, a growth mindset does appear to lead students to engage in the academic tasks presented to them in significantly different ways and at a level that goes beyond what typical remedial courses foster. These results provide evidence that changing students' psychological approaches to learning is needed in addition to teaching them new behaviors. As Schreiner (2010) notes, the behavioral and psychological aspects of engagement go hand-in-hand.

Implications for Policy and Practice

The results of these studies are relevant for any campus administrator who works directly or indirectly toward helping students succeed in terms of their retention, engagement, achievement, and development. In order to understand success, we must study success (Shushok & Hulme, 2006). The first study provides key elements to success by seeking to understand how students labeled as high risk in their transition to college overcame the odds and persisted to their senior year with excellent grade point averages. Colleges and universities need structures in place to monitor high-risk students throughout their tenure, particularly during the first two years of enrollment, ensuring their academic success and persistence. Although good curriculum, quality faculty, and cocurricular programs are all important for the success of college students, these components are not enough to help high-risk students thrive.

Understanding the academic strategies successful high-risk students use, how they use them, their involvements on and off campus, and the support systems they have in place, is essential in equipping high-risk students for success and persistence in college. Monitoring high-risk students should be part of the institutional retention plan and the direct responsibility of an individual, office, or advising system to determine whether or not (a) a realistic academic goal has been established by the student; (b) campus resources are being utilized to accommodate specific academic needs in a timely manner; (c) positive, engaged learning is occurring; (d) good academic practices are being employed along with consistent hard work; (e) an appropriate level of involvement in on- or off-campus activities is being maintained; and (f) a support network made up of peers on campus, a faculty or staff member, and family has been established. But identifying these deficits does not help students without also supplying ways to help increase their thriving. Therefore, administrators can use the three domains of thriving as a framework for analyzing what programs already exist and what programs are needed for students on an academic, intrapersonal, and interpersonal basis.

Knowing the psychological mindset of a student early in the collegiate experience is important for determining the motivation and the choices that will lead to success or failure. In addition to determining whether or not the institution is a student's first choice, colleges and universities should have a means for intentionally intervening on behalf of a student who lacks a positive disposition, a can-do attitude, determination to work hard, and confidence and belief in his or her ability to succeed. Institutional requirements for high-risk students will result in a greater positive impact on persistence if the students also employ a success mindset. In other words, achieving academic thriving in college for high-risk students comprises far more than remediating deficiencies.

So how do college faculty and administrators develop this success mindset in their students? A specific, practical place to start is to offer curricula, both in and out of the classroom, that promote a malleable view of intelligence. Although some in higher education may advocate for admitting only high-achieving students and getting out of their way, Light (2001) argues that colleges should attempt to get in the way of students—in a positive manner—to help them reach their goals. Scholars and practitioners must place more emphasis on how students view their own abilities, such as their intelligence, and whether those perceptions are constructive or detrimental to achieving desired outcomes.

Prior to presenting content on academically related skills for students, remedial programs could offer curriculum promoting a growth mindset. This content could be a mixture of psychology and neuroscience, with both areas used to increase motivation by demonstrating how the brain grows and changes. The curriculum can help students understand how their self-theories lead to either constructive or destructive behavior. The fixed and growth mindset paradigms can be explained along with the effects of each mindset as found in the literature. If such content were used to demonstrate the importance of effort in interpersonal, intrapersonal, and academic growth, then it would likely increase the motivation of academically high-risk students.

Although campus leaders can certainly initiate new programs aimed at promoting a growth mindset in high-risk students, administrators may also incorporate a growth mindset curriculum into currently existing programs. In this sense, a growth mindset becomes an amplifier to increase the benefit of evidence-based interventions (Robbins, Oh, Le, & Button, 2009). Remedial programs may be the ideal place to provide such amplification. Currently, the study skills offered by remedial programs may remain dormant in high-risk students due to mental filters that tell them they cannot change. A growth mindset can help remove such filters, thereby helping students see that significant change is not only possible, but worth the effort.

Rather than only attempting to gather more data on why students leave a particular institution, scholars and practitioners can also begin to learn why some students stay. Accordingly, the first study presented here should be replicated on campuses across the nation with those who, although labeled as academically high-risk upon admission, became successful outliers. Conducting focus groups of seniors who beat the odds at an institution is a valuable first step to understanding the emotional and behavioral resources a college or university should engender within in its students. There is little doubt that results from such attempts will overlap with the current findings.

Conclusion

Thriving in college students occurs at the intersection of academic engagement and performance, healthy relationships, and individual well-being. This chapter began by proposing that college student thriving is most important for those students at highest risk for academic failure. Colleges and universities label students as high risk if they have academic backgrounds that demonstrate lower high school achievement and college entrance test scores than those of their peers. Other characteristics, such as status as a first-generation student, also increase academic risk. From almost the beginning of higher education in the United States, remedial programs have been used to help academically high-risk students succeed, but recent and robust research indicates that these programs are not especially effective in four-year institutions. The lack of success from remedial programs may be due to their tendency to only focus on academic performance while ignoring the other vital components of thriving.

In order to help high-risk students thrive, scholars and practitioners must first understand what contributes to the success of high-risk students who achieve academic success. Then, it is important to implement appropriate interventions that can help promote these traits in other high-risk students. The two studies highlighted in the chapter addressed the importance of thriving for high-risk students and offered some insight into these two concerns. The first study sought to understand the experiences of academically successful graduating seniors who were labeled high risk when admitted to the institution as first-year students. One of the key results was that successful students who were once academically high risk possess a success mindset. The second study demonstrated how to use an intervention to change high risk students' mindsets and positively impact their success. The results of both studies, when combined with the existing literature on college student success, suggest that higher education scholars and practitioners must influence the way academically high risk students think about themselves in order to fuel thriving for this important student population.

References

Arendale, D. R. (2002). History of supplemental instruction (SI): Mainstreaming of developmental education. In D. B. Lundell, & J. L. Higbee (Eds.), *Histories of developmental education* (pp. 15-28). Minneapolis, MN: Center for Research on Developmental Education and Urban Literacy, General College, University of Minnesota.

Aronson, J., Fried, C. B., & Good, C. (2002). Reducing the effects of stereotype threat on African American college students by shaping theories of intelligence. *Journal of Experimental Social Psychology, 38*, 113-125.

Aronson, J., & Steele, C. M. (2005). Stereotypes and the fragility of academic competence, motivation, and self-concept. In A. J. Elliot & C. S. Dweck (Eds.), *Handbook of competence and motivation* (pp. 436-456). New York, NY: Guilford.

Attewell, P. A., Lavin, D. E., Domina, T., & Levey, T. (2006). New evidence on college remediation. *Journal of Higher Education, 77*, 886-924.

Bettinger, E., & Long, B. T. (2004). *Shape up or ship out: The effects of remediation on students at four-year colleges* (NBER Working Paper 10369). Cambridge, MA: National Bureau of Economic Research. Retrieved from the National Bureau of Economic Research website: http://www.nber.org/papers/w10369

Bettinger, E., & Long, B. T. (2008). *Addressing the needs of under-prepared students in higher education: Does college remediation work?* (NBER Working Paper 11325). Cambridge, MA: National Bureau of Economic Research. Retrieved from the National Bureau of Economic Research website: http://www.nber.org/papers/w11325

Blackwell, L. S., Trzesniewski, K. H., & Dweck, C. S. (2007). Implicit theories of intelligence predict achievement across an adolescent transition: A longitudinal study and an intervention. *Child Development, 78*(1), 246-263.

Boylan, H., & Saxon, D. (1999). *What works in remediation: Lessons from 30 years of research.* [Prepared for The League for Innovation in the Community College.] Retrieved from http://www.ncde.appstate.edu/reserve_reading/what_works.htm

Calcagno, J. C., & Long, B. T. (2008). *The impact of postsecondary remediation using a regression discontinuity approach: Addressing endogenous sorting and noncompliance* (NBER Working Paper 14194). Cambridge, MA: National Bureau of Economic Research. Retrieved from the National Bureau of Economic Research website: http://www.nber.org/papers/w14194

Chiu, C., Dweck, C. S., Tong, Y. Y., & Fu, J. H. (1997). Implicit theories and conceptions of morality. *Journal of Personality and Social Psychology, 73*, 923-940.

Creswell, J. W. (2007). *Qualitative inquiry and research design: Choosing among five approaches* (2nd ed.). Thousand Oaks, CA: Sage.

Dweck, C. S. (1999). *Self-theories: Their role in motivation, personality, and development.* Philadelphia, PA: Psychology Press.

Dweck, C. S. (2002). Beliefs that make smart people dumb. In R. Sternberg (Ed.), *Why smart people can be so stupid* (pp. 24-41). New Haven, CT: Yale University Press.

Dweck, C. S. (2006). *Mindset: The new psychology of success.* New York, NY: Random House.

Dweck, C. S., Chiu, C., & Hong, Y. (1995). Implicit theories and their role in judgments and reactions: A world from two perspectives. *Psychological Inquiry, 6*(4), 267-285.

Dweck, C. S., & Molden, D. C. (2005). Self-theories: Their impact on competence motivation and acquisition. In A. J. Elliot & C. S. Dweck (Eds.), *Handbook of competence and motivation* (pp. 122-140). New York, NY: Guilford.

Heine, S. J., Kitayama, S., Lehman, D. R., Takata, T., Ide, E., Leung, C., & Matsumoto, H. (2001). Divergent consequences of success and failure in Japan and North America: An investigation of self-improving motivations and malleable selves. *Journal of Personality and Social Psychology, 81*, 599-615.

Ishitani, T. T. (2006). Studying attrition and degree completion behavior among first-generation college students in the United States. *The Journal of Higher Education, 77*(5), 861-885.

Le, H., Casillas, A., Robbins, S. B., & Langley, R. (2005). Motivational and skills, social, and self-management predictors of college outcomes: Constructing the Student Readiness Inventory. *Educational and Psychological Measurement, 65*, 482-508.

Light, R. J. (2001). *Making the most of college: Students speak their minds.* Cambridge, MA: Harvard University Press.

Martorell, P., & McFarlin, I. (2007). *Help or hindrance? The effects of college remediation on academic and labor market outcomes.* Unpublished manuscript.

Moustakas, C. (1994). *Phenomenological research methods.* Thousand Oaks, CA: Sage.

Pascarella, E. T., Pierson, C. T., Wolniak, G. C., & Terenzini, P. T. (2004). First-generation college students: Additional evidence on college experiences and outcomes. *The Journal of Higher Education, 75*(3), 249-284.

Peterson, C. H., Casillas, A., & Robbins, S. B. (2006). The Student Readiness Inventory and the big five: Examining social desirability and college academic performance. *Personality and Individual Differences, 41,* 663-673.

Pike, G. R., & Kuh, G. D. (2005). First- and second-generation college students: A comparison of their engagement and intellectual development. *The Journal of Higher Education, 76*(3), 276-300.

Pizzolato, J. E. (2004). Coping with conflict: Self-authorship, coping, and adaptation to college in first-year, high-risk students. *Journal of College Student Development, 45,* 425-442.

Robins, R. W., & Pals, J. L. (2002). Implicit self-theories in the academic domain: Implications for goal orientation, attributions, affect, and self-esteem change. *Self and Identity, 1,* 313-336.

Robbins, S. B., Oh, I., Le, H., & Button, C. (2009). Intervention effects on college performance and retention as mediated by motivational, emotional, and social control factors: Integrated meta-analytic path analyses. *Journal of Applied Psychology, 94,* 1163-1184.

Schreiner, L. A. (2010). Thriving in the classroom. *About Campus, 15*(3), 2-10.

Shushok, F., & Hulme, E. (2006). What's right with you: Helping students find and use their personal strengths. *About Campus, 2*(4), 2-8.

Chapter 6

Beyond Sophomore Survival

Laurie A. Schreiner, Sharyn Slavin Miller, Tamera L. Pullins, and Troy L. Seppelt

Understanding the experiences of second-year students has recently become a topic of national interest for colleges and universities. Although the first documented use of the term *sophomore slump* occurred in 1956 (Freedman), it was not until the work of Schreiner and Pattengale (2000) that researchers and practitioners alike agreed that the sophomore experience includes daunting transitions. Sophomore students continue in general education courses, yet they experience a reduction in targeted programs and services provided by the institution (Gahagan & Hunter, 2009). They face pressure to declare a major, but report little interaction with faculty and peers in the classroom, and they report lower levels of motivation and satisfaction than students of other class levels (Schreiner, 2010a). The increased pressure and decreased support evident during the second year of college combine to create a difficult transition, and it is apparent that many sophomore students are not thriving in the face of these challenges.

This chapter explores this unique transition period by identifying the predictors of thriving for sophomore students. Doing so provides the information necessary to equip second-year students for positive functioning in the academic and interpersonal realms of their college experience and to support their overall well-being as individuals and as learners. After a brief literature review summarizing current research on the sophomore experience, the chapter focuses on the findings of two studies. The first, a quantitative study including information gathered from 41 four-year institutions, serves as the foundation for determining the significant predictors of thriving in the sophomore year. The second study is a qualitative exploration of the experiences of sophomores, some who are highly engaged and others who report low levels of engagement in their learning experiences. Together, the outcomes of these studies provide the framework for suggestions regarding institutional intervention in support of sophomore thriving.

The Sophomore Experience: Current Research and Literature

Research on the sophomore experience has tended to be primarily descriptive in nature, summarizing the unique challenges of the second year (Pattengale, 2000) or institutional responses to those needs (Tobolowsky & Cox, 2007). These challenges are not only academic, but also psychosocial in nature (Schaller, 2010a). As the collective attention of the institution shifts to the incoming class, sophomores face an intensified curriculum and academic performance demands, pressure to declare a major and choose a career, and shifting relationships and campus involvement—all in a context of increasing financial burdens and decreasing institutional support (Schreiner, 2010a). Qualitative studies have deepened existing knowledge of students' second-year experiences (Gansemer-Topf, Stern, & Benjamin, 2007; Gohn, Swartz, & Donnelly, 2001; Packard, 2005; Schaller, 2005), and quantitative studies of the sophomore experience have focused on students' satisfaction (Juillerat, 2000; Pullins, 2011) or predictors of their success (Graunke & Woosley, 2005; Schreiner, 2010a).

Studies of the second college year suggest that up to 25% of sophomores experienced slumping either academically, motivationally, or relationally (Schreiner, 2010a). For example, 20% of a national sample of more than 13,000 sophomores from 63 institutions reported that courses in their second year were worse or much worse than in their first year, 25% were getting lower grades than in their first year, and 18% stated their entire second-year experience was worse or much worse than their first-year experience (Schreiner, 2010c). Sophomores also reported declining satisfaction in almost every aspect of their campus experiences, a pattern Juillerat (2000) first identified and others have confirmed (Pullins, 2011; Schreiner, 2009).

Academic Challenges of the Sophomore Year

Although each year of college presents a new set of academic challenges and increasing rigor in the classroom, many of the academic demands of the second year are unique. Three of these are particularly salient for thriving in the sophomore year: (a) the reduced motivation experienced when taking general education courses that were avoided in the first year, (b) the challenge of engaging with faculty, and (c) the pressure to select an appropriate major.

Reduced motivation. Students often begin college highly motivated to succeed and eager to engage in all that the college experience has to offer. Institutional support to navigate the demands of the first year is commonplace (Barefoot, 2005), and often students have been permitted to postpone challenging general education courses until the second year. As sophomores, students may find themselves taking courses they avoided in the first year or other courses that fulfill graduation requirements but hold little interest for them and for which they see no practical use. The resulting lack of motivation may be compounded by indecision about a major or by the realization that nothing has aroused their curiosity yet (Schreiner, 2010b). They also realize they have a long road ahead of them. As one sophomore reported in a national study, "We're no longer the new kids on campus, but we're not getting out anytime soon either" (Schreiner, 2007).

Student-faculty interaction. One of the clearest findings in previous research on the second year is that satisfaction with faculty interaction is a strong predictor of sophomores' academic success and satisfaction with the total college experience (Graunke & Woosley, 2005; Keup, 2002; Schreiner, 2010a). Yet, such interaction can be more of a challenge in the second year because the small class sizes and intentional faculty interaction that often characterize the first-year experience are rarely continued into the sophomore year (Gahagan & Hunter, 2009). Too often, large introductory general education courses and courses taught by junior faculty or part-time instructors are the norm during this year (Schreiner, 2010b).

Selecting a major. Choosing a major is one of the primary tasks of the sophomore year, as timely graduation often depends on this task being completed before the second year ends. Thus, sophomores report intensifying pressure about choosing an academic major that will ultimately lead to a fulfilling career (Gore & Hunter, 2010; Schaller, 2005). Those who have not yet connected with a major may grapple with identifying and clarifying their sense of purpose and identity (Schaller, 2005, 2010b). For second-year students who have chosen a major, that decision may be revisited and questioned when they experience academic challenges in major courses or find that the courses are not what they expected (Gansemer-Topf et al., 2007).

Interpersonal Challenges in the Sophomore Year

Sophomores face particular challenges in interpersonal relationships because of the transition from carefully programmed social interactions provided during the first year to the more independently formed relationships characteristic of later stages of the college experience. Gansemer-Topf et al.'s (2007) qualitative study of the sophomore experience found that second-year students were experiencing a change in their social relationships. These residential students characterized newly formed social relationships as friendships of choice rather than convenience, in contrast to the first-year experience of social relationships that centered on the proximity offered by residence hall floors. Schaller (2010b) confirms that the primary interpersonal challenge of the sophomore year is to self-select the relationships that best fit who the student is becoming as a person.

For some sophomores, the lack of institutional support for networking with other students comes as an unpleasant surprise; they report that they are unsure how to make connections with their peers without such programming (Schreiner, 2010a). Campus involvement that was pervasive throughout their first-year experience becomes more difficult to balance with work obligations and increasing academic demands. As a result, the best strategy for sophomores is to be more selective in their commitments, choosing campus activities and organizations that are congruent with their major or interests (Schreiner, 2010a).

Emotional Challenges of the Sophomore Year

Although emotional challenges occur throughout the college experience, the transition into the sophomore year presents the unique challenge of coping with university systems that have shifted attention and support away from the student. As a result, sophomore satisfaction with university policies, services, and systems drops precipitously from the first year (Juillerat, 2000; Pullins, 2011). Second-year students who are able to find new ways of navigating the system and are able to reframe negative campus experiences are likely to be more successful.

Thriving in the Sophomore Year

Thriving is conceptualized in chapter 1 as "optimal functioning in three key areas that contribute to student success and persistence: (a) academic engagement and performance, (b) interpersonal relationships, and (c) psychological well-being" (pp. 4-5). Thriving in sophomores necessitates an ability to meet the unique challenges of the second year: reduced motivation, increased academic demands, decreased contact with faculty, the necessity of choosing a major, the selection of appropriate relationships and campus involvements, and diminished institutional support (Schaller, 2010b). The concept of thriving offers a framework for studying the sophomore year, as each aspect of the thriving model is comprised of malleable psychological qualities, meaning that these aspects of a student are amenable to change in response to a given situation or a specific intervention. Determining what aspects of the campus experience contribute most to sophomores' thriving could guide institutions in their design of programming and services for the second year.

Accordingly, two studies of the sophomore experience are described below. The first is a large-scale quantitative study of the predictors of thriving. The second study examines one element of thriving, engaged learning, and explores more fully the experiences and perceptions of what contributes to engagement in learning among sophomores from one institution. Two research questions guided the studies presented in this chapter:

- What are the significant predictors of thriving among sophomores at four-year institutions, after controlling for their demographic characteristics?
- What are the experiences that sophomores report as vital to their success and engagement in learning?

Each study and its findings will be described separately. Implications for practice and specific recommendations for institutions desiring to enhance thriving in the sophomore year will conclude the chapter.

Study 1: Predicting Thriving

A study of 4,845 traditional-aged sophomores from 41 four-year institutions across the United States formed the basis of analysis for the predictors of thriving in the sophomore year. The sample represented those who responded to all items on the Sophomore Experiences Survey, which was distributed online during the spring of 2010. The web-based instrument was designed to measure various aspects of the sophomore experience to include student thriving (chapter 1), frequency and satisfaction with faculty interaction, and levels of student involvement. Participating institutions were four-year colleges and universities who responded to an invitation through the sophomore-year experience listserv sponsored by the National Resource Center for The First-Year Experience and Students in Transition; 13 of the institutions were public and 28 were private. Table 6.1 outlines the characteristics of the participating

Table 6.1

Institutional Characteristics of the Sophomore Sample (N = 41)

Characteristic	*n*	%
Institutional Control		
Private	28	68.2
Public	13	31.8
Admissions Selectivity		
Open to all with high school diploma or equivalent	0	0.0
Majority of students admitted from bottom 50% of class	3	7.3
Majority of students admitted from top 50% of class	19	46.3
Majority of students admitted from top 25% of class	16	39.0
Majority of students admitted from top 10% of class	3	7.3
Size		
Under 5,000 students	20	48.7
5,000 – 9,999 students	9	21.9
10,000 – 14,999 students	4	9.8
15,000 – 19,999 students	6	14.6
20,000 or more students	2	4.9
Carnegie Classification		
Baccalaureate College—Arts and Sciences	14	34.1
Baccalaureate College—Diverse Fields	3	7.3
Master's Colleges and Universities (larger programs)	7	17.1
Master's Colleges and Universities (medium programs)	4	9.8
Master's Colleges and Universities (small programs)	3	7.3
Doctoral/Research University	0	0.0
Research Universities (high research activity)	6	14.6
Research Universities (very high research activity)	4	9.8
Residential (more than 75% of students live on campus)		
Yes	11	26.8
No	30	73.2

institutions, and Table 6.2 summarizes the demographic characteristics of the student participants. The sophomores in this sample were disproportionately White and female, so all data were weighted for these two variables in order to present a more accurate picture of college sophomores at four-year institutions.

A hierarchical multiple regression analysis was conducted to determine the significant predictors of thriving scores among these sophomores. This type of analysis allows the researcher to control statistically for demographic variables that may be related to the outcome of thriving but are not changeable once students arrive on campus, such as their gender, generation status, ethnicity, high school grades, and whether or not the institution was their first choice at enrollment. Once these demographic characteristics are controlled, then the unique contribution of particular campus experiences or perceptions can be determined.

Six blocks of variables were created to determine the unique contribution of each type of experience. The demographic characteristics were in the first block, followed by pervasive aspects of the student's campus experience, such as whether they lived on campus, worked on or off campus, had transferred into the institution, were certain of their major, or were an athlete and their level of concern over the amount of college debt they had accumulated. Levels of spirituality comprised block three, as previous research indicates that this aspect of a student's life contributes meaningfully to psychological well-being and positive student outcomes (Astin, Astin, & Lindholm, 2011). Furthermore, spirituality is a particularly notable contributor to thriving among students of color (Schreiner, Kitomary, & Seppelt, 2010). The amount and type of interaction with faculty, along with a student's satisfaction regarding such interactions, were variables in block four of the equation. Types of campus involvement, such as Greek organizations, campus groups, ethnic organizations, performing groups, student government, peer leadership, learning communities, and community service, comprised block five. A student's psychological sense of community was entered into the final block, based on Lounsbury and DeNeui's (1995) research indicating the importance of this variable in college student retention and satisfaction.

As can be seen in Table 6.3, this model explained 57% of the variation in sophomore thriving. The largest unique contribution to thriving was students' sense of community on campus. Interaction with faculty, being certain of one's major, level of spirituality, and concern about college debt explained a significant amount of the variation, as well. Surprisingly, campus

Table 6.2

Demographic Characteristics of the Sophomore Study Participants (N = 4,845)

Characteristic	*n*	%
Gender		
Female	3,350	69.1
Male	1,495	30.9
Generation		
First-generation	1,017	21.0
Not first-generation	3,828	79.0
Degree Aspirations		
None	90	1.8
Bachelors	965	19.9
Teaching credential	69	1.4
Masters	2,312	47.7
Doctorate	856	17.7
Medical or law	553	11.4
Institution was first choice at enrollment		
Yes	2,989	61.7
No	1,856	38.3
Housing		
On campus	3,145	65.8
Off campus	1,632	34.2
Race/Ethnicity		
African American	278	5.9
American Indian/Alaska Native	16	.3
Asian American/Pacific Islander	245	5.2
Caucasian	3,895	82.1
Latino/a	162	3.4
Multiethnic	150	3.2
Prefer not to respond	99	2.0
Transferred into the institution		
Yes	613	12.6
No	4,264	87.4
Athlete		
Yes	441	9.2
No	4,339	90.8
Work off campus		
Yes	1,544	31.9
No	3301	68.1

Table 6.3

Summary of Hierarchical Multiple Regression Analyses for Variables Predicting Thriving in Sophomores (N = 1,747)

Predictor variable	Engaged learning	Academic determination	Social connectedness	Diverse citizenship	Positive perspective	Thriving mean
	β	β	β	β	β	β
Block 1 R²	.03	.06	.02	.04	.02	.05
First choice	.08***	.05***	.06***	.03*	.09***	.09***
Gender	.05***	.09***	.02	.12***	.03	.08***
First-generation	.01	.01	-.06***	.01	.01	-.01
High school grades	.00	.14***	.06***	.06***	.06***	.09***
Degree aspirations	.14***	.13***	.05**	.10***	.07***	.14***
Asian	-.01	-.03	-.07***	-.04**	-.02	-.05***
Black	.01	.04**	.01	.09***	.06***	.06***
Latino/a	.01	.01	-.01	.00	.04**	.01
Block 2 R² Change	.06	.08	.05	.04	.08	.12
Work off campus	-.03	-.04*	.02	.02	.03*	.00
Work on campus	.07***	.02	.01	.05***	.02	.05***
Transfer student	.05***	.05***	-.06***	.00	.00	.01
Major certainty	.18***	.23***	.10***	.16***	.23***	.26***
Live on campus	.04*	.00	.05**	.05***	.03	.04**
Athlete	-.04**	-.03*	.05***	-.01	.01	-.01
Debt concern	-.14***	-.12***	-.17***	-.05***	-.14***	-.18***
Block 3 R² change	.01	.03	.01	.07	.12	.08
Spirituality	.11***	.16***	.12***	.28***	.34***	.29***

(Continued to p. 120)

(Continued from p. 119)

Predictor variable	Criterion variables					
	Engaged learning	Academic determination	Social connectedness	Diverse citizenship	Positive perspective	Thriving mean
	β	β	β	β	β	β
Block 4 R^2 change	.12	.07	.01	.06	.04	.12
Office hours	.01	.00	.02	.01	.00	.01
Faculty – career	.07***	.03*	.04*	.04**	.02	.06***
Faculty – social	.05***	-.03	-.01	.03	-.01	.01
Faculty – academic	.05**	-.01	.01	.04**	.01	.03
Faculty interaction	.30***	.26***	.09***	.20***	.19***	.31**
Advisor contact	-.02	.07***	.02	.03*	.05***	.04***
Block 5 R^2 change	.01	.01	.02	.05	.01	.03
Service-learning	-.02	.01	.01	-.01	.01	.00
Learning community	.01	.01	.01	.06***	.02	.03*
Greek organizations	-.071***	-.03	.03	-.06***	.01	-.04**
Performance groups	-.01	-.07***	-.08***	-.06***	-.04*	-.07***
Community service	.01	.04*	.03	.14***	.04**	.07***
Leadership	.03	.05**	.09***	.08***	.08***	.09***
Student organization	-.01	.02	.01	.04*	-.01	.01
Campus events	.01	.01	.09***	.05***	.04**	.05***
Peer leadership	.01	.02	.00	.05**	.01	.03
Student government	.00	-.01	-.04*	-.04*	-.01	-.02
Ethnic organizations	.01	-.05**	-.01	-.01	.01	-.02
Block 6 R^2 change	.06	.06	.12	.13	.12	.20
Sense of community	.29***	.29***	.41***	.43***	.40***	.52***
Total R^2	.28	.30	.24	.39	.37	.57

* $p < .05$. ** $p < .01$. *** $p < .001$.

involvement explained less than 3% of the variation in thriving, and students' demographic characteristics explained only 5% of the variation. Among the demographic characteristics that were significant predictors of thriving, high school grades and intent to pursue graduate study were the strongest predictors. Being African American was a positive predictor of thriving, while being Asian was a negative predictor. African American students' high levels of spirituality appeared to contribute most to their thriving. Among Asian students, lower levels of thriving appeared to be related to a lower reliance on spirituality as a coping mechanism and foundation for life, as well as less connection to the campus community, fewer supportive social networks, and feeling greater pressure to succeed academically.

After controlling statistically for these demographic characteristics, pervasive aspects of a student's sophomore year added another 11% to the explanation of the variation in their thriving levels. Specifically, being certain of one's major accounted for most of this variation. Being grounded in a major by the end of the sophomore year and feeling confident of that choice appears to be one of the most important aspects of sophomore thriving. Major certainty provides sophomores with a sense of purpose and direction, along with a potential network of friends who have similar academic interests and a connection to faculty who can guide them more specifically toward their future. Major certainty is also significantly predictive of sophomore grade point average (Graunke & Woosley, 2005). Thus, the findings confirm Schaller's (2010b) assertion that it is impossible to overstate the positive impact that being confident of one's major has on a sophomore.

Being a transfer student was positively associated with sophomore thriving, contrary to expectations (Ishitani, 2008). Further analysis revealed that transfer students were likely to report higher levels of effort and motivation, along with greater engagement in learning, openness to diversity, and desire to make a difference in the world. They were significantly less likely to have a supportive network of friends, however. It is possible that transfer students enter their new environment with a greater level of optimism and perceive their current university experience to be more positive than their first year, thus leading to higher levels of engagement and thriving.

Negative predictors of thriving included students' discouragement about the level of debt they were incurring to pay college bills, their status as an athlete, and living on campus. Two of these three findings were expected. For example, concern about one's future ability to pay growing school bills makes it difficult to be vitally engaged in the experiences that are creating those bills. The finding that athletes were less likely to be thriving academically is consistent with other research that has found lower levels of academic effort and engagement among this group of students (Umbach, Palmer, & Kuh, 2006), while their greater connection to friends and social networks contributed to higher levels of interpersonal thriving, as was expected.

In contrast to previous research that has documented the benefits of living on campus (Astin & Oseguera, 2005; Gahagan & Hunter, 2009; Pascarella & Terenzini, 2005), in this sample of sophomores, living on campus was negatively associated with thriving. Students living on campus reported less satisfaction with all aspects of their lives, were less open to diverse others, and were less confident of their ability to make a difference in the world. They also were less motivated to invest effort in their academic pursuits than those living off campus. This finding remains puzzling, although one possible explanation is that sophomores living on campus were less satisfied with their living arrangements than were those living off campus. In the open-ended comments at the end of the survey asking respondents what they would change about their sophomore year, a number mentioned the challenges of roommates or other aspects of campus housing.

Spirituality accounted for 8% of the variation in thriving, after controlling for the previous demographic characteristics and aspects of their sophomore year, with no significant differences between public and private institutions in the degree to which spirituality predicted thriving. This finding places spirituality as the third largest contributor to the variation seen in sophomores' levels of thriving. Spirituality was defined by three items reflecting a belief in a higher power beyond oneself and a reliance on that belief as a source of strength during difficult times and as a foundation for making life decisions. Lindholm (2010) notes that the sophomore year is a time for reflection on questions of life purpose and meaning, which is the heart of spirituality. Spirituality can also function as a coping skill that sustains students and leads to a positive perspective on life. In the study, students with high levels of spirituality also reported high levels of optimism and life satisfaction, along with greater openness to others who were different and higher motivation to make a contribution to society, all of which are consistent with major religious teachings and a sense of meaning and purpose in life (Chickering, Dalton, & Stamm, 2006; Lindholm, 2010). Particularly among African American students, spirituality appeared to function as a mediating variable for thriving, a lens through which other campus and life experiences were interpreted or reframed.

Interactions with faculty accounted for an additional 11% of the variance in thriving levels, after all the previous variables were controlled. This finding indicates that the more students interact with faculty, the greater the level of engagement in learning and investment of effort in academics they report; however, faculty interaction also contributed to their satisfaction with life and their optimism about the future, regardless of the type of student and their life circumstances during the sophomore year. As Noel (2007) found in her grounded theory study of high-achieving seniors, one of the primary ways that faculty impact students is by painting a picture of the future for them, helping them see options for their lives that they did not realize were possible. In the present study, conversations with faculty about career issues were the type of faculty interaction that contributed most to sophomore thriving, followed by conversations about academic issues. This finding is consistent with the developmental needs of sophomores who are engaged in what Schaller (2005) terms focused exploration, in which students are actively searching for insight into their future selves.

Once student demographic characteristics, life circumstances, spirituality, and faculty interaction were accounted for statistically, student involvement in campus activities and organizations explained little additional variation in their thriving. This finding comes as a surprise and stands in sharp contrast to Astin's (1984) assertions about the importance of involvement to student success. There are two possible explanations for this incongruence. One is that this particular sample of sophomores was highly involved on campus, and thus, there was not enough variation in their involvement to be significantly predictive of thriving. For example, almost 83% of the sample participated to some extent in campus events and three fourths of them were involved in student organizations. Students who self-reported as campus leaders comprised more than half the sample. This high level of involvement naturally restricts the predictive ability of the variable. A second explanation is that the type of involvement Astin advocated, and that continues to be encouraged in research by Kuh (2009) and others, is defined by learning-related activities rather than social activities. It is possible that the campus involvement many practitioners believe is beneficial to students is not as powerful as supposed. Very little research has been conducted on the contribution of campus involvement to student success, and most of that research connects such involvement to the development of peer relationships that promote retention and satisfaction (Fischer, 2007).

Finally, the largest contributor to sophomore thriving was students' sense of community on campus. This variable alone accounted for an additional 20% of the variation in thriving, over and above all the other variables discussed thus far. Students who experience a strong sense of community on campus feel they matter to the university and are part of a network of people who care about them, are committed to their growth and well-being, and are able to meet their needs (Lounsbury & DeNeui, 1995; Schreiner, 2010e). Cheng (2004) asserts that "what connects students with the community is not just small circles of friends who share personal interests; it is also effective programming and organized social opportunities" (p. 228). However, he discovered that student involvement in campus activities and groups did not foster a sense of community; rather, the largest contributor to a sense of community in his institution was a campus ethos centered around engagement in learning, an environment in which students felt accepted and valued and were encouraged to express their own opinions and beliefs.

This large-scale quantitative study of sophomores across multiple four-year public and private institutions demonstrated that a significant amount of the variation in students' thriving during the second year of college can be explained by a model that includes their demographic characteristics, quality of life on campus, spirituality, interaction with faculty, campus involvement, and sense of community on campus. The features of the campus experience that contribute most to sophomore thriving are primarily those aspects that enable a student to feel that the institution has been the right choice: a sense of community, interaction with faculty, and certainty about one's major.

Study 2: Exploring Sophomore Engagement in Learning

In the spring of their sophomore year, 23 students at a private, faith-based university were interviewed for 90 minutes each. The students participating in this study had taken the Sophomore Experiences Survey earlier in the semester and were identified as scoring in the highest or lowest deciles on levels of engaged learning. Of the 23 students interviewed, 10 had scored as highly engaged in learning and 13 had scored a low level of engagement. The interviewer was unaware of the students' scores on engaged learning until after the interview had been transcribed and coded. Students were asked questions about their experience as a sophomore, especially as it related to their levels of engagement on campus—interaction with faculty, classes they enjoyed, connection with friends, choice of major, and academic advising. Analysis of the student experiences produced several themes, including the importance of faculty interest in the student and interaction between the faculty and student outside of class, the importance of the students finding and making friendships through their major and required classes for their major, dissatisfaction with academic advising, and a sense of abandonment by their institution.

The belief that faculty were genuinely interested in them and that students had opportunities for high-quality interactions with faculty outside the classroom was a primary theme expressed by all of the participants. This theme was typified by one student who stated: "I love the teachers here. They are one of the reasons why I like staying here so much because it's a personal-type relationship....You can talk to them about anything." Students who had experienced a semester-long program where a small group of students and faculty studied, lived, and interacted daily with each other in the mountains experienced even more significant relationships with faculty. Students saw this program as the optimum model for faculty interaction:

> Being up there...it was wonderful because there is such a low ratio of faculty to students. Part of the program is that you eat dinner with your professors and part of it is to get to know your professors and have those mentoring relationships be more than just friendships. We also go on a backpacking trip for six days. Your professors are your leaders.

Students who had this kind of quality interaction also sought to have the same kind of meaningful interactions with faculty once they returned from the program: "Once I came back to main campus, I wanted that kind of special relationship with faculty, so I approached them and talked with them and connected outside of class."

The second theme that emerged from the student interviews was how friendships with peers, especially those in the same major and taking the same classes, contributed to their engaged learning. Without exception, all of the highly engaged participants talked about the deep relationships they had with "people from my major...we're all like a big family." They talked about "hanging out" with these friends, keeping each other motivated to stay at the school, and talking with each other about possible career choices and life after college.

Many of the low-scoring students talked about their disappointment with advising and their need for career counseling: "Advising was really stressful....I didn't really know what direction I wanted to go yet.... there wasn't advising as far as helping me figure out what I wanted to do....like, What are your interests?" Some described academic advisors as unhelpful because students expected advising to be oriented around choosing a major and an eventual career path, yet advisors focused mostly on course registration for the upcoming semester. In contrast, sophomores who were identified as thriving sought and received effective academic advising and career counseling.

A final theme that emerged from this study was that many of the sophomores felt abandoned by their institution, especially after being part of such a strong first-year experience. Many of the students felt negatively impacted by the requirement to move off campus so that first-year students could have their living spaces and described the difficulty they had in gathering together in a different living space:

> My freshman year was really easy for me to make friends because they all lived on my floor....This year...was definitely more difficult... it seemed like we got a lot of attention in the residence halls as freshmen, but once we became sophomores we lost housing priority and were really left to try and work things out on our own.

Another student had a similar experience, and described the same type of institutional abandonment: "I felt like I received a lot of attention as a freshman from everyone....Sophomore year all of that went poof! I was forced to move off campus to university apartments, and I never even met my RA the entire year."

An examination of these themes indicated that although all the sophomores had experienced many of the same challenges and perceived a lack of institutional support during their sophomore year, those who were highly engaged had found ways to connect to peers and faculty and to take the initiative to meet their own needs for advising and career counseling. This ability to proactively cope, seek out resources, and connect with others provides strategies that characterize thriving during times of transition.

Implications for Practice: Support for Sophomore Students

Weaving the themes from the qualitative study of sophomore engaged learning with the predictors of thriving found in the large national study of the second-year experience, there are two major implications leading to concrete recommendations for institutional policies and practices affecting sophomores.

Connections Matter

One of the clearest findings emerging from both studies in this chapter is that sophomores thrive when they are connected. Whether that connection is relational or cognitive, it serves to provide not only a source of support during transition but also a way of moving forward and gaining maximum benefit from the second year of college.

Sophomores who had significant and meaningful interactions with faculty were deeply impacted by those relationships and longed for them to continue. Keen disappointment with the lack of opportunity to interact with faculty was evident not only in student interviews but also in the open-ended comments that were part of the national survey. Peer connections were also paramount: seeking advice and assistance from peers, enjoying interaction with those in the same major or area of interest, and relying on peers for emotional support when challenges occurred.

The cognitive connections evident in both sophomore groups included linking what they were learning in class to what they already knew or to what interested them outside of class. Forging a cognitive connection between current circumstances and a future career was also a critical ingredient in a student's ability to thrive in a year when the pressure to choose a major was intensified. When this happened in the context of academic advising or a mentoring relationship with a faculty member, students were most likely to thrive. Collectively, these cognitive and relational connections, along with the broader connection to the university through the campus climate, combined to produce a sense of community that was highly predictive of the variation seen in sophomore thriving.

Spirituality was also linked to thriving among these sophomores. The regression analyses indicated that spirituality was a significant predictor of thriving, particularly in its contribution to a positive perspective. As defined in this study, spirituality is indicative of the sense of meaning and purpose that other researchers have postulated is so vital for sophomore success (Gardner, 2000; Lindholm, 2010; Schaller, 2010a). An implication of this finding is that the connections that matter to sophomore thriving are not only relational and cognitive, but also spiritual in nature, linking students' inner lives and their search for meaning and purpose with their academic pursuits and the relationships they develop.

Institutional Practices Affect Thriving

Sophomores' sense of community was the major predictor of their thriving at the end of the second year of college and is comprised of four aspects: (a) *membership*, or feelings of belonging; (b) *ownership*, or the ability to make a contribution and have a voice; (c) *relationship*, or positive interactions and shared emotional connections; and (d) *partnership*, or interdependence and commitment to a common goal (Schreiner, 2010e). Specific institutional policies and practices can impact each of these aspects, communicating to students the institution's commitment to their welfare, as well as the integrity of the institution, in the process. Equitable access to programs and services, transparency and fairness in administering policies and rules, and equal treatment and respect for students are examples of practices that can strengthen the sense of community on campus (Braxton, Hirschy, & McClendon, 2004).

Recommendations

Four specific recommendations arise from these implications. An institutional focus on any of these areas could significantly enhance sophomores' abilities to benefit from their second college year.

1. Connect sophomores to faculty in intentional and meaningful ways. Student-faculty interaction has numerous benefits that extend to all students, not just to sophomores (Kuh & Hu, 2001; Pascarella & Terenzini, 2005). Yet, in these studies sophomores experienced a distinct difference from the faculty interaction they had experienced in their first year. Larger classes, classes outside their major interest area, and required courses for the general education curriculum that were taught by adjuncts and part-time faculty combined to produce the perception that there was significantly less opportunity to interact with faculty. Thus, institutions desiring to enhance sophomore thriving might consider ways of intentionally connecting their sophomores with their faculty.

Forming student-faculty research partnerships is one example of a meaningful and intentional connection. Research by Nagda, Gregerman, Jonides, von Hippel, and Lerner (1998) demonstrated that the students who benefited most from such partnerships were sophomores and African American students. Wilson and Crowe (2010) point out that the sophomore year is the ideal time for student-faculty research partnerships, as "an early start fosters higher retention and a higher likelihood of pursuing a post-baccalaureate degree" (p. 181). However, Kim and Sax's (2011) study of student-faculty interaction and research engagement discovered that the impact of such interaction and research partnerships depended on the academic discipline. Their research is particularly instructive for institutional leaders and faculty developers, as they demonstrated that students were most likely to benefit from research with faculty in departments with a supportive and favorable faculty climate; clearly defined and communicated policies and expectations; and a well-organized curriculum with pedagogical practices that emphasized critical thinking and reasoning, integrating ideas from other courses, generating new ideas, and using facts and examples to support their viewpoints.

Yet, the classroom environment may be where students and faculty are most likely to interact. Cole (2007) identified specific in-class faculty behaviors that resulted in more positive effects of student-faculty interaction: "enthusiastically engaging students in the learning process, ...valuing students and their comments, ...and allowing students the opportunity to constructively challenge professors' ideas" (p. 276). Cole also notes that the type of relationship students develop with faculty affects their intellectual self-concept, as does the purpose for the interaction and the accessibility cues that faculty convey in class. In his study, students who developed mentoring relationships with faculty were more likely to report gains in their intellectual self-concept, while those whose interaction with faculty centered on a critique of their work were less likely to report gains.

2. Build community in and out of the classroom. At a time when commuting students represent almost 85% of all college students in the United States (Horn & Nevill, 2006), the classroom is the primary place for building a sense of community. Equipping faculty to use active and collaborative learning techniques and to capitalize on students' strengths and learning styles can ensure that the classroom becomes a place where sophomores feel a sense of belonging and connection. Forming learning communities, designing service-learning courses, and creating courses in the general education curriculum that target sophomores in smaller classes with approachable faculty can add to the likelihood that students will experience a sense of community in the academic environment.

Beyond the classroom, building community among second-year students can occur through sophomore programming; intentional interaction with other students and faculty in the major; and the selection of campus and community involvement that aligns with their interests, goals, and values. Carefully attending to institutional communication with students can build a sense of community, as well. Messages of welcome and inclusion, seeking student feedback and responding to their input, convey that sophomores are valued members of the campus community.

3. Focus sophomore advising on connecting present and future identities. The most poignant stories and comments from sophomores in our study were about their desire for the kind of academic advising relationship that would help them plan for the future. Advising was also the area where sophomores were least satisfied, and was a significant contributor to the variation in student thriving. Sophomores who were confident of the major they had chosen were highly likely to be thriving at the end of their second year.

Gordon (2010) suggests that academic advising targeted to the sophomore year should focus on three tasks: reviewing, immediate goal setting, and long-range planning. At the beginning of the sophomore year, offering students a chance to reflect on their previous year's experiences provides a foundation for goal setting in the second year. Immediate goal setting then focuses on the student's academic progress and choice of courses and goals for the year, while long-range planning involves setting goals for the remainder of the college experience and beyond. Aligning students' curricular and cocurricular goals with their life goals and career interests will enable sophomores to benefit most from the second year of college.

Academic advising is one of the best vehicles for addressing thriving in the sophomore year. Advisors who have been trained in a strengths-based approach that focuses on identifying students' assets, building hope, setting realistic goals, and helping students envision their future are best equipped to provide sophomores with the assistance they need (Schreiner, 2010d; Schreiner & Anderson, 2005). When students can envision a best possible self (Markus & Nurius, 1986), or the type of person they desire to become as a result of their college experience, and see how their strengths are pathways toward becoming that person, they are motivated to engage in the behaviors necessary to succeed.

4. Recognize spirituality as a pathway to thriving in sophomores. One of the most salient issues for the sophomore year is the search for meaning and purpose, as the pressure to declare a major intensifies and financial concerns may lead to a pivotal moment when students must decide whether they can justify the cost of a college education if they have not yet decided what they are doing with their lives (Schaller, 2010a). Spirituality, defined as "the search for ultimate purpose and truth" (Dalton, 2001, p. 18) can be a vital pathway to thriving in the sophomore year, as it provides students with a lens through which to view their current circumstances as well as their future. Lindholm (2010) notes that the sophomore year is a time in which students are likely to begin thinking more holistically about their lives; thus, campus opportunities and support for examining meaning and purpose can provide students with the resources they need for this transition.

In the present study, spirituality significantly contributed to the variation in sophomore thriving, particularly for students of color. Institutions can begin to help students explore the spiritual issues in their lives as a venue to thriving, especially among student populations for whom other venues, such as campus involvement, are not contributing to their overall well-being. For example, faculty can open the classroom dialogue for an exploration of meaning and purpose, and advisors can include a reflection on students' purpose as part of the process of goal-setting. Faculty development opportunities and new faculty orientation can provide training that equips professors to facilitate these dialogues. Cocurricular approaches can include creating times and spaces for spiritual reflection and meditation as part of an emphasis on wellness, hosting campus speakers and forums on spiritual issues, providing interfaith workshops on spirituality and religious diversity, and including discussions of spirituality in the residence life education programs and student leadership training programs.

An example of a multifaceted approach to spirituality is the Big Questions program at Carnegie Mellon University (Astin et al., 2011). Thirty faculty, in collaboration with residence life staff, meet weekly with students in small groups in the residence halls to engage in intentional dialogue around profound questions, such as the meaning of love, life, academic excellence, honor, democracy, respect, and diversity. This collaborative attention to students' inner lives and issues that are important to them communicates to students an abiding concern for their development as whole persons.

5. Examine institutional policies and practices from a sophomore perspective. Even a cursory examination of institutional practices that affect sophomores leads to the conclusion that second-year students are often last in line. Course registration timing and access, housing policies, financial aid distribution, campus parking, and class schedules are examples of areas where an institution may be unintentionally disadvantaging the sophomore student.

Including sophomores on campus committees, assessing sophomore satisfaction, and conducting sophomore focus groups about their experiences with campus services are ways the institution can communicate to sophomores that they matter to the institution, a practice that Braxton et al. (2004) note is vital for student retention. Providing user-friendly mechanisms for sophomores to address the financial issues that create a barrier to their thriving and success is also a step an institution can take to communicate concern for students' welfare in the second year.

Finally, a culture of service excellence across the bureaucratic structures of the institution can enhance sophomore thriving, as well. Bean (2005) notes that bureaucratic exchanges should be seen as learning opportunities that can enhance students' academic and social integration, as well as their loyalty to the institution, yet too often serve to further alienate the student. For example, students who feel they learned how to navigate the system effectively in the process of being helped are more likely to feel positively about the institution; whereas, students who feel powerless and treated like a number are likely to experience negative emotions and to share their dissatisfaction with others. Institutions concerned about the sophomore slump can encourage staff to see the key role they play in influencing student perceptions of the institution as well as in creating an environment conducive to student thriving.

Conclusion

Despite the burgeoning research about the success of sophomore students, they remain in many ways the *invisible students* (Schreiner & Pattengale, 2000). This chapter focused on both quantitative and qualitative research to support recommendations that would enable a greater percentage of sophomores to not only return as juniors, but thrive as well. A clear institutional focus on building a campus community where sophomores experience a sense of belonging and ownership in a context of healthy relationships and meaningful partnerships with faculty and other students is the foundation for addressing the needs of these students. Academic advising that connects their present to their future and helps sophomores set not only educational goals but life goals builds on that solid foundation by equipping students with pathways to success in the second year. As institutions enrich the connections available to sophomores and energetically support their progress toward a positive future, students experiencing the transitions of the sophomore year gain the visibility necessary to help them thrive.

References

Astin, A. W. (1984). Student involvement: A developmental theory for higher education. *Journal of College Student Personnel, 25,* 297-308.

Astin, A. W., Astin, H. S., & Lindholm, J. A. (2011). *Cultivating the spirit: How college can enhance students' inner lives.* San Francisco, CA: Jossey-Bass.

Astin, A. W., & Oseguera, L. (2005). Pre-college and institutional influences on degree attainment. In A. Seidman (Ed.), *College student retention: Formula for student success* (pp. 245-276). Bolton, MA: Anker.

Barefoot, B. O. (2005). Current institutional practice in the first college year. In M. L. Upcraft, J. N. Gardner, & B. O. Barefoot (Eds.), *Challenging and supporting the first-year student: A handbook for improving the first year of college* (pp.47-66). San Francisco, CA: Jossey-Bass.

Bean, J. P. (2005). Nine themes of college student retention. In A. Seidman (Ed.), *College student retention: Formula for student success* (pp. 215-244). Bolton, MA: Anker.

Braxton, J. M., Hirschy, A. S., & McClendon, S. A. (2004). *Understanding and reducing college student departure* (ASHE-ERIC Higher Education Report Vol. 30, No. 3). San Francisco, CA: Wiley.

Cheng, D. X. (2004). Students' sense of campus community: What it means and what to do about it. *NASPA Journal, 41,* 216-232.

Chickering, A. W., Dalton, J. C., & Stamm, L. (2006). *Encouraging authenticity and spirituality in higher education.* San Francisco, CA: Jossey-Bass.

Cole, D. (2007). Do interracial interactions matter? An examination of student-faculty contact and intellectual self-concept. *The Journal of Higher Education, 78*(3), 249-281.

Dalton, J. C. (2001). Career and calling: Finding a place for the spirit in work and community. In M. A. Jablonski (Ed.), *The implications of student spirituality for student affairs practice* (New Directions for Student Services No. 95, pp. 17-25). San Francisco, CA: Jossey-Bass.

Freedman, M. (1956). The passage through college. *Journal of Social Issues, 12*(4), 13-28.

Fischer, M. J. (2007). Settling into campus life: Differences by race/ethnicity in college involvement, college satisfaction, and outcomes. *Journal of Higher Education, 78*(2), 125-161.

Gahagan, J., & Hunter, M. S. (2009). Residential learning in the sophomore year. In M. Hunter, B. Tobolowsky, J. Gardner, S. Evenbeck, J. Pattengale, M. Schaller, & L. A. Schreiner (Eds.), *Helping sophomores succeed: Understanding and improving the second-year experience* (pp. 189-202). San Francisco, CA: Jossey-Bass.

Gansemer-Topf, A., Stern, J., & Benjamin, M. (2007). Examining the experiences of second-year students at a private liberal arts college. In B. F. Tobolowsky & B. E. Cox (Eds.), *Shedding light on sophomores: An exploration of the second college year* (Monograph No. 47, pp. 31-48). Columbia, SC: University of South Carolina, National Resource Center for The First Year Experience and Students in Transition.

Gardner, P. (2000). From drift to engagement: Finding purpose and making career connections in the sophomore year. In L.A. Schreiner & J. Pattengale (Eds.), *Visible solutions for invisible students: Helping sophomores succeed* (Monograph No. 31, pp. 67-77). Columbia, SC: University of South Carolina, National Resource Center for The First-Year Experience and Students in Transition.

Gohn, L., Swartz, J., & Donnelly, S. (2001). A case study of second-year student persistence. *Journal of College Student Retention, 2*(4), 271-291.

Gordon, V. N. (2010). Academic advising: Helping sophomores succeed. In M. Hunter, B. Tobolowsky, J. Gardner, S. Evenbeck, J. Pattengale, M. Schaller, & L. A. Schreiner (Eds.), *Helping sophomores succeed: Understanding and improving the second-year experience* (pp. 83-98). San Francisco, CA: Jossey-Bass.

Gore, P., & Hunter, M. (2010). Promoting career success in the second year of college. In M. Hunter, B. Tobolowsky, J. Gardner, S. Evenbeck, J. Pattengale, M. Schaller, & L. A. Schreiner (Eds.), *Helping sophomores succeed: Understanding and improving the second-year experience* (pp. 99-113). San Francisco, CA: Jossey-Bass.

Graunke, S. & Woosley, S. A. (2005). An exploration of factors that affect the academic success of college sophomores. *College Student Journal, 39*(2), 367-376.

Horn, L., & Nevill, S. (2006). *Profile of undergraduates in U.S. postsecondary education institutions: 2003-04, With a special analysis of community college students* (NCES 2006184). Washington, DC: Office of Educational Research and Improvement, U.S. Department of Education. Retrieved from http://nces.ed.gov/pubsearch/pubsinfo.asp?pubid=2006184

Ishitani, T. T. (2008). How do transfers survive after "transfer shock"? A longitudinal study of transfer student departure at a four-year institution. *Research in Higher Education, 49*(5), 403-419.

Juillerat, S. L. (2000). Assessing the expectations and satisfaction of sophomores. In L.A. Schreiner & J. Pattengale (Eds.), *Visible solutions for invisible students: Helping sophomores succeed* (Monograph No. 31, pp. 19-30). Columbia, SC: University of South Carolina, National Resource Center for The First-Year Experience and Students in Transition.

Keup, J. (2002). The impact of curricular interventions on intended second-year enrollment. *Journal of College Student Retention, 7*(1-2), 61-89.

Kim, Y. K., & Sax, L. J. (2011). Are the effects of student-faculty interaction dependent on academic major? An examination using multilevel modeling. *Research in Higher Education, 52*(6), 589-615.

Kuh, G. D. (2009). What student affairs professionals should know about student engagement. *Journal of College Student Development, 50,* 683-706.

Kuh, G. D., & Hu, S. (2001). The effects of student-faculty interaction in the 1990s. *Review of Higher Education, 2,* 309-332.

Lindholm, J. A. (2010). Spirituality, meaning making, and the sophomore-year experience. In M. Hunter, B. Tobolowsky, J. Gardner, S. Evenbeck, J. Pattengale, M. Schaller, & L. A. Schreiner (Eds.), *Helping sophomores succeed: Understanding and improving the second-year experience* (pp. 203-214). San Francisco, CA: Jossey-Bass.

Lounsbury, J., & DeNeui, D. (1995). Psychological sense of community on campus. *College Student Journal, 29,* 270-277.

Markus, H., & Nurius, P. (1986). Possible selves. *American Psychologist, 41,* 954-969.

Nagda, B. A., Gregerman, S. R., Jonides, J., von Hippel, W., & Lerner, J. S. (1998). Undergraduate student-faculty research partnerships affect student retention. *Review of Higher Education, 22*(1), 55-72.

Noel. P. M. (2007). *Still making a difference in the person I am becoming: A study of students' perceptions of the faculty who make a difference in their lives* (Doctoral dissertation). Available from ProQuest Dissertations and Theses database. (UMI No. 3287752)

Packard, B. (2005). Mentoring and retention in college science: Reflections on the sophomore year. *Journal of College Student Retention, 6*(3), 290-300.

Pascarella, E. T., & Terenzini, P. T. (2005). *How college affects students: A third decade of research.* San Francisco, CA: Jossey-Bass.

Pattengale, J. (2000). Policies and practices to enhance sophomore success. In L. A. Schreiner & J. Pattengale (Eds.), *Visible solutions for invisible students: Helping sophomores succeed* (Monograph No. 31, pp. 31-46). Columbia, SC: University of South Carolina, National Resource Center for The First-Year Experience and Students in Transition.

Pullins, T. L. (2011). *Predicting the retention of college sophomores: The importance of satisfaction* (Unpublished doctoral dissertation). Azusa Pacific University, Azusa, CA.

Schaller, M. A. (2005). Wandering and wondering: Traversing the uneven terrain of the second college year. *About Campus, 10*(3), 17-24.

Schaller, M. A. (2010a). College sophomores: The journey into self. In M. Hunter, B. Tobolowsky, J. Gardner, S. Evenbeck, J. Pattengale, M. Schaller, & L. A. Schreiner (Eds.), *Helping sophomores succeed: Understanding and improving the second-year experience* (pp. 66-81). San Francisco, CA: Jossey-Bass.

Schaller, M. A. (2010b). Understanding the impact of the second year of college. In M. Hunter, B. Tobolowsky, J. Gardner, S. Evenbeck, J. Pattengale, M. Schaller, & L. A. Schreiner (Eds.), *Helping sophomores succeed: Understanding and improving the second-year experience* (pp. 13-29). San Francisco, CA: Jossey-Bass.

Schreiner, L. A. (2007). [Student comments from the 2007 Sophomore Experiences Survey]. Unpublished raw data.

Schreiner, L. A. (2009). *Linking student satisfaction and retention.* Retrieved from Noel-Levitz, Inc. website: https://www.noellevitz.com/NR/rdonlyres/A22786EF-65FF-4053-A15A-CBE145B0C708/0/LinkingStudentSatis0809.pdf

Schreiner, L. A. (2010a). Factors that contribute to sophomore success and satisfaction. In M. Hunter, B. Tobolowsky, J. Gardner, S. Evenbeck, J. Pattengale, M. Schaller, & L. A. Schreiner (Eds.), *Helping sophomores succeed: Understanding and improving the second-year experience* (pp. 43-65). San Francisco, CA: Jossey-Bass.

Schreiner, L. A. (2010b). The critical role of faculty and faculty development in sophomore success. In M. Hunter, B. Tobolowsky, J. Gardner, S. Evenbeck, J. Pattengale, M. Schaller, & L. A. Schreiner (Eds.), *Helping sophomores succeed: Understanding and improving the second-year experience* (pp. 129-145). San Francisco, CA: Jossey-Bass.

Schreiner, L. A. (2010c, November). *The Sophomore Experiences Survey: Latest findings and implications.* Paper presented at the annual conference of Students in Transition, Houston, TX.

Schreiner, L. A. (2010d). Thriving in the classroom. *About Campus, 15*(3), 2-10.

Schreiner, L. A. (2010e). Thriving in community. *About Campus, 15*(4), 2-11.

Schreiner, L. A., & Anderson, E. (2005). Strengths-based advising: A new lens for higher education. *NACADA Journal, 25*(2), 20-29.

Schreiner, L. A., Kitomary, A., & Seppelt, T. L. (2010, February). *Predictors of thriving among first-year students of color.* Presentation at the 29th Annual Conference on The First-Year Experience, Denver, Colorado.

Schreiner, L. A. & Pattengale, J. (2000). *Visible solutions for invisible students: Helping sophomores succeed* (Monograph No. 31). Columbia, SC: University of South Carolina, National Resource Center for The First-Year Experience and Students in Transition.

Tobolowsky, B. F., & Cox, B. E. (2007). Findings from the 2005 National Survey on Sophomore Initiatives. In B. F. Tobolowsky & B. E. Cox (Eds.), *Shedding light on sophomores: An exploration of the second college year* (Monograph No. 47, pp. 13-30). Columbia, SC: University of South Carolina, National Resource Center for The First-Year Experience and Students in Transition.

Umbach, P. D., Palmer, M. M., & Kuh, G. D. (2006). Intercollegiate athletes and effective educational practices: Winning combination or losing effort? *Research in Higher Education, 47*(6), 709-733.

Wilson, K. J., & Crowe, M. (2010). Undergraduate research: A powerful pedagogy to engage sophomores. In M. Hunter, B. Tobolowsky, J. Gardner, S. Evenbeck, J. Pattengale, M. Schaller, & L. A. Schreiner (Eds.), *Helping sophomores succeed: Understanding and improving the second-year experience* (pp. 177-188). San Francisco, CA: Jossey-Bass.

Chapter 7

Transfer Students: Thriving in a New Institution
Eric J. McIntosh and Denise D. Nelson

Whether a student moves between two-year colleges, four-year institutions, or from a two-year college to a four-year college or university, transferring between institutions of higher learning is often tumultuous. Townsend (2008) describes the experience of transfer students as a double transition during which they must first navigate the processes required to move from one institution to another and then adjust to the academic, social, and behavioral expectations of that new environment. Despite the enormity of such a transition, transfer students may seem uniquely positioned for collegiate success; after all, they have "already survived college life" (p. 73), demonstrating some level of academic success by virtue of accumulated course credit. Research indicates, however, that recent transfer students tend to lag in both academic performance (Glass & Harrington, 2002; Ishitani, 2008) and engagement (Ishitani & McKitrick, 2010; National Survey of Student Engagement, NSSE, 2008). The goal of this book is to provide college educators with strategies to create environments where students in transition can thrive. Given the challenges of the transfer experience, facilitating success for the students within this transitional population requires new, more informed efforts on the part of the institutions that serve them. This chapter will describe the transfer student experience, report the results of a study regarding thriving within this population, offer several suggestions for equipping transfer students to thrive in their new institutions, and identify three exemplar transfer student support and transition programs.

In comparison to native students—those who have been continuously enrolled at the same institution—transfer students are less likely to persist to graduation (Ishitani, 2008; Li, 2010; Wirt et al., 2003). They also report lower overall engagement scores than their counterparts (NSSE, 2008) and are significantly less likely than their peers to engage in activities such as research with faculty, study abroad programs, internships, and senior capstone projects (McCormick, Sarraf, BrckaLorenz, & Haywood, 2009). Another unsettling consequence of the transition experienced by transfer students is commonly referred to as transfer shock. This phenomenon, which describes a dip in transfer students' grades during their first semester at their receiving institution, was first explored by Hills (1965). More recent research (Glass & Harrington, 2002; Ishitani, 2008) confirms that transfer shock persists in contemporary student populations.

The numerous areas in which transfer students lag behind their native peers suggest that transferring between institutions is inherently challenging. Students who are less likely to graduate, demonstrate lower engagement and involvement with the college environment, and suffer academically in the term following their transfer are unlikely to experience the academic, interpersonal, and intrapersonal well-being associated with thriving (Schreiner, Pothoven, Nelson, & McIntosh, 2009). Accordingly, as institutions aspire to equip all students to thrive, transfer students require particular attention.

Understanding the Transfer Challenge

Practitioners and researchers in higher education have long recognized that the experiences of transfer students differ from those of students who enter an institution their first year and persist to graduation along a smooth trajectory. Despite this recognition, the diversity of experiences within the transfer population often remains unacknowledged and underresearched (Herzog, 2005). Transfer students are not only transitioning from two-year colleges to bachelor's granting four-year institutions, but also between four-year institutions. Townsend and Dever (1999) describe another subgroup of those who transfer as the swirling student. They note that this type of student "may swirl upward from a two-year to a four-year school, float laterally from one two-year school to another two-year school, or spin downward from a four-year to a two-year school" (p. 5). As an example, a swirling student may first be enrolled part time, later enrolled full time, and at another time marked as a stop out or drop out. Whether students transfer in predictable ways or swirl from one institution to another and back again, multiple entries to and exits from different institutions limit schools' capacity to identify irregularities in academic progress that may signal a student's need for intervention.

Adelman (1999, 2005) found that students who had transferred were less likely to graduate and required more time to complete their degree than native peers. A U.S. Government study (Enzi, Boehner, & McKeon, 2005) showed that vertical transfer students require the most time to complete their degrees (5.4 years), whereas horizontal transfers complete in 5.1 years. Native students who persist within one institution graduate, on average, most quickly at 4.4 years. Purposeful upward transfer from a two- to a four-year institution is positively associated with degree attainment (Adelman, 2005); however, Li (2010) reports that students who break enrollment are 70% less likely to graduate than students who persist within a single institution.

Not only is the picture grim for transfer students in the aggregate, but a study of transfer students of color at the University of Missouri found that such students were significantly less likely to complete a degree than their Caucasian transfer peers (Eimers & Mullen, 1997). Hispanic students were 11% less likely to attain a degree regardless of their educational pathway (Li, 2010). Although all transfer students of color have been shown to exhibit more difficulty in degree attainment, an ethnographic study of Hispanic students identified unique barriers, including undocumented immigrant status, traditional gender roles within their culture, and being less likely to perceive the need for and value of a baccalaureate degree (Alexander, Garcia, Gonzalez, Grimes, & O'Brien, 2007). One study indicated that minority students are more likely to swirl and transfer among institutions (Rab, 2004). Research findings revealing that students of color who transfer fare even worse than White transfer students on campus should compel institutions to act on their behalf, especially when considering the increased desire to provide access and opportunity for underrepresented populations.

Student Engagement and Transfer Behavior

Nearly 30 years ago, it was conjectured that transfer students lacked the desire to engage in campus life (Astin, 1982). Since that time, engagement has garnered increasing attention (Banta & Kuh, 1998; Carini, Kuh, & Klein, 2006; Kinzie & Kuh, 2004; Kuh, 2003a, 2003b) and has been identified as a critical component of student success in college (Astin, 1993b; Carini et al., 2006; Pace, 1980; Pascarella & Terenzini, 2005). In fact, a 2008 study (Allen, Robbins, Casillas, & Oh) identified social connectedness and college commitment as two primary mitigating factors influencing the decision of students to persist, transfer, or dropout. Presumably, the reason students transfer is to find an institution better suited to their needs or desires

(Choy, 2002); however, movement among institutions may inhibit transfer student engagement both academically and socially, ultimately impeding the ability of these students to thrive in the college environment.

Astin's (1984, 1993b) involvement theory links physical and mental time devoted to student learning with success. Adding to the theoretical foundation of the engagement dialogue was Pace's (1969, 1979, 1980, 1984) research on the relationship between student effort and student learning. As a result, much of the engagement literature is focused on the amount of time students spend involved in activities, such as the use of the campus library and other support resources and interactions with faculty, predictive of success (Kuh, 2003a). Current studies indicate that transfer students are less engaged on campus (Ishitani & McKitrick, 2010; McCormick et al., 2009). Campus participation and engagement with faculty are theoretically linked to student retention (Tinto, 1993), and lower transfer student scores on the National Survey of Student Engagement (NSSE) benchmarks in these areas are indicative of transfer student disengagement (McCormick et al., 2009).

One potential side effect of low involvement is the diminished opportunity for transfer students to form social bonds within their institution, a problematic issue due to the importance of social connection in student adjustment to university life. From the outset of contemporary research regarding persistence and degree attainment (Tinto, 1975), social integration has been recognized as essential for success. Further, student satisfaction has been shown to be negatively impacted by underdeveloped interpersonal relationships (Astin, 1993b). A recent NSSE (2009) report indicates that transfer students are less integrated socially than their native peers, suggesting that they are also less likely to experience the positive outcomes associated with integration.

Pascarella and Terenzini (2005) questioned whether social connections among university students have a direct or indirect effect on persistence. In 2008, Allen et al. discovered that social connection and college commitment do indeed demonstrate direct effects on persistence. The same study also found indirect effects of academic motivation and precollege academic preparedness on college persistence.

From Engaging to Thriving

Although student engagement in the activities and behaviors associated with positive outcomes is undeniably worthy of study, researchers (Bean, 2005; Bean & Eaton, 2002) have called for a deeper investigation into the psychological processes that motivate students to engage. Understanding both outward student behavior and the internal factors that precede such behavior allows researchers and practitioners in higher education to more knowledgably facilitate holistic student success. This comprehensive approach includes academic factors, but it also acknowledges the importance of personal well-being and healthy relationships with others as vital components of a successful student experience. Accordingly, researchers (Schreiner, McIntosh, Nelson, & Pothoven, 2009; Schreiner, Pothoven et al., 2009) have sought to explore these psychosocial factors through the construct of thriving.

Thriving conceptualizes student behavior, including engagement and persistence, as psychologically motivated (Bean & Eaton, 2002) and may offer insight into the experiences of transfer students as a unique population. Similar to, and linked conceptually with, the positive psychology concept of flourishing (Keyes & Haidt, 2003), student thriving is indicative of a fulfilling university experience. Thriving students feel they belong within their institutional communities and are fully engaged intellectually, socially, and emotionally. All of these contributing factors facilitate students' academic success and persistence, as well as their well-being as thriving individuals (Schreiner, Pothoven et al., 2009). Ongoing research is needed to explore differences in thriving among various student groups in order to help meet the needs of specific groups as they are discovered. A recent study provides a better understanding of the struggles that inhibit transfer student thriving and offers insight for practitioners who desire to create or revise programming to better meet the needs of this important student group.

The Thriving Project

In the spring of 2009 undergraduate students at 27 public and private colleges and universities across the United States participated in the Thriving Quotient research project. The Thriving Quotient is a reliable and valid 35-item instrument designed to measure the three domains of interpersonal, intrapersonal, and academic student thriving. The instrument was developed in an effort to measure malleable psychosocial processes that enable students to succeed in college (Schreiner, McIntosh et al., 2009) and is described more fully in chapter 1. Among the 5,339 participants from 18 private and nine public institutions who participated in this study, 614 (11.5%) were transfer students (Table 7.1).

Table 7.1

Demographic Characteristics of the Transfer Study Participants ($N = 5{,}339$)

Characteristic	Nontransfers ($n = 4{,}725$)	%	Transfers ($n = 614$)	%
Gender				
Female	3,286	70.0	416	68.1
Male	1,409	30.0	195	31.9
Institution was first choice at enrollment				
Yes	3,269	69.9	344	56.5
No	1,408	30.1	265	43.5
Generation				
First-generation	932	19.9	164	36.8
Not first-generation	3,761	80.1	447	73.2
High school grades				
Mostly *A*s	2,234	47.6	218	35.6
*A*s and *B*s	1,729	36.8	242	39.5
Mostly *B*s	382	8.1	81	13.2
*B*s and *C*s	279	5.9	50	8.2
Mostly *C*s	50	1.1	18	2.9
*C*s and *D*s	19	.4	3	.5
Hours worked off campus per week				
None	3,243	69.5	341	56.0
Less than 5	244	5.2	36	5.9
6-10	326	7.0	42	6.9
11-15	296	6.3	37	6.1
16-20	284	6.0	68	11.2
21-25	212	4.5	67	11.0
26-30	31	.7	7	1.1
More than 30	29	.6	11	1.8
Hours worked on campus per week				
None	2,686	57.4	430	70.6
Less than 5	286	6.1	17	2.8
6-10	820	17.5	55	9.0
11-15	569	12.2	60	9.9
16-20	197	4.2	29	4.8
21-25	62	1.3	9	1.5
26-30	15	.3	2	.3
More than 30	45	1.0	7	1.1

(Continued on p.143)

(Continued from p.142)

Characteristic	Nontransfers ($n = 4,725$)	%	Transfers ($n = 614$)	%
Housing				
On campus	3,158	68.9	300	51.5
Off campus	1,425	31.1	282	48.5
Race/Ethnicity				
African American	89	1.9	15	2.5
American Indian/Alaska Native	71	1.5	9	1.5
Asian American/Pacific Islander	202	4.4	41	6.9
Caucasian	3,897	84.8	472	79.7
Hispanic	212	4.6	34	5.7
Multiracial	123	2.7	21	3.5

Data Analysis and Results

There were three phases of data analysis in this study of transfer students. First, the measurement model of college student thriving that had been established by Schreiner, McIntosh et al. in 2009 was tested for its ability to fit the data from this transfer student sample in order to determine whether thriving in transfer students could be conceptualized in the same way as it had been for native students in previous studies. Using structural equation modeling, the thriving model was determined to be a good fit for transfer students (CMIN = 1229.347, df = 452, CFI = .914, RMSEA = .05), indicating that thriving could indeed be conceptualized in the same way as for native students, as a higher order construct comprised of Academic Determination, Engaged Learning, Positive Perspective, Social Connectedness, and Diverse Citizenship.

Second, a hierarchical multiple regression analysis was conducted to determine the predictors of thriving for this group of transfer students. Six separate multiple regression analyses were conducted, one for each scale of the Thriving Quotient (chapter 1) and one for sum scores on the instrument as a whole, since thriving had been determined to be a higher order construct. The blocks of the regression analyses were determined based on the literature and Astin's I-E-O model (1993a) of inputs, environment, and outcomes, as well as on a previous model constructed by Schreiner, Nelson, McIntosh, and Edens (2011). Entering student characteristics comprised block 1 of the equation, institutional features were entered into block 2, then in block 3 were aspects of the students' current campus experiences, such as their living arrangement, hours worked off campus, and whether or not they were an athlete. Block 4 contained three items assessing spirituality, as literature indicated this variable was a significant predictor of student outcomes (Astin, Astin, & Lindholm, 2011), block 5 was comprised of faculty interaction and satisfaction, and block 6 contained campus involvement items. The final block contained the items measuring a sense of community on campus (Schreiner, 2006), to determine the extent to which this variable added to an understanding of transfer thriving after campus involvement, faculty interaction, and all prior variables had been taken into consideration.

The results indicated that 50.3% of the variation in transfer students' total scores on the Thriving Quotient could be explained by the model (Table 7.2). The most significant predictor of transfer student thriving was their amount of interaction with faculty, followed by their sense of community on campus and their level of campus involvement. The model could account for 21% to 38% of the variation in each of the scales of the Thriving Quotient; Engaged Learning and Academic Determination could be explained best by the model (Table 7.2).

The same hierarchical multiple regression analysis was conducted with the nontransfer students in the sample (Table 7.3), revealing key areas of difference in the predictors of thriving as well as in the amount of variation that could be explained by the model. Specifically, a much greater amount of the variation in Academic Determination (37% vs. 23%) among transfer students could be explained by the model, while a smaller amount of the variation in Social Connectedness could be explained by the transfer model (21% vs. 28%). The predictors of thriving were similar, except in five areas: (a) age was a more significant predictor of thriving in transfer students than in native students; (b) hours worked off campus, athlete status, and living on campus were significant predictors for native students, but not for transfers; (c) faculty interaction was significant for both samples, but explained much more of the variation in transfer student thriving than was seen in native students; (d) campus activities contributed much more to the variation in transfer student thriving than in native students, but student organizations contributed less; and (e) psychological sense of community on campus, while the most significant predictor for both samples, contributed less in the transfer student model than in the native student model.

In order to explore some of the differences between transfer and nontransfer students more thoroughly, independent sample *t*-tests were conducted to compare not only the scale scores on the Thriving Quotient, but also involvement, faculty interaction, and sense of community items, as these were areas that contributed differentially to the thriving models. Table 7.4 displays the results of those analyses. Social Connectedness was the only Thriving

Table 7.2

Summary of Hierarchical Regression Analysis for Variables Predicting Outcomes of Thriving in Transfer Students (N = 542)

Variable	Thriving quotient β	Engaged learning β	Diverse citizenship β	Academic determination β	Positive perspective β	Social connectedness β
Step 1						
Age	.156***	.194***	.029	.112**	.084*	.103*
Student of color	.048	.06	.067	.024	.002	-.011
First choice of college	.005	.083*	-.025	-.01	-.020	-.057
R^2	**0.063**	**0.119**	**0.010**	**0.039**	**0.018**	**0.007**
Step 2						
Public institution	-.003	-.124***	.060	-.005	.034	.096*
Two-year college	.024	.062	-.019	.042	.046	-.084*
R^2 Change	**0.019**	**0.045**	**0.003**	**0.016**	**0.016**	**0.006**
Step 3						
Hours worked off campus per week	.01	-.030	.054	.018	.065	.017
Athlete	-.041	-.022	-.002	.015	.066	-.007
Live on campus	-.041	-.049	-.006	.012	-.009	-.105*
R^2 Change	**0.006**	**0.006**	**0.005**	**0.003**	**0.012**	**0.003**

(Continued to p. 146)

(Continued from p. 145)

Variable	Thriving quotient β	Engaged learning β	Diverse citizenship β	Academic determination β	Positive perspective β	Social connectedness β
Step 4						
Spirituality1	.005	.023	-.021	.028	.065	-.104*
Spirituality2	.266	.187	.431	-.067	.223	.161
Spirituality3	-.255	-.196	-.386	.020	-.218	-.096
R² Change	**0.002**	**0.001**	**0.005**	**0.002**	**0.009**	**0.009**
Step 5						
Faculty interaction (amount)	.200***	.164**	.013	.218***	.205***	.109
Faculty satisfaction	.005	.053	.057	-.075	-.020	-.030
R² Change	**0.211**	**0.125**	**0.100**	**0.130**	**0.136**	**0.046**
Step 6						
Campus activities	.269***	.202***	.209***	.356***	.132***	-.011
Student organizations	.061	.040	.126**	.008	.043	-.020
R² Change	**0.081**	**0.045**	**0.070**	**0.120**	**0.023**	**0.001**
Step 7						
Community1	.327***	.266***	.310***	.284***	.176***	.061
Community 2	-.002	-.069	-.008	.003	.084	.027
Community 3	.178***	.041	.180***	-.049	.173***	.394***
R² Change	**0.12**	**0.043**	**0.109**	**0.063**	**0.083**	**0.136**
Total R²	**0.503**	**0.384**	**0.302**	**0.373**	**0.295**	**0.207**

$* p < .05. ** p < .01. *** p < .001.$

Table 7.3

Summary of Hierarchical Regression Analysis for Variables Predicting Outcomes of Thriving in Nontransfer Students (N = 4,302)

Variable	Thriving quotient β	Engaged learning β	Diverse citizenship β	Academic determination β	Positive perspective β	Social connectedness β
Step 1						
Age	.047***	.053***	.031**	.016	.006	.056***
Student of color	.003	.003	.069***	-.031*	-.018	-.025
First choice of college	-.007	-.004	-.016	.004	.006	-.017
R²	**0.024**	**0.043**	**0.010**	**0.012**	**0.007**	**0.004**
Step 2						
Public institution	-.044***	-.147***	-.023	.017	.026	.045**
Two-year college	.102***	.142***	.015	.110***	.013	.039**
R² Change	**0.031**	**0.073**	**0.005**	**0.017**	**0.003**	**0.001**
Step 3						
Hours worked off campus per week	.044***	.021	.045***	.034**	.053***	.002
Athlete	-.042***	-.077***	-.066***	-.024	.018	.047***
Live on campus	-.031**	-.016	-.004	-.004	-.051***	-.049***
R² Change	**0.000**	**0.004**	**0.003**	**0.000**	**0.002**	**0.005**

(Continued to p. 148)

(Continued from p. 147)

Variable	Thriving quotient β	Engaged learning β	Diverse citizenship β	Academic determination β	Positive perspective β	Social connectedness β
Step 4						
Spirituality1	.008	.005	.007	.021	-.008	-.001
Spirituality2	.036**	.024	.047**	.017	.041**	-.006
Spirituality3	.020	.008	.001	.018	.024	.028
R² Change	**0.007**	**0.004**	**0.006**	**0.005**	**0.006**	**0.001**
Step 5						
Faculty interaction (amount)	.148***	.162***	.038	.162***	.097***	.025
Faculty satisfaction	.128***	.185***	.072***	.066***	.058**	.011
R² Change	**0.178**	**0.174**	**0.062**	**0.098**	**0.078**	**0.025**
Step 6						
Campus activities	.030**	.029**	.003	.057***	.008	-.003
Student organizations	.126***	.089***	.182***	.060***	.067***	.031**
R² Change	**0.046**	**0.019**	**0.062**	**0.016**	**0.019**	**0.012**
Step 7						
Community 1	.294***	.271***	.313***	.264***	.150***	-.059***
Community 2	.077***	.004	-.032	.020	.194***	.160***
Community 3	.224***	.038**	.209***	.070***	.165***	.444***
R² Change	**0.198**	**0.071**	**0.144**	**0.081**	**0.145**	**0.232**
Total R²	**0.483**	**0.388**	**0.291**	**0.231**	**0.262**	**0.280**

*$p < .05$. **$p < .01$. ***$p < .001$.

Table 7.4
Results of Independent t-Test Comparison Between Transfer and Nontransfer Students

Variable	M	SD	t	df	p
Factor 1 – Engaged Learning			0.047	5337	0.963
Transfers	4.25	0.78			
Nontransfers	4.25	0.76			
Factor 2 – Diverse Citizenship			-0.171	5337	0.864
Transfers	4.54	0.66			
Nontransfers	4.55	0.62			
Factor 3 – Academic Determination			0.683	5337	0.495
Transfers	4.67	0.73			
Nontransfers	4.65	0.69			
Factor 4[a] – Positive Perspective			-0.111	754.27	0.912
Transfers	4.30	0.90			
Nontransfers	4.31	0.83			
Factor 5[a] – Social Connectedness			-2.878	760.21	0.004
Transfers	3.88	1.25			
Nontransfers	4.03	1.17			
How involved are you in campus events and activities?			-1.026	5344	.305
Transfers	4.64	1.09			
Nontransfers	4.84	4.67			
Given my current goals, this institution is a good fit for me. [a]			-.21	753.45	.834
Transfers	4.87	1.22			
Nontransfers	4.88	1.11			
How involved are you in a fraternity or sorority?[a]			-5.612	878.84	.000
Transfers	1.46	1.24			
Nontransfers	1.78	1.64			

(Continued to p. 150)

(Continued from p. 149)

Variable	M	SD	t	df	p
How many hours per week do you work OFF campus? (Likert 1-8) [a]			7.301	711.48	.000
Transfers	2.57	2.06			
Non-Transfers	1.94	1.64			
How many hours per week do you work ON campus? (Likert 1-8)			-3.537	5287	.000
Transfers	1.87	1.53			
Nontransfers	2.10	1.50			
How much time per week do you spend on leadership responsibilities in student organizations? [a]			-6.80	798.98	.000
Transfers	1.72	1.10			
Nontransfers	2.04	1.19			
Rate your satisfaction with the amount you are learning in college. [a]			-2.84	734.37	.005
Transfers	4.63	1.12			
Nontransfers	4.76	0.96			
How sure are you of your major? [a]			-.818	755.99	.414
Transfers	5.00	1.37			
Nontransfers	5.05	1.28			
Rate your satisfaction with your overall experiences on this campus so far. [a]			-3.926	746.15	.000
Transfers	4.53	1.18			
Nontransfers	4.73	1.05			
How involved are you in music or theatre performance groups on campus? [a]			-2.23	768.64	.026
Transfers	1.97	1.57			
Nontransfers	2.12	1.66			

(Continued to p. 151)

(*Continued from p. 150*)

Variable	M	SD	t	df	p
Met informally or socially with a faculty member outside of class or office hours			.674	5295	.500
Transfers	2.57	1.57			
Nontransfers	2.52	1.52			
How involved are you in student organizations on campus?			-10.57	5314	.000
Transfers	2.68	1.68			
Nontransfers	3.45	1.70			
I am confident that the amount of money I'm paying for college is worth it in the long run.			-2.17	5336	.030
Transfers	3.99	1.45			
Nontransfers	4.12	1.36			
Being a student here fills an important need in my life.			-0.603	752.27	.547
Transfers	4.62	1.22			
Nontransfers	4.65	1.11			
I feel like I belong here.			-2.628	757.40	.009
Transfers	4.55	1.30			
Nontransfers	4.69	1.21			
I have friends on this campus upon whom I can depend.			-9.021	721.43	.000
Transfers	4.51	1.31			
Nontransfers	5.00	1.06			

Note. Items measured by 1-6 Likert scale unless otherwise specified.

[a] The *t* and *df* were adjusted because equal variances were not assumed.

Quotient scale score where transfer students responded significantly differently than native students. Transfers were also significantly different in their
campus experiences and life circumstances, working off campus more hours
per week and not working on campus as much; being less involved in student
organizations, particularly in Greek organizations and in the performing arts;
and being less likely to have a leadership role on campus. Overall, they were less
satisfied with the institution and particularly with their learning and not as
likely to perceive their tuition as a worthwhile investment. Among the sense
of community items, transfer students were most different from nontransfer
students in their sense of belonging and of having friends on campus upon
whom they could depend.

Discussion and Implications

Despite a dearth of tracking information regarding transfer students,
several important features of the transfer experience have been established.
Transfer students face logistical challenges in the transfer of their earned
credit, social challenges in the creation of connections with new peers, and
academic challenges in a longer path toward graduation and a decreased likelihood of degree attainment. They are less satisfied than other students with
their peer interaction and with the institution in general. To help address
these disparities between transfer students and the nontransfer population,
colleges and universities must embrace the importance of transfer students
as a valuable component of the student body, actively seeking to understand
and meet their needs.

The findings from the transfer thriving study described in this chapter
highlight the importance of social connectedness for students who transfer
into an institution. Transfer students' thriving is partially a function of their
age, but once age is accounted for, the largest contributors are their interaction with faculty, their sense of community on campus, and their involvement in campus activities. However, due to the greater number of hours that
transfer students work off campus, these off-campus commitments may
compel transfer students to divide their attention in ways that discourage or
prevent the time investment required for building connections with individuals and organizations on their new campus. When transfer students are able
to participate in campus activities, they report higher levels of thriving and a
stronger sense of community.

The picture of the transfer students in this sample describes students who
are older, are more likely to live and work more hours off campus, and are less
involved in campus activities and student organizations than their nontransfer

peers. Their total thriving scores are no different from nontransfer students, but their Social Connectedness scores are significantly lower, as is their sense of community on campus, their satisfaction with the institution, and their perception that their tuition is a worthwhile investment. For those who are highly thriving, faculty interaction and campus involvement have combined to foster the goal setting, self-regulated learning, and sense of control over the demands placed upon them that are represented in their Academic Determination scores.

As Horn (2006) notes, following the paths of transfer students through postsecondary education is complicated by the fact that the U.S. Department of Education only tracks the enrollment of full-time, first-time-in-college students through the Integrated Postsecondary Education Data System (IPEDS). Because transfer students are not included in national reporting, they often are overlooked in regard to campus experiences and retention. Campus administrators should begin to more fully include transfer students in the conversation regarding student retention and success. When campuses begin to better understand the behavior of their transfer students, they will be more appropriately equipped to identify and rectify gaps in programming or interventions directed toward this important population. The implications arising from these findings are thus threefold: (a) well-designed programming for transfer students should offer opportunities for involvement and integration, not only with peers but also with faculty; (b) building a sense of community among transfer students can enhance their ability to thrive; and (c) productive programs should ease the academic transition between schools and provide structures that facilitate the logistical aspects of transfer.

1. Foster social integration and involvement by emphasizing social connections and student-faculty interaction. Transfer students need opportunities for involvement. Because transfer students report more off-campus commitments than their native peers, campuses should seek to offer a variety of opportunities specifically catered to a busy student schedule. Although evidence suggests that too few transfer students are taking advantage of such opportunities, the literature is also overwhelmingly supportive of the role that campus involvement plays in enriching the student experience. Encouraging participation likely entails devising transfer-friendly campus clubs, organizations, and activities by offering multiple options for meeting times or locations. Challenging administrators to better understand the transfer experience will assist them in making the necessary changes to existing organizations or programs in order to be certain that transfer students are not overlooked.

Providing socialization venues is key for positive social integration of incoming transfer students (Lanaan, 2007). Integration opportunities should involve not only other transfers, but nontransfer peers as well. Student leaders on campus should be aware of the needs of transfer students and be prepared to assist in their integration. Whether campuses highlight transfer-specific student leaders or begin by raising the profile of the transfer student experience with existing student leaders, these individuals are socially and culturally integrated at the institution. They are therefore a valuable resource for including transfer students in the campus culture in meaningful ways.

Such peer interaction and involvement in campus activities and organizations is likely to strengthen transfer students' sense of community by building shared emotional connections and interdependent relationships among students. But the contribution of student-faculty interaction to thriving among transfer students is even greater than the contribution of their campus involvement. For this reason, attending to the ways in which transfer students are connected to faculty upon their arrival to campus can be an important process in helping more transfer students thrive.

The benefits of student-faculty interaction are well-established in the literature (Cole, 2007; Kuh & Hu, 2001; Lundberg & Schreiner, 2004; Pascarella & Terenzini, 2005). In the present study, such student-faculty interaction was the greatest contributor to thriving among transfer students. This interaction explained transfer students' Academic Determination, Positive Perspective, and Engaged Learning especially well. Helping transfer students connect to faculty, particularly in their major area of interest, shortly after their arrival to a new campus could provide the foundation for both academic and social integration into the community. Providing an orientation to the major for transfer students each semester, encouraging faculty advisors to attend specifically to the needs of transfer students, and establishing student-faculty research teams that are accessible to transfer students could not only ease the transition to a new campus, but also encourage goal-setting, social connections, and a vision for the future that will enable more transfer students to thrive.

2. Build a sense of community through membership and ownership. In chapters 1 and 3, a sense of community is highlighted as critical to all students' perception that they are thriving in college. With transfer students, two particular aspects of a sense of community that are under the institution's control can be fostered through intentional actions taken with transfer students upon arrival.

Foundational to a sense of community on campus is the feeling that one belongs, or what Schreiner (2010) labels membership. For most native students, there are rituals, symbols, and rites of passage, such as orientation, that mark entrance to the university and communicate that the student is now an official member of that learning institution. Transfer students, however, are often not afforded the same attention or rituals to mark their joining the institution. Thus, one way for institutions to enhance transfer students' sense of belonging is through transfer orientations, ceremonies or welcome receptions that are just for transfers, and special attention from university leaders.

Ownership is the component of a sense of community that signifies voice and contribution (Schreiner, 2010). Students with a strong sense of community feel they matter to the institution, believe that their opinion counts, and perceive the institution as responsive to their needs. This concept is similar to what Braxton, Hirschy, and McClendon (2004) refer to as an institution's commitment to students' welfare, which they have demonstrated is reliably associated with social integration into the institution. Providing transfer students with the opportunity to participate in the decision-making process and to give input to the institution about their needs builds a sense of ownership about the university, while also helping students to thrive.

3. Ease the academic transition by creating structures to help with the logistical aspects of transferring. Any student who has transferred has likely experienced frustration with the complexity of moving academic credits from one institution to another. Helping students navigate these complexities will certainly ease in their transition. In particular, providing knowledgeable advisors who are familiar with articulation agreements can help transfer students apply prior credit appropriately, choose a reasonable course load, and understand the requirements for timely degree completion.

For most campuses, some modifications to existing programs could create more accessible opportunities for transfer students to use important services such as advising. Advising services could be offered during nontraditional times of the day (e.g., early morning or evening) or via telephone or nontraditional formats such as video or text chat. Such possibilities create opportunities for transfer students to meet their academic needs while honoring their personal commitments.

Universities and colleges should focus on equipping advisors with the tools and training required not only to assist transfer students but also to evaluate their needs according to their unique prior experiences. Although academic experiences are of greatest concern, more personal experiences are also relevant. In addition to supplying expert advisors for help with technical issues, providing students with mentors and cultural guides is both appropriate and instrumental to a healthy transfer transition.

Programming for Transfer Thriving

Transfer students who feel as though they belong at their institutions, interact more frequently with faculty, perform well academically, and feel their transferred credits are appropriately applied are positioned well to thrive. As noted in chapter 1 of this volume, transitions can be facilitated by accurate information, social support, the perception that the transition is an opportunity for growth, and the use of proactive coping skills. Three institutions—the University of Michigan, Vassar College, and the University of North Texas—offer initiatives that meet transfer needs and assist in a successful transition. Examining these programs supplies concrete examples of programs worth emulating and allows practitioners to examine effective policies for transfer students.

Enhancing Social Connections

Programming at most universities and colleges is specifically intended to ease the transition of first-year students to campus life. Because transfer students are not first-time enrollees, they are often overlooked for such programming. Although all transfer students have some kind of previous campus experience, universities and colleges should not forget that transfer students have little to no experience on their new campus. It is within such programmed orientations that traditional students make social connections with peers and faculty and gain familiarity with the campus community.

Much like first-year students, transfer students must be intentionally introduced to campus opportunities. Clubs and organizations should be clearly described, particularly where leadership roles may be available, and performing arts groups should advertise their willingness to accept new members. Campus gathering places, including the student union building, the library, and dining or recreational facilities, should be highlighted when transfer students are oriented to campus. Transfer students may simply be unaware of the numerous opportunities for involvement and social interaction offered by their new institution. Some exemplars of effective initiatives are highlighted in the following section.

University of Michigan. The College of Literature, Science, and Arts (LSA) at the University of Michigan in Ann Arbor, Michigan, offers a mentoring program called Transfer Connections for incoming LSA transfer students. Students who register for the Transfer Connections program are able to take part in campus activities and are introduced to campus life by peer mentors. Peer mentors are supervised by professional staff and matched with incoming transfer students to develop relationships and provide opportunities for conversation and other social connections or activities. The mission of Transfer Connections is "to ease the transition of transfer students into the University of Michigan" (Office of New Student Programs, 2011).

A program such as Transfer Connections provides students the important opportunity to build the social connections that are the hallmarks of retention (Tinto, 1975, 1993). Mentor-mentee relationships for transfer students have been recommended for some time (Laanan, 1996); however, many institutions still lack such programs. Transfer Connections supports transfer students on campus by identifying key faculty and staff allies who are empathetic to the unique experience of the transfer population and are willing to supplement the peer mentoring system as needed. The program not only provides students an immediate social and support network, but also updates transfer students through a regular newsletter designed to address their needs and interests.

The LSA at the University of Michigan has created a unique presence for Transfer Connections on its website. Visibility and accessibility on the web also increases the profile of this program and its reach to incoming transfer students. Pictures of participating staff and faculty are posted online, along with contact information, photographs of social events, and informative material regarding the program.

The University of Michigan Transfer Connections program includes four features that could be easily employed at other institutions. First, transfer students are matched with peer mentors who provide assistance as new students navigate the institution, offices, and social environment. Mentors could be drawn from either the native student population or from among students who have successfully transferred to the institution. The important characteristic of peer mentors is their willingness to help familiarize transfer students with their new setting. Second, University personnel are given an opportunity to participate in the program by advertising their willingness to serve as resources for transfer students within their departments or work areas.

In addition, the program can be promoted with relative ease because of its useful website. Online information about the program, staff, and events offers transfer students maximum opportunity to learn about the program's mission and its benefits. Finally, the transfer student program is intentionally distinct from orientation programs for first-year students. This clear differentiation conveys to transfer students that the institution recognizes their prior college experience and seeks to support the application of that experience within a new social and learning environment.

Easing Academic Transitions

The academic environment of an institution provides the setting within which social connections are formed, yet integrating transfer students into the campus community through the academic structure poses clear challenges. Townsend and Wilson (2006) found that, over time, native students lost motivation to intentionally include transfer students in study groups, collaborative learning, and other learning groups—a behavioral trend specifically uninviting toward transfer students. Regular contact with faculty is also vital to transfer students' success, as students who perceive that faculty are approachable may experience a less traumatic academic transition because they feel welcome to communicate with their professors both within and beyond the classroom (Laanan, 2007). Programming such as the pretransfer initiative at Vassar College, which is designed to prepare students academically for the transfer process, may minimize transfer shock by offering community college students opportunities for forming relationships with faculty before they begin full-time enrollment at their new institution.

Vassar College in Poughkeepsie, New York, has a unique pretransfer program called Exploring Transfer (Vassar College, 2011). For five weeks during the summer, Vassar College provides New England community college students the opportunity to enroll in six credits of university-level coursework as an introduction to pursuing studies at a four-year college. The program, which has been facilitating such introductions for community college students for the past 20 years, focuses specifically on students from underrepresented populations. In addition to offering an opportunity for students to experience the academic level of four-year studies, Exploring Transfer (ET) helps address the challenges present for transfer students of color (Alexander et al., 2007; Eimers & Mullen, 1997; Rab, 2004) by providing access to mentors and faculty who can assist their adjustment to a new campus. This unique introductory program is free for participants and has served more than 1,000 students since its inception.

Courses in the ET program are cotaught by community college and Vassar faculty. Students participating in the program move into campus housing at Vassar and are immersed in an intensive introduction to four-year studies. This program provides access for vertical transfers to experience firsthand how the demands at a four-year institution differ from those at the community college level.

The ET program provides a tangible example of a program specifically designed to meet the academic needs of transfer students. Among students who transferred from community colleges to four-year institutions, students' perception of four-year institutions was predictive of their successful academic integration after transferring (Laanan, 2007). Students who participate in Exploring Transfer are not obligated to transfer to Vassar; program participants have transferred to four-year institutions of all types.

The central lesson offered by Vassar College's Exploring Transfer program is that there is no substitute for experience. Providing community college students with an opportunity to experience the academic environment of a four-year institution prior to enrollment enables them to better understand the level of preparation required for success within that environment. Even for schools that lack the resources to offer intensive learning experiences like Exploring Transfer, identifying opportunities for cooperative teaching arrangements between community college and university faculty could expose students at two-year colleges to the academic rigor characteristic of four-year institutions. The focus of the Vassar program on students from underrepresented populations suggests that institutions could consider offering support to transfer students of color beyond the services or programs offered to all transfer students.

University of North Texas. Exposure to the academic expectations of the university learning environment is clearly beneficial to students who are likely to transfer. Programs that facilitate this sort of exposure help students form appropriate academic expectations for their new academic setting. Entering that setting, however, may present significant logistical challenges. Students who encounter difficulty with the transfer process itself are, at best, frustrated or dissatisfied and, at worst, discouraged from transfer altogether.

Articulation agreements have been previously mentioned as tools for easing the transition of transfer students to their new campus. The University of North Texas (2010) in Denton, Texas has developed an online tool for determining course transfer eligibility from other Texas institutions. This tool simplifies the process of identifying which courses will count toward their degree goals at the University of North Texas, and the online nature of the program makes the necessary information convenient to access. In a 2007 qualitative study, Alexander et al. found that Hispanic transfer students reported that familial involvement in the transfer process was crucial to campus adjustment. At an institution such as the University of North Texas, cultural sensitivity to the needs of underrepresented student groups is important in meeting the needs of the campus constituency. Offering an online tool allows students to gather information early, discuss it with their families if they wish to do so, and interact with professional transfer counselors in the initial stages of their transfer plans.

One set of recommendations (Rhine, Milligan, & Nelson, 2000) proposes that universities and colleges identify university-bound community college students early and work with those students to ensure their courses will transfer to a four-year school. The University of North Texas transfer program is an example of how effective articulation agreements, common course number-ing, and common core curriculum can assist in easing the transfer student experience. Successful transfer students are more likely to have taken courses specifically designated as suitable for transfer (Hagedorn, Cypers, & Lester, 2008). Although this fact seems intuitive, it demonstrates why potential transfer students must be made aware of the transferability of courses.

Poor articulation processes result in a loss of academic credit in the transition from one school to another. Repeating coursework at a four-year institution that was completed in community college is not only frustrating to students, but it also represents wasted time and is likely to diminish students' belief that their tuition dollars are well-spent. Accordingly, campuses should work to enable transfer of credit from feeder institutions whenever possible, even if specific articulation agreements are not in place. Developing tools such as the one in use at the University of North Texas is more straightforward for campus professionals working in states where legislated articulation agreements exist, but the lack of such agreements should not prevent colleges from easing the logistics of transfer.

The University of North Texas offers two important lessons, especially to institutions without extensive articulation agreements. First, four-year universities and colleges should provide easy online access to transfer requirements. Courses that transfer without difficulty should be listed, and courses that are unlikely to meet transfer requirements should be clearly identified, as well. If transferability is judged on a case-by-case basis, criteria for transferability should be described in detail. Offering this information as early as possible allows students to interact with their personal support networks and to ask questions of institutional representatives. When campuses provide clear information, competent professionals, and time to evaluate the best course of action, they demonstrate their high regard for the needs of transfer students.

Conclusion

In order for transfer students to transition well to a new institution and thrive within it, concerted effort is required on the part of the college or university that serves them. Given the growth in two-year college enrollment and the anticipated continual growth in vertical transfer, it seems wise for campuses to encourage a culture friendly to transfer students. The findings of the thriving study align with concerns in the literature (McCormick, 1997; McCormick et al., 2009; NSSE, 2008) about the social engagement of transfer students, and also align with Tinto's (1993) assertion that social connections, with faculty as well as peers, are critical to student retention. Despite the known challenges faced by transfer students as they attempt to integrate into campus culture (McCormick, 1997; McCormick et al., 2009), it is important that they find a sense of belonging on campus and feel as though their new environment is a good fit for them (Schreiner, 2009).

The recommendations offered in this chapter are intended as pragmatic solutions for supporting students throughout their transfer experiences. Among these suggestions are providing peer mentors and trained faculty or staff advisors to assist transfers in their social and academic adjustments, exposing students as early as possible to the academic rigor of the new institution, and communicating articulation requirements and processes clearly. In addition to easing the logistical challenges of changing institutions, these suggestions encourage student success by addressing one or more of the areas that comprise holistic thriving. The centrality of social connectedness highlights initiatives such as the University of Michigan's Transfer Connections program, which supports thriving through opportunities to build relationships with peers and university personnel. The Exploring Transfer pretransfer experience program at Vassar College also fuels connectedness by introducing students to the faculty and peers awaiting them at the four-year institution; further, it facilitates academic thriving by providing students with a glimpse into the expectations of their anticipated learning environment. Finally, articulation tools such as the one described at the University of North Texas relieve some of the stressful uncertainty associated with the transfer process, allowing students a sense of ownership regarding the transition and freeing them to enjoy a positive perspective about their institution and about themselves as learners.

Transfers must know that their chosen institution believes them to be important and seeks to support their success. The campus environment must intentionally welcome this student population, ease the mechanics of their transition into the community, and successfully present opportunities for involvement. When campuses embrace a culture responsive to transfer student needs, the transfer population will inevitably benefit from the experience. Perhaps more importantly, the entire campus community can thrive as all of its populations are well served.

References

Adelman, C. (1999). *Answers in the tool box: Academic intensity, attendance patterns, and bachelor's degree attainment.* Jessup, MD: U.S. Department of Education.

Adelman, C. (2005). *The toolbox revisited: Paths to degree completion from high school through college.* Jessup, MD: U.S. Department of Education.

Alexander, B. C., Garcia, V., Gonzalez, L., Grimes, G., & O'Brien, D. (2007). Barriers in the transfer process for Hispanic and Hispanic immigrant students. *Journal of Hispanic Higher Education, 6*(2), 174-184.

Allen, J., Robbins, S. B., Casillas, A., & Oh, I.-S. (2008). Third-year college retention and transfer: Effects of academic performance, motivation, and social connectedness. *Research in Higher Education, 49*(7), 647-664.

Astin, A. W. (1982). *Minorities in higher education.* San Francisco, CA: Jossey-Bass.

Astin, A. W. (1984). Student involvement: A developmental theory for higher education. *Journal of College Student Personnel, 25,* 297-308.

Astin, A. W. (1993a). *Assessment for excellence: The philosophy and practice of assessment and evaluation in higher education.* Westport, CT: The American Council on Education/Oryx Press.

Astin, A. W. (1993b). *What matters in college? Four critical years revisited.* San Francisco, CA: Jossey-Bass.

Astin, A. W., Astin, H. S., & Lindholm, J. A. (2011). *Cultivating the spirit: How college can enhance students' inner lives.* San Francisco, CA: Jossey-Bass.

Banta, T. W., & Kuh, G. D. (1998). A missing link in assessment. *Change, 30*(2), 40-46.

Bean, J. P. (2005). Nine themes of college student retention. In A. Seidman (Ed.), *College student retention* (pp. 215-244). Westport, CT: Praeger.

Bean, J. P., & Eaton, S. B. (2002). A psychological model of college student retention. In J. M. Braxton (Ed.), *Reworking the student departure puzzle* (pp. 48-61). Nashville, TN: Vanderbilt University Press.

Braxton, J. M., Hirschy, A. S., & McClendon, S. A. (2004). *Understanding and reducing college student departure* (ASHE-ERIC Higher Education Report, Vol. 30, No. 3). San Francisco, CA: Jossey-Bass.

Carini, R., Kuh, G. D., & Klein, S. (2006). Student engagement and student learning: Testing the linkages. *Research in Higher Education, 47*(1), 1-32.

Choy, S. P. (2002). *Access and persistence: Findings from 10 years of longitudinal research on students* (EDO-HE-2002-02). Washington, DC: American Council on Education.

Cole, D. (2007). Do interracial interactions matter? An examination of student-faculty contact and intellectual self-concept. *The Journal of Higher Education, 78*(3), 249-281.

Eimers, M., & Mullen, R. (1997). Transfer students: Who are they and how successful are they at the University of Missouri? *College and University, 72*(3), 9-19.

Enzi, M. B., Boehner, J. A., & McKeon, H. P. (2005). *Transfer students: Postsecondary institutions could promote more consistent consideration of coursework by not basing determinations on accreditation* (GAO-06-22). Washington, DC: U.S. Government Accountability Office.

Glass, J. C., & Harrington, A. R. (2002). Academic performance of community college transfer students and "native" students at a large state university. *Community College Journal of Research and Practice, 26*(5), 415-430.

Hagedorn, L. S., Cypers, S., & Lester, J. (2008). Looking in the review mirror: Factors affecting transfer for urban community college students. *Community College Journal of Research and Practice, 32*(9), 643-664.

Herzog, S. (2005). Measuring determinants of student return vs. dropout/stopout vs. transfer: A first-to-second year analysis of new freshmen. *Research in Higher Education, 46*(8), 883-928.

Hills, J. R. (1965). Transfer shock: The academic performance of the junior college transfer. *Journal of Experimental Education, 33*(3), 201-215.

Horn, L. (2006). *Placing college graduation rates in context: How 4-year college graduation rates vary with selectivity and the size of low-income enrollment* (NCES 2007161). Washington, DC: U.S. Department of Education.

Ishitani, T. T. (2008). How do transfers survive after "transfer shock"? A longitudinal study of transfer student departure at a four-year institution. *Research in Higher Education, 49*(5), 403-419.

Ishitani, T. T., & McKitrick, S. A. (2010). After transfer: The engagement of community college students at a four-year collegiate institution. *Community College Journal of Research and Practice, 34*(7), 576-594.

Keyes, C. L. M., & Haidt, J. (2003). *Flourishing: Positive psychology and the life well-lived.* Washington, DC: American Psychological Association.

Kinzie, J., & Kuh, G. D. (2004). Learning from campuses that share responsibility for student success. *About Campus, 9*(5), 2-8.

Kuh, G. D. (2003a). *The National Survey of Student Engagement: Conceptual framework and overview of psychometric properties.* Retrieved from http://nsse.iub.edu/pdf/conceptual_framework_2003.pdf

Kuh, G. D. (2003b). What we're learning about student engagement from NSSE. *Change, 35,* 24-32.

Kuh, G. D., & Hu, S. (2001). The effects of student-faculty interaction in the 1990s. *Review of Higher Education, 2,* 309-332.

Laanan, F. S. (1996). Making the transition: Understanding the adjustment process of community college transfer students. *Community College Review, 23*(4), 69-84.

Laanan, F. S. (2007). Studying transfer students: Part II: Dimensions of transfer students' adjustment. *Community College Journal of Research and Practice, 31*(1), 37-59.

Li, D. (2010). They need help: Transfer students from four-year to four-year institutions. *Review of Educational Research, 33*(2), 207-238.

Lundberg, C., & Schreiner, L. (2004). Quality and frequency of faculty-student interaction as predictors of learning: An analysis by student race/ethnicity. *Journal of College Student Development, 45*(5), 549-565.

McCormick, A. C. (1997). *Transfer behavior among beginning postsecondary students: 1989-94.* (NCES 97266). Washington, DC: U.S. Department of Education.

McCormick, A. C., Sarraf, S. A., BrckaLorenz, A., & Haywood, A. M. (2009). *Examining the transfer student experience: Interactions with faculty, campus relationships, & overall satisfaction.* Paper presented at the Association for the Study of Higher Education Annual Conference, Vancouver, Canada.

National Survey of Student Engagement (NSSE). (2008). *Promoting engagement for all students: The imperative to look within.* Bloomington, IN: Indiana University Center for Postsecondary Research.

National Survey of Student Engagement (NSSE). (2009). *Assessment for improvement: Tracking student engagement over time—annual results 2009.* Bloomington, IN: Indiana University Center for Postsecondary Research.

Office of New Student Programs. (2011). *Transfer connections.* Retrieved from http://www.onsp.umich.edu/transfer_students/mentorship/

Pace, C. R. (1969). *College and University Environment Scales (CUES) technical manual* (2nd ed.). Princeton, NJ: Educational Testing Service.

Pace, C. R. (1979). *Measuring outcomes of college: Fifty years of findings and recommendations for the future.* San Francisco, CA: Jossey-Bass.

Pace, C. R. (1980). Measuring the quality of student effort. *Current Issues in Higher Education, 2,* 10-16.

Pace, C. R. (1984). *Measuring the quality of college student experiences.* Los Angeles, CA: UCLA, Higher Education Research Institute.

Pascarella, E. T., & Terenzini, P. T. (2005). *How college affects students: A third decade of research.* San Francisco, CA: Jossey-Bass.

Rab, S. Y. (2004). *Swirling students: Putting a new spin on college attrition.* (Unpublished doctoral dissertation). University of Pennsylvania, Philadelphia, PA.

Rhine, T. J., Milligan, D. M., & Nelson, L. R. (2000). Alleviating transfer shock: Creating an environment for more successful transfer students. *Community College Journal of Research and Practice, 24*(6), 443-453.

Schreiner, L. A. (2006). [Psychological sense of community on campus index]. Unpublished raw data.

Schreiner, L. A. (2009). *Linking student satisfaction and retention.* Retrieved from https://www.noellevitz.com/NR/rdonlyres/A22786EF-65FF-4053-A15A-CBE145B0C708/0/LinkingStudentSatis0809.pdf

Schreiner, L. A. (2010). Thriving in community. *About Campus, 15*(4), 2-11.

Schreiner, L. A., McIntosh, E. J., Nelson, D., & Pothoven, S. (2009). *The Thriving Quotient: Advancing the assessment of student success.* Paper presented at the Association for the Study of Higher Education Annual Conference, Vancouver, Canada.

Schreiner, L. A., Nelson, D., McIntosh, E. J., & Edens, D. (2011). *The Thriving Quotient: A new vision of student success.* Paper presented at the annual conference of the National Association of Student Personnel Administrators, Philadelphia, PA.

Schreiner, L. A., Pothoven, S., Nelson, D., & McIntosh, E. J. (2009). *College student thriving: Predictors of success and retention.* Paper presented at the Association for the Study of Higher Education Annual Conference, Vancouver, Canada.

Tinto, V. (1975). Dropout from higher education: A theoretical synthesis of recent research. *Review of Educational Research, 45*(1), 89-125.

Tinto, V. (1993). *Leaving college: Rethinking the causes and cures of student attrition* (2nd ed.). Chicago, IL: University of Chicago Press.

Townsend, B. K. (2008). "Feeling like a freshman again": The transfer student transition. In B. O. Barefoot (Ed.), *The first year and beyond: Rethinking the challenge of collegiate transition* (New Directions for Higher Education No. 144, pp. 69-77). San Francisco, CA: Jossey-Bass.

Townsend, B. K., & Dever, J. T. (1999). What do we know about reverse transfer students? In B. K. Townsend (Ed.), *Understanding the impact of reverse transfer students on community colleges* (New Directions for Community College No. 106, pp. 5-13). San Franciso, CA: Jossey-Bass.

Townsend, B. K., & Wilson, K. (2006). "A hand hold for a little bit": Factors facilitating the success of community college transfer students to a large research university. *Journal of College Student Development, 47*(4), 439-456.

University of North Texas. (2010). *Transfer guides.* Retrieved from http://essc.unt.edu/registrar/articulation/

Vassar College. (2011). *Exploring Transfer.* Retrieved from http://eter.vassar.edu/

Wirt, J., Choy, S., Provasnik, S., Rooney, P., Sen, A., & Tobin, R. (2003). *The condition of education* (NCES 2003067). Washington, DC: U.S. Department of Education.

Chapter 8

Thriving in the Senior-Year Transition
Michelle C. Louis and Eileen Hulme

Compared to the extensive body of literature that exists on first-year college students, research on college seniors is in relative infancy. However, there is a growing recognition of the need to strengthen the educational value of the senior year through developing new programs, policies, and structures aimed at preparing students for the roles and responsibilities they will assume upon graduation (Gardner & Van der Veer, 1998). The most prominent subjects addressed in writings on the senior year are students' thoughts and experiences regarding career-related issues (Bowers, Dickman, & Fuqua, 2001; Hettich, 2010; Hurst & Good, 2009; Long, Sowa, & Niles, 1995; Wood, 2004; Young, 2000) and postgraduation plans (Allen & Taylor, 2006). Another segment of the literature delineates the contours of seniors' experiences by focusing on the ways in which the final year of college is laden with challenges. One author notes that the senior year can be marked by grieving as peer relationships change and students lose the security of a familiar environment and perhaps their college identities (Vickio, 1990). The adjustments that are associated with the senior year transition, including changes in living arrangements, social networks, and support systems, can create heightened stress and ambiguity (Eckel, 1994). To further describe the nature of some of these difficulties, researchers have studied the predictors of attrition in college seniors (Mohr, Eiche, & Sedlacek, 1998), and others have created instruments to determine which concerns are most salient for this population (Pistilli, Taub, & Bennett, 2003; Taub, Servaty-Seib, & Cousins, 2006).

Although it is valuable to understand the concerns and challenges of senior students and how to address them effectively, a focus solely on challenges creates only a partial understanding of the senior-year experience and generates an incomplete set of strategies for enriching it. The foundational assumption of this chapter is that valuable insights can be derived from exploring the experiences, behaviors, and attitudes of students who thrive during the senior-year transition. This chapter therefore offers a snapshot of some of the characteristics and perspectives of a sample of seniors who are thriving at exceptionally high levels and then offers suggestions for institutions desiring to enhance these functional student attributes. The participant characteristics that are the focus of this chapter are amenable to change, consistent with the conceptualization of thriving used throughout this book. The central themes emerging from this qualitative study are situated in the context of relevant literature at the close of the chapter.

A Model of Thriving in the Senior Year

Participants

A purposeful sampling method was used to identify a sample of traditionally aged students who were demographically diverse and pursuing undergraduate degrees in assorted fields at a variety of institutional types across the country. In an effort to locate a national sample of students distinguished by academic achievement, leadership, community engagement, and sense of purpose, recent recipients of the Truman Scholarship, a prestigious award given annually to approximately 60 students nationwide in recognition of exceptional academic achievement and leadership potential, were invited to participate in the study.

The 22 traditionally aged college seniors in the sample included 17 women, five men, and one transgendered student hailing from a variety of institutional types, with nine participants enrolled in public universities and 13 attending private institutions. There were 15 White students, three who self-identified as multiracial, one African American, and one Asian American; two of the participants were first-generation college students. The Truman Scholarship Foundation indicates that their award recipients typically exhibit several characteristics: (a) cumulative collegiate grade point average of 3.8 or higher; (b) demonstrated leadership potential as exhibited through campus or civic engagement and service; and (c) commitment to ongoing leadership and public service through involvement careers in government, the nonprofit or advocacy sectors, education, or elsewhere in the public service. The sample consisted of students who were in their second year of the Truman program, meaning that they would graduate from college within a few weeks of initial contact for the study. Though somewhat small, this sample was fitting for the purpose of studying thriving, as it was national in scope and consisted of a diverse group of college seniors who had scored exceptionally high on the Thriving Quotient (Schreiner, McIntosh, Nelson, & Pothoven, 2009).

The decision to examine this subgroup of exceptional thrivers as opposed to a more representative sample of college seniors was informed by a philosophical stance that aligns with the emerging field of positive psychology. Scholars in this area seek to expand the scope of inquiry within the broader field of psychology, believing that there are insights that can only be gleaned from an explicit focus on the rigorous study of optimal human functioning, as this endeavor provides insight into human potential and the conditions that promote it (Gable & Haidt, 2005; Seligman & Csikszentmihalyi, 2000).

Procedures

In partnership with the Truman Scholarship Foundation, Truman Scholars were contacted via e-mail and invited to participate in this research. Interested students were asked to respond to two sets of interview questions, separated in time by approximately one year, which provided an understanding of the participants' perspectives during the transition out of college. The first set of interviews were 60 to 90 minutes in duration and were conducted in person, utilizing a semistructured approach with questions addressing past experiences, present attitudes and behaviors, and future aspirations. Clarifying or probing questions were used, as appropriate, and the responses were audio recorded for subsequent verbatim transcription. The second round of interviews occurred via telephone or in written form, according to each participant's preference, approximately one year after the first set of interviews. These second phone interviews were approximately 60 to 90 minutes in duration, and participants who opted to provide written feedback were asked to provide detailed responses to the questions.

This research adopted a grounded theory approach (Strauss & Corbin, 1998) to understand the experiences and perspectives of highly thriving seniors and sought to construct a preliminary theory of thriving in the senior year of college. Verbatim transcripts were used as the basis for content analysis. The researchers grouped data according to codes and then sought to identify recurring themes that captured prevalent patterns or ideas shared by multiple participants, a process called *convergent analysis* (Patton, 2002). However, the researchers were interested in divergence as well, which required an examination of data that differed from the common themes. By also attending to these dissimilar perspectives, the study was able to capture a comprehensive picture of how the participants experienced thriving. Throughout the data analysis, the researchers sought to identify contextual or environmental antecedents as well as intrapersonal consequences of thriving among the sample.

To enhance the trustworthiness of the study, transcripts were coded independently so that observations could be triangulated. Over several months, codes and themes identified in the data analyses were discussed, which generated a set of emerging themes that would be explored in greater detail during follow-up interviews.

Findings

The central findings of this study are best reported as a series of central phenomena that emerged as the data were coded and analyzed. Although each participant articulated a unique personal background and perspective, this section highlights the beliefs, attitudes, and behaviors that characterized this sample of thriving seniors. Curiosity, drive, and passion constitute the central phenomena of the researchers' emerging theory of thriving in the senior year, and in the section that follows, each of these concepts will be described through illustrative participant quotations.

Curiosity

The most striking and ubiquitous characteristic of the students in this study was their insatiable curiosity. This quality has been linked to the tendency to process information more deeply and with greater retention and to persist in goal pursuits despite challenges (Silvia, 2006). Kashdan and colleagues (2009) posit that curiosity is comprised of two distinct factors: *stretching* (the desire to seek new experiences and information) and *embracing* (a proclivity to appreciate and engage with the novel, unpredictable nature of life). Both of these components of curiosity were evidenced by the participants as they described their continual pursuit of novel learning experiences, willingness to place themselves in uncomfortable but potentially growth-inducing situations, and desire to ask questions and engage in ongoing dialogue with others who would challenge their thinking. In the emerging model of thriving during the senior year, these attitudes and behaviors were characterized as outcomes or consequences of the participants' curious inclinations. Many of the participants described how they faced uncertainty and responded to failure in ways that supported their curiosity by enabling them to pursue new experiences and opportunities without being immobilized by fear or overly preoccupied with their initial performance. These contributors to thriving are described in greater detail below.

Embracing uncertainty. Each of the participants identified goals that they intentionally chose to pursue even when personal success was not assured. When asked how they were able to engage these situations despite their unknown conclusions, many of the students described their common practice of embracing and valuing the opportunities embedded within challenging situations. The attitude reflected in the interviews was not merely a tolerance of uncertainty and ambiguity but was instead a realization that uncertainty is a valuable and universal part of the human experience. One participant reflected this perspective when she asked, "What really is certain? I don't feel like the issue is being leery of taking on something uncertain; the problem really is the notion that *anything* is certain...facing uncertainty is a daily task one just becomes accustomed to." Another participant described how the unpredictable nature of life is part of what makes it a "beautiful journey," noting that "even when you fail and bad things happen, it's just part of the epic journey that you're on... I think if we just all sat back in fear, nothing would ever happen in our world or country."

Students' recognition that uncertainty is inevitable allowed them to respond to unpredictable situations in a unique way, frequently referring to these moments in their lives using terms such as "exciting" and "energizing." Several students indicated that these uncertain situations were interesting and laden with opportunities for personal development, and that the challenges they presented created a venue for growth. One participant described why he often sought to place himself in such situations, explaining that "If I only did what I knew I would succeed at, my life would be much less rich and meaningful."

Participants associated their embrace of uncertainty with the resulting ability to be unabashedly and relentlessly curious, a perspective that supported a rigorous and ongoing pursuit of new knowledge through asking questions and critically reevaluating preconceived ideas:

> The most important secret to my success in college was living in inquiry. I was constantly asking how I could discover a more comprehensive view of any picture or lesson, or how I could become a better student, public speaker, community member, and person.

Based upon these observations, a student's attitude of viewing uncertainty as something positive was classified as an antecedent to the development of curiosity in the emerging model of thriving during the senior year.

In addition to adopting this perspective in their own approach to college, students often described how faculty who modeled the value of asking questions and avoiding overconfidence in espoused perspectives had fueled their curiosity. This inquisitive stance created a tone of productive uncertainty within the classroom, which students believed augmented their own engagement with course topics. One student described a professor who nurtured student curiosity by highlighting the complex and uncertain nature of the subject matter:

> he didn't just give the answers. He said, "There are no answers, this is complex; this is a complex problem. You have to read; you have to think about these things." ... He never said, "This is how it is." He said, "Maybe it's like this, but I don't know. What do you think?" And it was just so stimulating in the way he ran the class and then told us that there were no definite answers and that "This is not a black and white issue. You have to figure out what you think..." And I just loved that. I ended up reading more for this class than I ever read for any class in my entire life!

Several other participants echoed the idea that they were more likely to engage in course material when they were challenged to find their own answers to relevant questions embedded within the subject matter, as this process allowed their inquisitiveness to drive their learning. Many of the Truman scholars indicated that they were most impressed by faculty who valued good questions as much as profound answers, and who interacted with their students and their field of expertise in a dynamic, fluid way. One student offered the following advice for faculty seeking to prompt curiosity within students:

> Be willing to change and seriously grapple with the issues your students care about and the ideas your students bring to the table. Professors who teach the same course with the same reading list and the same assignments and the same exams will not spark curiosity. Curiosity is contagious, and professors' passions, whether they see it or not, will have an impact on students. Be interested in the material, keep it fresh for yourself, keep being curious and exploring and learning, and it will have a broader impact.

The curiosity described by these Truman scholars led them to become psychologically present in the learning process and to engage it in meaningful ways, which was an important aspect of their experience of thriving. Engaged learners ask questions, continue to think about course content outside of class, and connect what they are learning to what interests them (Schreiner & Louis, 2011), each of which implies an energized and proactive stance to learning.

Acceptance of failure as a learning opportunity. Many of the students who were interviewed had succeeded in remarkably ambitious endeavors throughout their college experience, yet the participants were also readily able to describe significant failures. One of the notable features of the thriving seniors we interviewed was that these failures were not paralyzing; instead, students leveraged them to inform the use of new approaches, which often facilitated the attainment of future goals. This perspective was perhaps possible because of the ways that the students perceived their failures and the meaning they extracted from them. A common theme among the participants was their tendency to normalize failure and to view it as a part of the learning process as opposed to framing it as enduring indictment on the lack of personal ability. For example, one scholar noted,

> Certainly [failure] affects me just like it would affect any other person. But the difference is that even as it's affecting me, I'm already thinking, "Okay, so this failed. How can I move past it? How can I turn around what I've just learned and start moving forward again?" ... For me, even though failures personally affect me just as they would affect anybody, there's this sense of like, "Okay, now I have even more information about what is going to work next time."

Participants described how their failures informed the use of new approaches for achieving their goals. This stance aligns with Weiner's (1985) attribution theory, which suggests that people who believe that their failures are due to situational factors, such as the use of incorrect strategies, are more likely to persevere in the face of setbacks than are individuals who believe that failures can be ascribed to lack of ability.

Students' approaches to learning through failure are also resonant with Dweck's (1999) description of an incremental self-theory, which espouses the belief that people are capable of meaningful change through effort. Individuals who adopt this mindset tend to set goals related to growth and increasing personal competence as opposed to focusing on merely demonstrating their abilities. This growth-minded attitude increases the likelihood that such individuals will seek challenging endeavors, even if those efforts may reveal personal deficiencies (Hong, Chiu, Dweck, Lin, & Wan, 1999). People with an incremental self-theory desire and attend to performance feedback because they believe that such information is instrumental in helping them learn and improve in the future (Dweck, Mangels, & Good, 2004). Participants illustrated this concept with statements such as "if you fail, you have still gained some solid experience for next time" and "failing is okay. You are not defined by one event or one action, but all of them help define your perspectives and help make you stronger."

The ability to attribute failures to factors under one's control is the foundation of an optimistic explanatory style (Seligman, 1990) that is implicit in the *positive perspective* element of thriving. Having a positive perspective toward life enables students to reframe negative events and perceive failure as a learning opportunity (Schreiner, 2010). Several participants described failure in ways that were somewhat similar to their perspectives on uncertainty, viewing both as inevitable and potentially valuable parts of their experience as learners:

> Failure is in some sense just like a standard by-product of trial and error...It's sort of like a scientific method in that way or in the sense that you'll have all of these failed experiments, but the information that you're gathering from those failed experiments will be the drivers of your one successful experiment. I very much see [failure] as great information-gathering... Success stories that we all love and know are stories of people who have failed and struggled and have emerged victorious at the end because they were so driven by whatever they had learned from their failures that they were able to then apply it and push past it and become successful.

It was common for these thriving seniors to note that this attitude provided a buffer against discouragement when their efforts had not produced desired outcomes, helping them to view setbacks as a natural by-product of attempting difficult endeavors. This attitude enabled them to attempt to achieve challenging goals without fearing the failure that might result, and this persistence in spite of difficulty or failure is characteristic of the *academic determination* component of thriving (Schreiner et al., 2009). Moreover, many of the participants indicated that they fully expected *failure*, that it should not be feared, and that success is defined not by the absence of failure but instead by one's ability to persevere when encountering inevitable obstacles. One student advised his peers that they "should not be afraid to fail, because you will fail; and when you fail, try to learn and use failure as a source of motivation for what you want to attain." This fearless approach not only emboldened these students' attempts to realize ambitious goals by prescribing a positive, adaptive response to failure; it also served as an engine for driving their curiosity because it helped make performance considerations a more peripheral determinant of the activities with which they would engage.

Deliberately facing fears and allowing oneself to experience discomfort. Although these students normalized failure and emphasized that it should not be feared, participants also acknowledged that they encountered challenges and opportunities in college that did make them feel intimidated or fearful. It was common for these thriving individuals to suggest, however, that such situations should be pursued instead of avoided. Many of the students described how they deliberately sought out opportunities that made them uncomfortable, believing that such occasions offered venues for acquiring new skills, improving performance, and learning new information. Emblematic of this perspective, one individual reflected, "I've pushed myself to do the things that scare me the most. I've pursued...all of the things that intimidate me because I realize I'll only be satisfied if I jump into the fire and face my fears." Another student advised that "if you go through college and you don't find yourself in a situation where you are challenged or feel uncomfortable, then you're really not getting a lot out of it...those specific times are when you really grow up."

This sample of thriving seniors viewed uncomfortable, novel situations as challenging instead of threatening and spoke about them as laden with potential for growth as opposed to replete with opportunities for failure. The participants described how viewing challenges through a positive lens made it more likely that they would proactively engage unfamiliar situations instead of fearing them, an observation that aligns with Elliot's (1999) description of how approach and avoidance motivation prompt different behavioral tendencies. These students were more strongly driven by the approach motivation of imagining what they could gain from participating in new experiences than they were by the motivation to avoid discomfort. When paired with the propensity to perceive setbacks as learning tools, these students were equipped to maximize their college experience and the postcollege transition.

Drive and Passion

In addition to curiosity, the elements of drive and personal passion for specific pursuits appeared as central phenomena in the theory of thriving in the senior year. These two phenomena, although conceptually distinct, were so strongly interconnected in participants' responses that they are described together here.

Responding to an inquiry about which personal characteristics had led to her success, one student stated, "Drive! It's my drive." Many participants described their ongoing efforts to achieve levels of optimal personal performance, an endeavor that often required working harder than many of their peers and persevering in situations when others simply gave up. In addition, behavioral examples indicative of participants' drive include the large number of students who had two majors or were engaged in significant acts of public service. One individual described how she successfully completed 27 credit hours of coursework in one semester at a highly selective university.

For many participants, it appeared that their drive to work hard actually increased their confidence in their ability to be successful. Several Truman scholars emphasized that their academic success was primarily a result of effort as opposed to innate ability. One female participant stated, "The [characteristic leading to personal success] would just be being very driven. I don't consider myself extremely intelligent, but I have confidence that I can work through anything that I have to." It is apparent from this study that drive is a characteristic common to all the seniors interviewed, but it would be inaccurate to suggest that these thriving seniors were distinguished exclusively by their drive. These students' determination was inextricably linked to a deep sense of intrinsically motivated passion.

Intrinsic motivation. During a period in American higher education in which many college students focus on course grades as the primary indicator of academic success, the thriving seniors who participated in this study represented a divergent attitude. When asked if they were more motivated by external factors (e.g., achieving high grades or approval from others) or internal factors (e.g., a sense of passion or joy of learning), the Truman scholars indicated a significant bias toward intrinsic motivation as prompting their actions. One student noted, "I never used to check my final grades. I didn't know what my GPA was until my junior year when I was asked to apply for scholarships." Several seniors indicated that although both internal and external factors affected their motivation, internal factors had the greatest lasting influence on their behaviors.

> I think in college I was more motivated by internal factors, but some of the internal factors were affected by the external. For instance, I certainly enjoyed internally the attention I received for being a "smart" person or for succeeding...But overall, I think it was my internal desire to keep improving and to learn new things that kept me motivated.

Several participants revealed that they were intrinsically motivated at the outset of their undergraduate experience; however, the majority expressed an increase in internal motivation as they progressed through their college years. One student described his shift in motivation by stating, "I found work I was truly passionate about in college and that shifted a lot of my motivation inward." Participants noted that course grades, awards, and parental expectations all exerted a basic level of influence, yet it was clear that these high thrivers believed that their deep passions were the foundation for their intrinsically motivated drive.

Passion behind the drive. The thriving students in this study were clearly people who held a coherent set of strong beliefs. Many believed that their college experience should be driven by their convictions and not by external factors.

> I think a lot of students that I saw coming through the honors program had this end goal of like, they were going to be a Rhodes scholar. I was like, "No! You have to do what you're passionate about and if that leads you to wanting a degree from Oxford...then apply for a Rhodes scholarship."

When asked to give advice to incoming students, many were quick to offer counsel such as, "Try new things and pursue those that you are most passionate about. Passion is the driver for success, not the name of your degree."

The passionate convictions of the participants appeared to have two basic aims: service to the greater good, and to a lesser degree, fulfillment of personal potential. In describing the dual aims of personal passion, one scholar asserted, "I am motivated to be the best person I can be and to make a positive difference." One criterion for selection as a Truman scholar is involvement in public service. Therefore, it is possible that references to the passion found in the service to others may not be found as frequently among other thriving students. Whether they were working to create a more sustainable campus or providing health care for underserved populations, these students believed in the power of their passions. The following statement is representative of this commitment expressed by the majority of the participants: "the number one factor that has gotten me to where I am today is that I am driven about something that isn't my own personal success… that mission, that goal, is much bigger than I am." The desire to make a difference in others' lives, to see beyond themselves, and to enrich their communities is integral to Schreiner and colleagues' (2009) conceptualization of thriving. What they refer to as *diverse citizenship* was clearly depicted in the Truman scholars' commitment to goals that extended beyond their own personal success.

Various participants also reported a passionate drive toward realizing their potential. Phrases such as "becoming the best person I can be," "outdoing myself," "prove to myself," "internal drive to keep achieving," and "proactively seeking opportunities to better myself" were recurrent themes throughout the transcripts. Many students mentioned a desire to "push" themselves and to have others impel them toward their full capability. One student remarked, "I kind of wanted to be that person in the classroom that now I've come to find out everyone hates, but that wants the professor to push us harder and make us think more and write more and do more." For a majority of the scholars, a passion to reach their full potential appeared to be a distinguishing factor of their intrinsic drive.

Based upon this study, the directionality of drive and passion is not clear. The question remains whether drive is a consequence of passion or whether existing internal drive is an antecedent of developing a sense of passion. The convergent analysis suggested that for most participants, innate drive was a catalyst for exploration and ultimately helped determine their passions and sense of purpose. Yet, one student described an experience of having minimal drive until discovering a passion and noted that that her motivation and engagement increased once she could use them in the service of something that truly excited her. Regardless of the directionality, the passions of the Truman scholars had four identifying characteristics: they (a) were enhanced through self-awareness, (b) generated a love of learning, (c) became a filter for decision making, and (d) engendered a sense of purpose. In the theory of thriving in the senior year, self-evaluation is conceptualized as an antecedent that contributes to the identification of students' passions. Within this model, consequences or outcomes of knowing one's passion include a sense of purpose, having a filter for making decisions, and enjoyment of the learning process.

Passions enhanced through self-awareness. Many students described how taking the time to be personally reflective helped them discern their passions and develop and maintain a sense of clarity related to their values and goals.

This sentiment was expressed by one Truman scholar who noted, "I think constant self-evaluation is very important. In college, it is really easy to get stuck in tracks that actually deter one from what is more fulfilling to oneself." It was common for participants to describe valuing relationships with an advisor or professor who had helped stimulate increased self-awareness throughout their college years. These thriving students' levels of self-reflection were evident in their exceptionally thoughtful and reasoned responses to the inquiries made into their personal lives throughout the interview process.

Passions generated a love of learning. The love of learning was consistently linked to the passionate drive found within the students interviewed. One scholar discussed the dilemma of being in a major that was not aligned with her passions.

> I just always sort of loved being in school and being a nerdy kid who loved all of that. But I was unhappy, not passionate about the topic, and trying to, of course, talk with professors and learn more about the material, but ultimately realizing that it wasn't for me. And so when I had the opportunity to take some public health courses and realize that it was just this combination of everything that I loved from communications to science to thinking about social histories...that was a huge boon.

One student indicated that learning was the focus of her ambition and motivation. She stated, "ambition is what drives me to learn in the things that I'm doing... in my current job, I had a conversation with my boss and I said 'I want this to be the hardest job that I've ever had,'" describing how her work became most meaningful if it could offer new challenge, insight, or opportunities for personal growth that would support her efforts to contribute in her areas of passion.

Passions provided a filter for decision making. The awareness of their passions influenced the participants' decisions regarding the use of their time. This influence was notable when one student summarized how she prioritized her time and determined the things to which she would apply herself in college: "I spent my energy on things that excited me, things I was passionate about. Obviously, it is important to build a respectable résumé and develop connections, but I think those things come naturally if you first stay engaged and passionate." Several students noted that they tended not to be involved indiscriminately in multiple campus organizations, but to instead invest great effort in a few deliberately selected commitments.

Passions engendered a sense of purpose. The passion that appeared to drive the Truman scholars in college also provided many with a deeper sense of purpose in life. One student commented on his sense of purpose when he stated

> I think people have certain callings in their life. Some are content to not be associated with others or to have no impact on other people. I think my calling, something that I've found to be residual with me, is an urge to engage others and to move other people and to be involved in things that shape other people's lives.

This sense of purpose found in their passions shaped for many how they conceptualized their lives after college. The causes they had championed in college informed the direction for their continued community involvement.

Recommendations

This study of high-thriving college seniors offers multiple implications for negotiating the transition from college to employment or graduate education. As previously discussed, the same characteristics that enable students to thrive during college are also important in their adaptation to the roles they will assume after graduation. The following recommendations describe strategies that institutions might adopt to develop curiosity, drive, and passion within their students, three notable qualities present in the thriving college seniors in the study.

1. Recognize that preparation for a successful transition out of college begins during a student's first year. If colleges and universities are serious about ensuring a successful transition from their institutions, efforts to develop the personal qualities necessary to facilitate that change will begin early in a student's collegiate career. Although seniors may benefit from exposure to topics, such as financial literacy and career planning, many of the challenges that recent college graduates encounter are psychosocial in nature. An essential question that designers of first-year programs might raise is, What do we need to teach new students to enable them to thrive in their lives after college? This question raises deeper and more fundamental concerns regarding the purpose of a college degree. It positions the university to graduate individuals who are prepared to make significant contributions in their professional and personal lives. Committees created to focus on the senior-year transition should begin by determining how educators can foster the psychosocial capabilities and practical skills that will help students successfully navigate their postgraduation responsibilities throughout college.

2. Focus on the development of curiosity through increasing students' mindfulness. An observation of young children makes it apparent that curiosity is a central aspect of human nature. However, for many individuals, years of structure, rules, obligations, and routine have diminished their innate desire for exploration and novelty seeking (Kashdan, 2009). As the data in this study reveal, curiosity is an essential characteristic of students who are thoroughly engaged in their academic experience.

Improving a student's level of mindfulness provides one avenue for increasing curiosity. Langer (1997) defines mindfulness as "the continuous creation of new categories; openness to new information; and an implicit awareness of more than one category" (p. 4). Mindlessness, in contrast, may be characterized as going through the motions of life in an unreflective and routine manner. Engaging academic environments teach a healthy skepticism of existing knowledge through dialogue that is accepting of divergent opinions. If students have been taught to enter into unfamiliar environments with the goal of creating new mental frameworks and experiencing the richness of unique people and perspectives, they will develop greater levels of mindfulness and will be more likely to find the transition from the collegiate culture invigorating as opposed to overwhelming.

Mindfulness is the foundational construct in the *focused attention* component of engaged learning (Schreiner & Louis, 2011) that characterizes thriving college students. Mindfulness may be cultivated by focusing on the inner experience or on the outward conditions of the current moment. The development of mindfulness stands in sharp opposition to some of the cultural forces that have shaped a distracted generation of college students. Text messaging, online social networking, and mobile computing have created significant deterrents to a focus on the present moment. Rather than disavowing current technologies, educators must use these tools to increase mindfulness. For example, students in a leadership course could be asked to use social media to communicate with other students in the class when they observe servant leadership occurring on campus. This type of activity may help students become more aware of the leadership exhibited in the current moment, which otherwise may go unnoticed. However, it is not enough to merely teach students to be more aware of their current circumstance. Kashdan (2009) notes that "it's not about whether we pay attention, but how we pay attention to what is happening in the present" (p. 3). An openness to ideas, experiences, and current realities provides students a strong mental and emotional foundation from which to approach change.

Students must be encouraged to enter situations with an open mind as opposed to imposing a preexisting mental framework that might limit their understanding of the richness of the present moment. As the seniors noted in the interviews, faculty who presented course topics in ways that communicated a value for dialogue and exploration offered students an opportunity to question assumptions inherent in the subject matter. When students are free to develop and articulate their own points of view, learn in a climate that encourages asking questions, and are given opportunities to explore topics of personal interest, the learning becomes personally relevant, increasing the possibility for mindfulness. On the other hand, courses taught in a manner that precludes questions make students less likely to take a mindful approach to learning.

Courses and programs focusing specifically on teaching mindful attention have emerged on some college campuses throughout the last decade. Counseling centers have begun to offer outreach programs that combine mindfulness and academic success strategies, and living-learning communities have developed workshops promoting mindful awareness ("Counseling Center," 2010). The University of California, Los Angeles' Mindful Awareness Research Center (2011) offers online courses and workshops for faculty, staff, and students seeking to develop or improve their mindfulness. These types of programs represent a first step toward developing the kind of focused attention that prompts greater levels of curiosity and leads to engaged learning.

3. Promote exploration and thoughtful risk taking. Inherent in students' transitions from college is an increased degree of uncertainty. During this time, individuals are likely to ask questions, such as Where will I live? Which career suits me? Will I be successful in graduate school? How will I find a social support system? How one copes with this ambiguity may be the difference between a successful or difficult transition. Curious individuals are able to mitigate the negative stress associated with college graduation by embracing the uncertainty found in a transition, viewing it as intriguing or energizing. Kashdan (2009) suggests that:

> When we experience curiosity we are willing to leave the familiar and routine and take risks, even if it makes us feel anxious and uncomfortable. Those who deal better with novelty, who function more optimally in a world that is unpredictable, uncertain, and unstable, I call "curious explorers." Curious explorers are comfortable with the risks of taking on challenges. In fact, the most curious among us actually lust for the new. (p. 7)

The desire to explore and effectively manage one's fears regarding the uncertainty was evident in the highly thriving students we studied and is essential to thriving in the midst of a transition. If seniors frame graduation as an opportunity for advanced exploration as opposed to primarily a period of loss or threat, they are likely to experience fewer negative emotions and lower levels of stress. Although seniors may still experience a season of loss, that time period may be shortened if they have a greater tolerance and appreciation for risk taking.

Institutions may challenge their students to take calculated, productive risks in several ways. The first possibility is for institutional leaders to systemically support study in cultures and countries that represent divergent values and customs. Other possibilities include promoting cross-disciplinary study through program requirements and elective selection, encouraging affiliation with student organizations outside one's existing experience, and creating a cultural ethos in student life and academic programming that prompts students to take educationally beneficial risks. In addition, institutions could help students connect with mentors who encourage movement beyond what is comfortable while providing the interpersonal support necessary for successful completion of and reflection on the undertaken risk.

4. Provide opportunities for participation in appreciative advising to help students identify their passions. Many students depart from colleges and universities without a well-developed sense of their passions and future aspirations, yet developing a sense of purpose is considered a major developmental task for students (Chickering & Reisser, 1993). It is therefore important for educators to adopt a proactive approach to encouraging students to define their passions and create an attainable plan to achieve their goals. One method that may facilitate this outcome is appreciative advising, an approach to the advising process based upon the tenets of appreciative inquiry. Appreciative inquiry is a paradigm that uses a constructivist model to identify and mobilize the assets and positive features of individuals and organizations through asking questions that focus on potential building instead of problem solving (Cooperrider & Srivastva, 1987; Cooperrider & Whitney, 2000). Appreciative advising uses open-ended questions to help students identify their strengths and interests, generate positive images of the future, and establish high personal standards for achievement (Bloom, Hutson, & He, 2008). In short, appreciative advising prompts students to explore their individual passions.

The University of North Carolina at Greensboro (UNC-G) is a pioneer in integrating appreciative advising throughout their Student Academic

Services division. Programs serving students on academic probation employ the Appreciative Advising Inventory (AAI; Bloom et al., 2008) and review the results in subsequent advising sessions. Since the inception of the program, the institution has noted more than a 20% increase in retention of their at-risk student population (Kamphoff, Hutson, Amundsen, & Atwood, 2007). In addition, the implementation of the appreciative advising curriculum in the University's first-year experience program has been associated with an increase in UNC-G's overall first-year student to sophomore retention rate and academic performance as measured by grade point average (Hutson & Atwood, 2006).

Career counseling plays a valuable role in identifying possible occupational opportunities, but developing a sense of purpose that may transcend a specific career is a more in-depth developmental process that can be facilitated by a meaningful advising relationship embodying an appreciative perspective. When students understand their unique strengths and passions, they are well positioned to form personally relevant and authentic goals, which contribute to a sense of meaning and promote flourishing (Emmons, 2003). The positive emotions associated with having a clear sense of purpose may facilitate thriving during the transition to postcollege life because the pleasure in what lies ahead is most fully experienced by those who have a hopeful expectation of the contributions they will make in the future.

5. Develop practices that encourage intrinsic motivation and reduce students' dependence on extrinsic rewards. Intrinsic motivation is based on "active engagement with tasks that people find interesting and that, in turn, promote growth" (Deci & Ryan, 2000, p. 233). This type of motivation is evident in people who are highly curious and who pursue a wide range of interests. Intrinsic motivation was pervasive among the highly thriving students in this study.

Research suggests that the pursuit of intrinsically motivated goals promotes well-being (Emmons, 2003). However, the current American educational system has often emphasized extrinsic rewards as an incentive for student learning. Despite decades of research indicating that the provision of such rewards can substantially undermine intrinsic motivation (Deci, Koestner, Ryan, & Cameron, 2001), colleges and universities continue to focus on external motivators for student learning by emphasizing grades, academic awards, and the earning potential associated with particular academic majors or careers.

A shift in focus from extrinsic to intrinsic motivation would require significant changes in educational practices, most notably in curriculum design, pedagogy, and academic advising. An extensive body of research indicates that providing choice increases intrinsic motivation in most situations (see Patall, Cooper, & Robinson, 2008 for a review). Colleges and universities interested in improving their students' level of intrinsic motivation must begin by optimizing the opportunities students have to follow their own interests. One implication for curriculum design is that students should be encouraged to explore various options before determining an academic major (Hettich & Helkowski, 2005). During an era in which policy makers and constituents are focused on timely degree completion, this exploration must occur within the context of providing a range of viable electives within each major and allowing margin in the degree requirements for minors and double majors. Pedagogically, the change required to promote intrinsic motivation among a greater percentage of students is twofold: (a) the provision of choice in assignments and (b) the reconceptualization of the faculty role from one of an expert dispensing knowledge to that of a designer of learning opportunities that help students connect knowledge to lived experiences (Barr & Tagg, 1995). Allowing students choices in how they demonstrate mastery of course objectives enhances their intrinsic motivation by meeting their need for autonomy. Structuring learning experiences in ways that encourage the meaningful processing that is the hallmark of engaged learning fosters what Ryan and Deci (2000) call *authentic motivation*, as it meets students' needs for competence and relatedness, two fundamental drivers of self-determined behavior.

Academic advising that supports intrinsic motivation would consistently expose students to opportunities to align their curricular and cocurricular choices with their interests and passions. Such advising would also encourage a fuller exploration of potential majors and careers in the context of life goals, personal values, and relevant skill sets (Hettich, 2010). The challenge to equip graduating students with the curiosity, passion, and intrinsic motivation to successfully navigate the transition from college into a fast-paced world replete with choices demands a critical examination of existing educational practices.

Conclusion

This study of students who are thriving at exceptionally high levels during the senior year transition provides insight into the kinds of attitudes and behaviors that characterize such individuals. The research described here indicates that students who thrive during the final year of college are distinguished by their curiosity and passionate drive, characteristics that can be influenced by institutional efforts to create a context for thriving during the senior year and throughout the transition into the roles students will assume in their lives after graduation. This chapter offers several recommendations that provide a framework for determining practical action steps to promote thriving during the senior year transition. Institutions may vary in the specific strategies deemed most appropriate for their particular students; however, educational leaders seeking to orchestrate an environment conducive to student thriving may benefit from considering how to prepare students for the transition out of college beginning in the first year. A reconsideration of curriculum design, pedagogical practices, and the nature of academic advising may be necessary to develop institutional practices that are likely to nurture intrinsic motivation. Creating a climate that fosters curiosity, promotes exploration and purposeful risk taking, and helps students identify their passions throughout their college experience can equip students to thrive as they transition to postcollegiate life.

References

Allen, J. K., & Taylor, K. (2006). The senior year transition: Women undergraduates search for a path. *Journal of College Student Development, 47*(6), 595-608.

Barr, R. B., & Tagg, J. (1995). From teaching to learning—a new paradigm for undergraduate education. *Change, 27*(6).

Bloom, J., Hutson, B., & He, Y. (2008). *The appreciative advising revolution.* Champaign, IL: Stipes Publishing.

Bowers, P. J., Dickman, M. M., & Fuqua, D. R. (2001). Psychosocial and career development related to employment of graduating seniors. *NASPA Journal, 38*(3), 326-347.

Chickering, A. W., & Reisser, L. (1993). *Education and identity* (2nd ed.). San Francisco, CA: Jossey-Bass.

Cooperrider, D. L., & Srivastva, S. (1987). Appreciative inquiry in organizational life. In W. Pasmore & R. Woodman (Eds.), *Research in organization change and development* (Vol. 1, pp. 129-169). Greenwich, CT: JAI Press.

Cooperrider, D. L., & Whitney, D. (2000). A positive revolution in change: Appreciative inquiry. In D. L. Cooperrider, P. F. Sorensen, Jr., D. Whitney, & T. F. Yaeger (Eds.), *Appreciative inquiry: Rethinking human organization toward a positive theory of change* (pp. 3-27). Champaign, IL: Stipes Publishing.

Counseling center offers mindfulness meditation workshops. (2010, March 31) *Baylor University Lariat.* Retrieved from http://www.baylor.edu/lariat/news.php?action=story &story=71831

Deci, E. L., Koestner, R., Ryan, R. M., & Cameron, J. (2001). Extrinsic rewards and intrinsic motivation in education: Reconsidered once again. *Review of Educational Research, 71*(1), 1-27.

Deci, E. & Ryan, R. (2000). The "what" and "why" of goal pursuits: Human needs and the self-determination of behavior. *Psychological Inquiry, 11*(4), 227-268.

Dweck, C. S. (1999). *Self-theories: Their role in motivation, personality, and development.* Philadelphia, PA: Psychology Press.

Dweck, C. S., Mangels, J. A., & Good, C. (2004). Motivational effects on attention, cognition, and performance. In D. Y. Dai & R. J. Sternberg (Eds.), *Motivation, emotion, and cognition: Integrative perspectives on intellectual functioning and development* (pp. 41-55). Mahwah, NJ: Lawrence Erlbaum.

Eckel, P. (1994, July). *Building community in the freshman and senior year: Completing the cycle of student-institution involvement.* International Conference on The First-Year Experience, Dublin, Ireland.

Elliot, A. (1999). Approach and avoidance motivation and achievement goals. *Educational Psychologist, 34*, 169-189.

Emmons, R. A. (2003). Personal goals, life meaning, and virtue: Wellsprings of a positive life. In C. L. Keyes & J. Haidt (Eds.), *Flourishing: Positive psychology and the life well-lived* (pp. 105-128). Washington, DC: American Psychological Association.

Gable, S. L., & Haidt, J. (2005). What (and why?) is positive psychology? *Review of General Psychology, 9*(2), 103-110.

Gardner, J. N., & Van der Veer, G. (1998). The emerging movement to strengthen the senior experience. In J. N. Gardner & G. Van der Veer (Eds.) *The senior year experience: Facilitating integration, reflection, closure, and transition* (pp. 3-20). San Francisco, CA: Jossey-Bass.

Hettich, P. I. (2010). College-to-workplace transitions: Becoming a freshman again. In T. W. Miller (Ed.) *Handbook of stressful transitions across the lifespan* (pp. 87-109). New York, NY: Springer.

Hettich, P. I., & Helkowski, C. (2005). *Connect college to career: A student's guide to work and life transitions.* Belmont, CA: Thomson Wadsworth.

Hong, Y., Chiu, C., Dweck, C. S., Lin, D., & Wan, W. (1999). Implicit theories, attributions, and coping: A meaning system approach. *Journal of Personality and Social Psychology, 77*, 588-599.

Hurst, J. L., & Good, L. K. (2009). Generation Y and career choice: The impact of retail career perceptions, expectations, and entitlement perceptions. *Career Development International, 14*(6), 570-593.

Hutson, B. L., & Atwood, J. A. (2006, November). *Outcome evaluation to support a freshman orientation program.* Paper presented at the annual meeting of the American Evaluation Association, Portland, OR.

Kamphoff, C. S., Hutson, B. L., Amundsen, S. A., & Atwood, J. A. (2007). A motivational/ empowerment model applied to students on academic probation. *Journal of College Student Retention: Research, Theory, and Practice, 8*(4), 397-412.

Kashdan, T. B. (2009). *Curious? Discover the missing ingredient to a fulfilling life.* New York, NY: Harper Collins.

Kashdan, T. B., Gallagher, M. W., Silvia, P. J., Winterstein, B. P., Breen, W. E., Terhar, D., & Steger, M. F. (2009). The curiosity and exploration inventory-II: Development, factor structure, and psychometrics. *Journal of Research in Personality, 43*(6), 987-998.

Langer, E. (1997). *The power of mindful learning.* New York, NY: Addison Wesley.

Long, B. E., Sowa, C. J., & Niles, S. G. (1995). Differences in student development reflected by the career decisions of college seniors. *Journal of College Student Development, 36*(1), 47-52.

Mohr, J. J., Eiche, K. D., & Sedlacek, W. E. (1998). So close, yet so far: Predictors of attrition in college seniors. *Journal of College Student Development, 39*(4), 343-354.

Patall, E. A., Cooper, H., & Robinson, J. C. (2008). The effects of choice on intrinsic motivation and related outcomes: A meta-analysis of research findings. *Psychological Bulletin, 134*(2), 270-300.

Patton, M. Q. (2002). *Qualitative research & evaluation methods* (3rd ed.). Thousand Oaks, CA: Sage.

Pistilli, M. D., Taub, D., & Bennett, D. E. (2003). Development of the Senior Concerns Survey: An exploratory factor analysis. *Journal of The First-Year Experience & Students in Transition, 15*(1), 39-52.

Ryan, R. M., & Deci, E. L. (2000). Self-determination theory and the facilitation of intrinsic motivation, social development, and well-being. *American Psychologist, 55*(1), 68-78.

Schreiner, L. A. (2010). The Thriving Quotient: A new vision for student success. *About Campus, 15*(2), 2-10.

Schreiner, L. A., & Louis, M. C. (2011). The Engaged Learning Index: Implications for faculty development. *Journal on Excellence in College Teaching, 22*(1), 5-28.

Schreiner, L. A., McIntosh, E. J., Nelson, D., & Pothoven, S. (2009, November). *The Thriving Quotient: Advancing the assessment of student success.* Paper presented at the annual meeting of the Association for the Study of Higher Education, Vancouver, Canada.

Seligman, M. E. P. (1990). *Learned optimism.* New York, NY: Knopf.

Seligman, M. E. P., & Csikszentmihalyi, M. (2000). Positive psychology: An introduction. *American Psychologist, 55*(1), 5-14.

Silvia, P. J. (2006). *Exploring the psychology of interest.* New York, NY: Oxford University Press.

Strauss, A., & Corbin, A. (1998). *Basics of qualitative research: Techniques and procedures for developing grounded theory* (2nd ed.). Thousand Oaks, CA: Sage Publishers.

Taub, D. J., Servaty-Seib, H. L., & Cousins, C. (2006). On the brink of transition: The concerns of college seniors. *Journal of The First-Year Experience & Students in Transition, 18*(2), 111-132.

University of California at Los Angeles (UCLA) (2011). *Mindful Awareness Research Center.* Retrieved from http://marc.ucla.edu

Vickio, C. J. (1990). The good-bye brochure: Helping students to cope with transition and loss. *Journal of Counseling and Development, 68*(5), 575-577.

Weiner, B. (1985). An attribution theory of achievement motivation and emotion. *Psychological Review, 92,* 548-573.

Wood, F. B. (2004). Preventing post-parchment depression: A model of career counseling for college seniors. *Journal of Employment Counseling, 41*(2), 71.

Young, R. R. (2000). I've always wanted to be a ..., but now I'm not so sure: A survey of students' career plans. *College & University, 76*(2), 9-16.

Chapter 9

Recommendations for Facilitating Thriving in Transitions
Laurie A. Schreiner, Denise D. Nelson, and Michelle C. Louis

This book focuses on the many transitions that students encounter during the college experience, beginning with the transition from high school to college and continuing through the transition from college to the world of work or graduate school. In each of these transition points, a student's ability to not only survive the transition but thrive during it has been emphasized. Thriving implies making the most of an experience, emerging from a transition stronger and better prepared for the next phase of life.

As outlined in the first chapter, successful transitions have five distinguishing hallmarks: students (a) perceive them as positive opportunities for growth, (b) use proactive coping skills during the transition, (c) have the social and practical support they need, (d) access resources in a timely manner for information and assistance, and (e) emerge from the transition having grown in personally significant ways. Throughout the book, the chapter authors have applied the construct of thriving, with its expanded perspective on student success, as a framework for helping students move successfully through transitions in college in ways that further their growth and enable them to benefit more fully from their college experience.

In closing this book, we synthesize the recommendations offered throughout, providing a blueprint for helping students navigate the numerous transitions of college life. We have organized the recommendations into the three major elements of thriving: academic, interpersonal, and intrapersonal thriving.

Enhancing Academic Thriving

Academic thriving encompasses student engagement in the learning process, as well as students' goal direction, investment of effort, and ability to manage life in a way that supports academic success. The following recommendations highlight specific ways that institutions can foster academic thriving during transitions.

In the classroom:
- Give students a sense of control over the demands of their courses by teaching effective strategies for success in each class. Encourage students to set learning rather than performance goals.
- Use reflective writing, class discussion, or other exercises to help students frame academic performance as the result of appropriately applied effort rather than innate levels of intelligence.
- Foster student-faculty interaction through undergraduate research opportunities.
- Fuel intellectual curiosity by modeling enthusiasm for learning; help students view challenges or failures as building blocks for future success.
- Support intrinsic motivation by offering students a range of alternative assignments or methods of evaluation within a class or throughout a course of study.
- Connect transfer students with faculty in their major through small-group orientation sessions or faculty-student work teams.
- Explore each student's strengths and their unique contributions to the shared learning experiences within a classroom.
- Employ active-learning techniques to connect with a variety of learning styles and encourage high levels of engagement.
- Offer challenging assignments with clearly described expectations.
- Give students timely, frequent, and constructive feedback regarding their work.

In advising:
- Adopt strengths-based or appreciative advising practices that help students consider how their strengths can be mobilized and developed during college.
- Teach students goal direction by using academic advising as the vehicle for hope building.
- Assign students' first-year seminar instructors as their academic advisors throughout the first year.

- Expose students to the possibility of graduate education and encourage them to revisit their initial degree goals in light of their career aspirations and college experiences.

In curricular and cocurricular programming:

- Offer learning communities built around a variety of social issues or intellectual topics to permit self-selection into immersive learning experiences that address issues of significant personal interest.

- Educate faculty and students about the harmful effects of expecting students of color to speak on behalf of their ethnic or cultural group.

- Publicize transfer policies including articulation agreements and transferability requirements to support the ongoing academic work of transfer students.

- Offer summer preview courses for students considering vertical transfer from a two-year college to a four-year institution.

Enhancing Interpersonal Thriving

Interpersonal thriving encompasses healthy relationships and social connections in students' lives, but also their openness to difference and their desire to make an impact in the community around them. The following recommendations can help bolster students' interpersonal thriving during key transition points:

- Link students not only to others who are experiencing the same transition, but also to peers who have successfully navigated that transition.

- Include peer instructors as coteachers within first-year seminars or courses to offer relational, as well as academic, connections.

- Design peer mentorship programs and campus leadership opportunities specifically for transfer students or encourage transfers to pursue existing opportunities by initiating transfer-friendly meeting schedules.

- Create supportive relationships for students of color, either one-on-one or in group settings, with peers who can mentor new students in the midst of daily intercultural transitions; promote ethnic organizations across campus.

- Offer guidelines for healthy levels of involvement in campus activities and organizations to encourage participation without burnout.

- Design learning communities that permit students to bond with one another through shared living arrangements or linked courses as they learn together. Organize learning communities in ways that encourage commuter student involvement.

- Offer service-learning activities that encourage peer collaboration and allow students to work alongside those from unfamiliar cultures or circumstances.

- Include nonresidential students, adult learners, and transfer students in cocurricular community-building activities that are often reserved for residential first-year students.

- Encourage student input and feedback regarding campus programming, especially from often overlooked groups, such as sophomores and transfer students.

- Host a special campus welcome reception for transfer students in order to convey their importance to the institution; encourage a variety of student organizations to participate.

Enhancing Intrapersonal Thriving

Intrapersonal thriving refers to the positive perspective that thriving students possess. This perspective, comprised of realistic optimism and a strong sense of well-being, enables students to remain motivated and persist during difficult challenges. Foundational to all aspects of thriving, this positive perspective can be enhanced by the following institutional efforts during key transition periods in students' lives:

- Communicate openly with students and their families about how to positively engage the growth opportunities associated with specific transitions.

- Teach students about the psychological processes that impact their success in order to help them gain a sense of control.

- Equip students to understand and develop their unique strengths to support success in all aspects of their college lives.

- Create a spiritually supportive environment with opportunities for students to examine questions of meaning and purpose in their lives.

- Use advising appointments to help students set long-term personal and academic goals and plans for reaching them; focus on students' strengths and interests.

- Support healthy exploration by designing activities in classroom or advising settings that urge students to consider numerous possible scenarios for their lives after graduation, including unfamiliar or daunting possibilities.

- Leverage appreciative advising and strengths development techniques to guide students in recognizing and exploring their passions.

Campuswide Recommendations

We close this book with a series of broad recommendations for institutions to consider as they seek to enhance thriving among their students during the many seasons of transition that characterize the college years. The aforementioned specific recommendations for helping students thrive academically, interpersonally, or intrapersonally will be more easily implemented within a campus culture where student transitional issues are understood and where thriving is perceived as a valued goal for the undergraduate experience. The following recommendations address the campus ethos and shared institutional goals:

Clearly define student success holistically in terms of student thriving—and measure student thriving at key transition points. This book articulates a new vision for student success that reaches beyond some of the commonly cited indices of success, such as high levels of academic performance and persistence to graduation. Although these factors are important, seeking to produce thriving among students requires that educators' scope of concern extends also to a consideration of other factors, such as students' ability to form and maintain healthy relationships, their commitment to make a contribution to their community, and their response to challenging circumstances. To advance the goal of promoting student thriving requires that student success be defined more broadly, and that this more holistic approach is supported by assessment strategies that reflect this perspective. Simply stated, when institutions embrace the charge to invest in students' holistic growth, they will employ assessment techniques that reflect this value and that provide information on thriving-related indicators. In addition, because thriving is a dynamic state, we recommend that institutional leaders pay particular attention to high-stress transition points at which they can systematically measure and track student success by examining it from academic, interpersonal, and intrapersonal perspectives. Part of this assessment strategy may require the initiation of a comprehensive monitoring system designed to support students in transition and to identify opportunities to intervene on their behalf. In adopting this approach, we recommend a consideration of not only how to support those students who may be struggling but also how to augment the positive experiences of those who are thriving.

Design all campus programs from a long-term perspective that includes life after college, so that students perceive transition periods within the context of a bigger picture. Normalizing some of the challenges associated with transitions, helping students understand their current transitions within a broader context, and increasing students' awareness of resources that are available to them during a transition are all strategies for facilitating smooth transitions throughout the college years. As postsecondary educational leaders identify the skills and attributes they hope for their graduates to possess, we recommend that these desired endpoints inform the nature of the educational experience from the very beginning of students' time on campus. Planning for success in postcollegiate life requires that educators consider how each aspect of the campus environment serves to advance or detract from their students' abilities to develop the personal qualities that will serve them well beyond college.

Assess students' strengths at entrance and design programs with ongoing development of those strengths as a goal. As students transition into college, having an understanding of the personal strengths they bring into that environment may be a critical feature of a smooth transition in which students are able to gain a sense of confidence and competence in responding to some of the challenges they will encounter on campus. Students who are aware of their strengths can more readily mobilize and develop them during their college years. In addition, when students are challenged to nurture their existing strengths, they can be more intentional about leveraging them when they engage in coursework and cocurricular activities.

Chapter 2, which focuses on strengths development, notes that a strengths program may be most impactful when it is planned and implemented by representatives from several functional areas of campus working in collaboration to create a strategy for seamless strengths development. This type of group is also well positioned to integrate a strengths perspective into multiple aspects of the curricular or cocurricular experience, thereby facilitating the development of students' strengths throughout the undergraduate years. In some situations, designing a comprehensive campuswide strategy to achieve this objective may require the addition of new initiatives. However, instead of merely adopting a discrete or stand-alone strengths program, many institutions may benefit considerably from an exploration of how to infuse a strengths perspective into existing programs or services on campus, such as advising, academic support services, and leadership development.

Final Thoughts

The overarching intention of this book is to present thriving as a holistic model of student success that is a viable and realistic institutional goal, despite the challenges that confront students throughout their college years. By offering research-based recommendations for practice, we have sought to respond to the struggles inherent in specific transitions with helpful strategies for equipping students to overcome them. Creating an environment in which students can thrive requires a foundational commitment to holistic student wellness. Communicating that commitment to prospective and current students, their families, institutional alumni, faculty, and staff is the first step toward creating a thriving campus that facilitates positive student transitions. Our hope is that the ideas presented here will catalyze reflection, dialogue, and action among educators committed to creating campus climates that enable all students to thrive.

Index

Note: Page references with a *t* indicate tables.

A

AAC&U. *See* Association of American Colleges and Universities (AAC&U)

academic advising. *See also* faculty interaction
academic thriving enhanced by, 192–193
appreciative, 29, 183–184, 192, 195
assessment phase, 29–30
envisioning phase, 30
planning phase, 30–31
second-year students, 126, 127, 130
steps in, 29–31
strengths development perspective, 28–31
supporting intrinsic motivation, 184–185, 186
teaching phase, 31
transfer students, 155–156
as vehicle for transition strategies, 14

academic determination, 6–7
components, 13, 91
first-year students, 54
high-risk students, 87, 90, 94
senior-year students, 174–175
for strengths development, 24, 26
transfer students, 153, 154

academic environment, xxiv, 70, 158–159, 181. *See also* institution

academic integration, xv, 43–44, 74, 159

ACT program. *See* American College Testing (ACT) program

active learning, 25, 192

Adelman, C., 138–139

advising. *See* academic advising

African American students. *See also* students of color, at PWIs
alienation feelings, 67–68
campus environment satisfaction, 70
compositional diversity satisfaction, 71
first-year experience example, 65–66
peer stereotypes, 68
perceptions about campus racial climate, 72–73
racial discrimination, 67–68, 72
second-year thriving predictors, 121
sense of belonging, 65–66, 69, 72
spirituality, 122–123
thriving predictors for, 74–75

Alexander, B. C., 160

Allen, J., 27, 140

Allen, W., 67, 70

alma mater day, 56

American College Testing (ACT) program, 99

Analysis of Covariance (ANCOVA), 99

H

Harper, S. R., xxii, 70
Harter, J. K., 21
Hausmann, L., 74
Hershberger, S. L., 72
Higher Education Act of 1965, 88
high-impact educational practices, 22
high-risk students, 87–110
  academic strategies of successful, 93,
    94, 105
  campus involvement, 93, 95
  effect of historic policies on, 88
  first-generation students, 88, 107
  growth mindset, 96–97, 98–100,
    106–107
  importance of thriving for, 87, 90–92
  mindset study, 95–100, 104–105,
    107–108
  phenomenological study of, 92–95,
    100, 104, 107–108
  policy and practice recommendations
    for, 105–107
  positive perspective, 93, 100
  remedial education and, 88–92, 107
  self-perceptions, 91
  success mindset development, 93–94
  supportive relationships, 93, 95
  vs. at-risk students, 88
Hills, J. R., 138
Hispanic students. See Latina/o
    students
Holland, J. L., xxiv
hope building, 14, 30, 192
Horn, L., 153
Hoyle, R. H., 74
Hulme, E., ix
Hurtado, S., 68, 70, 72, 73

I

I-E-O model. See Inputs-Environment-
    Outcomes (I-E-O) model

Implicit Theory of Intelligence Scale, 99
Inputs-Environment-Outcomes
    (I-E-O) model, 42, 48, 50, 143
institution. See also academic
    environment
  creating diverse learning environment
    in, 76–81
  diversity supported by, 76–77
  goals of, 34, 37
  positive framing of transitions, 9–11
  student commitment to, 43
  support structures, 11–13, 44
Integrated Postsecondary Data System
    (IPEDS), 153
interactionalist theory of retention, xv
interventions, 14
  academic advising, 14
  academic determination, 6, 7, 13, 24
  classroom, 13
  curriculum design, 13, 14–15
  diverse citizenship, 11, 12–13
  engaged learning, 6, 13–14, 24
  faculty development, 13–14
  first-year seminars, 12, 54
  growth mindset, 98–100
  high-risk students, 92, 96, 104
  hope building, 14, 30, 192
  institutional, 11–12
  living-learning communities, 12–13,
    15
  peer mentoring, 10, 12
  positive perspective, 7, 9, 10–11, 14
  service-learning courses, 12
  social connectedness, 11–12
  strengths, 22, 35
  students of color, 81
  transfer students, 138
intrinsic motivation, 25, 26. See also
    authentic motivation
  academic advising supporting, 184–
    185, 186
  curriculum design implication, 185

support during, 9, 11–13

types, 1

Truman Scholarship Foundation, 168, 169

U

UNCG. *See* University of North Carolina at Greensboro (UNCG)

underrepresented students, xxii, 69–70, 158, 159, 160. *See also* students of color, at PWIs

University of California, Los Angeles, 182

University of Michigan, 156, 157–158, 161

University of North Carolina at Greensboro (UNCG), 183-184

University of North Texas, 156, 159–161

Upcraft, M. L., 42

V

Values in Action Inventory of Strengths, 22–23, 29

Vassar College, 156, 158–159, 161–162

Vetter, D., ix

Villareal, P., 70

virtues, 23

von Hippel, W., 128

W

Weiner, B., 173

Welcome Week activities, 53

well-being, 141

first-year students, 58

importance of, 141

intrapersonal, xviii, 5, 94, 114

intrinsic motivation and, 184

perspectives on, xii, 6

strengths-oriented approach, 19, 23, 30

students of color, 67, 72, 73

White students

background variables as thriving predictors for, 73–74, 81

campus environment satisfaction, 70

perceptions about campus racial climate, 72–73

sense of belonging, 72

Whitt, E. J., 2

Wilson, K. J., 128, 158

Wolniak, G. C., 88

About the Authors

Eileen Hulme is executive director of the Noel Academy for Strengths-Based Leadership and Education and a professor in the doctoral programs in Higher Education at Azusa Pacific University (APU). She possesses more than 30 years of experience in higher education administration. Prior to joining APU in 2005, Hulme served as the chief student affairs officer at Baylor University, George Fox University, and the University of Houston-Clear Lake. Hulme, a 2001 Fulbright Scholar in higher education administration, has taught at the graduate level for the past 10 years and codirected the master's in Student Services Administration program at Baylor. In her role as vice president for student life at Baylor, she was responsible for creating the first major strengths program at a doctoral granting university. Currently, she consults with more than 20 institutions a year on topics related to positive student development and a strengths-oriented approach to higher education.

Jillian Kinzie is associate director at Indiana University Center for Post-secondary Research and NSSE Institute for Effective Educational Practice. Prior to this, she served on the faculty and coordinated the University's master's program in higher education and student affairs. She conducts research and leads project activities on effective use of student engagement data to improve educational quality and is currently coprincipal investigator on the Spencer Foundation funded project, Learning to Improve: A Study of Evidence-Based Improvement in Higher Education. Kinzie earned her PhD from Indiana University in higher education with a minor in women's studies. She is co-author of *Student Success in College: Creating Conditions that Matter* and *One Size Does Not Fit All: Traditional and Innovative Models of Student Affairs Practice.* She serves on the editorial board of the *Journal of College Student Development* and is an advisory board member of the National Resource Center for The First-Year Experience and Students in Transition.

Michelle C. Louis is an adjunct assistant professor of psychology and organizational leadership at Bethel University, teaching undergraduate and master's-level students. She is associate editor at *The Journal of Positive Psychology* and sits on the strengths advisory board at The Gallup Organization. She also served as a postdoctoral fellow at the Noel Academy for Strengths-Based Leadership and Education at Azusa Pacific University. She holds a master's degree in counseling psychology from Bethel University and a PhD in higher education with an emphasis in organizational leadership from Azusa Pacific University.

Eric J. McIntosh is dean of students at The King's University College, an independent liberal arts undergraduate university in Edmonton, Canada. As dean, he serves as chief student affairs officer and oversees all cocurricular programs at the University. He holds a BA from Bethel University, an MA in higher education from Geneva College, and a PhD in higher education from Azusa Pacific University. McIntosh's research interests include transfer student integration and issues related to access, success, and spirituality in higher education.

Sharyn Slavin Miller is an associate professor and program director for the master's in College Counseling and Student Development program at Azusa Pacific University. She received her master's and PhD degrees from the University of Southern California (USC). She has served in many administrative positions in her 35-year career, including the director of the Career Development Center at USC. It was in this role that she became interested in sophomore students and their ability to thrive and transition successfully into their second year. She currently serves on the NASPA National Board as the director of the Research Division and recently served on the NASPA Research and Scholarship Task Force to develop the *NASPA Research and Scholarship Agenda for the Student Affairs Profession.*

Denise D. Nelson is an instructional services librarian at Point Loma Nazarene University (PLNU) where she has been a member of the library faculty since 2004. She is conducting dissertation research toward the completion of a PhD degree in higher education at Azusa Pacific University (APU), examining predictors of undergraduate thriving. Nelson's co-authored conference papers on thriving have been presented at the annual conferences of the Association for the Study of Higher Education (2009) and NASPA (2011). As a result of her ongoing interest in college student success, she was awarded the 2009 Student Success Advocate scholarship by the APU doctoral faculty in higher education. Nelson holds an MS in library and information science from Drexel University and a BA in literature from PLNU.

Kristin Paredes-Collins is the associate editor of *Christian Higher Education: A Journal of Research, Theory, and Practice*. Prior to her appointment with the *Journal*, she served as director of admissions at Pepperdine University. She regularly hosts college essay writing workshops for high school seniors. Her research interests include campus climate for diversity at religious institutions, student spirituality, and access and equity in the college admission process. Recent publications explore the unique intersection between race and spirituality. Paredes-Collins holds a PhD in higher education from Azusa Pacific University and an MA in education from Pepperdine University.

Tamera Pullins is the associate academic vice president at Southwestern College in Winfield, Kansas, where she has served in both student and academic affairs since 1998. In her current role, she oversees the institution's academic support services, providing leadership for the student success center, services for students with disabilities, and faculty advising. She also serves students who are on academic probation as an academic coach. Previously, she held residence life positions at Southwestern College and Texas Christian University. Her research interests include sophomore retention and satisfaction. Pullins earned her BS from Kansas State University, MEd from Texas Christian University, and PhD in higher education leadership from Azusa Pacific University.

Laurie A. Schreiner is professor and chair of the doctoral programs in higher education at Azusa Pacific University. She has taught for 30 years, after receiving her PhD in community psychology from the University of Tennessee. She is co-author of the Student Satisfaction Inventory and has co-authored such books as *StrengthsQuest: Discover and Develop Your Strengths in College and Beyond* (2006) and *Helping Sophomores Succeed* (2010), along with numerous journal articles, including a three-part series on college student thriving for *About Campus* (2010). She is co-editor of the peer-reviewed research journal *Christian Higher Education* and has served on the advisory board of the National Resource Center for The First-Year Experience and Students in Transition and the editorial board for the *Journal of The First-Year Experience & Students in Transition*. Author of the *Thriving Quotient*™, she maintains an active research program on college student thriving.

Troy L. Seppelt is director of residence life at Colorado Mesa University and has been a student affairs professional for more than 13 years. In addition to his interest in the experiences of sophomore students, he has presented on the predictors of thriving for first-year students of color and the importance of appropriate preparation for student affairs professionals; he also advocates for a curricular approach to both residence life and student affairs work. Seppelt currently serves on the Directorate Body of the Commission for Housing and Residence Life for ACPA and is on the steering committee for the ACPA Residential Curriculum Institute. He received his BA from the University of Minnesota, Morris, his MA in administration of college student affairs from Western Michigan University, and is currently a doctoral student in higher education leadership at Azusa Pacific University.

Rishi Sriram spent eight years as a higher education and student affairs administrator before beginning his current role as assistant professor and program coordinator of the Higher Education and Student Affairs graduate program at Baylor University. As an administrator, he played a key role in the development of all living-learning programs at Baylor University, as well as the establishment of a faculty-in-residence program. His administrative work has won him a NASPA Excellence Award (Gold Honoree) and a Promising Practices Award from the NASPA Student Affairs Partnering with Academic Affairs Knowledge Community. His research interests include student affairs practice and college student retention, engagement, achievement, and development. Sriram currently serves on the editorial boards of the *Journal of Student Affairs Research and Practice*, the *Journal of The First-Year Experience & Students in Transition,* the *Journal of College and University Student Housing*, and as chair of the Graduate Education and Research Commission for the Texas Association of College and University Student Personnel Administrators (TACUSPA).

Deb Vetter has served for 12 years as associate dean of student affairs at Asbury University overseeing student success initiatives, such as short-term and extended orientation seminars and peer mentoring for first-year students, support for high-risk students, and intercultural programs. Vetter's nearly 30 years in student affairs include positions in career development, leadership development, and student activities. As an adjunct faculty member, she has taught leadership development, career development, and the theory and practice of teaching in higher education. She has held leadership roles with ACPA, presented at national conferences on topics related to student success, and received the 2011 Azusa Pacific University Higher Education Department Student Success Advocate Award. She holds a BA in psychology from Ohio Wesleyan University, an MA in college student personnel from Bowling Green State University, and is completing a PhD in higher education at Azusa Pacific.